THE SOUTH AFRICAN ECONOMY

What are the macroeconomic prospects for South Africa from 1994 until the new millennium? Two frameworks of macroeconomic modelling, associated with the World Bank and IMF, are used here to generate three scenarios, believed to represent the range of possible future directions of the South African economy. The study demonstrates that there is room for a developmental state, addressing the legacies of Apartheid such as poverty and inequality, within the confines of a stable macroeconomy.

Although the scenarios produced may seem specific to South Africa, the methodology outlined is just as applicable to the policy-making process elsewhere. The IMF's Financial Programming and the World Bank's Revised Minimum Standard Model were central to many macroeconomic management studies of the 1980s, which focused on stabilization and structural adjustment. This study shows for the first time how they can be quantitatively applied and illustrates their strengths and weaknesses.

Therefore, this volume can serve as a textbook in development economics courses. Moreover, the modelling skills acquired from this book will be equally relevant to those studying macroeconomic development and to government and aid practitioners involved in policy work.

Finn Tarp is currently Associate Professor at the Institute of Economics at the University of Copenhagen. Formerly with the United Nations, he worked as an economist for almost a decade in Southern Africa. **Peter Brixen** is an Economist at the Danish Economic Council and has worked extensively on applied general equilibrium models and development economics.

Routledge Studies in Development Economics

1. **Economic Development in the Middle East**
   Rodney Wilson

2. **Monetary and Financial Policies in Developing Countries**
   Growth and Stabilization
   Akhtar Hossain and Anis Chowdhury

3. **New Directions in Development Economics**
   Growth, Environmental Concerns and Government in the 1990s
   Edited by *Mats Lundahl and Benno J. Ndulu*

4. **Financial Liberalization and Investment**
   Kanhaya L. Gupta and Robert Lensink

5. **Liberalization in the Developing World**
   Institutional and Economic Changes in Latin America, Africa and Asia
   Edited by Alex E. Fernández Jilberto and André Mommen

6. **Financial Development and Economic Growth**
   Theory and Experiences from Developing Countries
   Edited by Niels Hermes and Robert Lensink

THE SOUTH AFRICAN ECONOMY

Macroeconomic prospects for the medium term

Finn Tarp and Peter Brixen

London and New York

First published 1996
by Routledge
11 New Fetter Lane, London EC4P 4EE

Simultaneously published in the USA and Canada
by Routledge
29 West 35th Street, New York, NY 10001

Typeset in Garamond by
J&L Composition Ltd, Filey, North Yorkshire
Printed and bound in Great Britain by
TJ Press (Padstow) Ltd, Padstow, Cornwall

British Library Cataloguing in Publication Data
A catalogue record for this book is available from the British Library

Library of Congress Cataloging in Publication Data
Tarp, Finn, 1951–
The South African economy: macroeconomic prospects for the medium term/Finn Tarp and Peter Brixen.
p. cm. — (Routledge studies in development economics, ISSN 1359–7884: no. 7)
Includes bibliographical references and index.
1. South Africa—Economic conditions—1991—Econometric models.
2. South Africa—Economic policy—Econometric models.
3. Economic forecasting—South Africa—Econometric models.
I. Brixen, Peter, 1963– . II. Title. III. Series.
HC905.T374 1996 96–14479
330.968′064—dc20 CIP
ISBN 0–415–14260–1
ISSN 1359–7884

CONTENTS

FIGURES

TABLES AND BOXES

TABLES

BOXES

PREFACE

The motivation to write this study in which we develop and use basic macroeconomic modelling tools to explore the complex development problems and medium-term perspectives of South Africa draws on many sources of inspiration and experience.

First, much has been said and written on the role of the IMF and the World Bank in the context of stabilization and structural adjustment programmes in sub-Saharan Africa and elsewhere during the last 15 years. Yet, with a few notable exceptions, little effort has been made to putting the Financial Programming (FP) and Revised Minimum Standard Modelling (RMSM) approaches, associated with the two Bretton Woods institutions, squarely into the public domain. This is surprising since these frameworks have played an important role and continue to inform at least some of the actors in country analytic work. We felt it was a challenge to help rectify this by (a) fully documenting how the two models can be operationalized, using GAMS as our basic computer language, and (b) applying the FP and RMSM tools in an inherently consistent manner, which goes beyond standard practice.

It is our hope that we have compiled a volume that can serve as a basic teaching text in quantitative development economics programmes and as a set of guidelines for practitioners involved in applied analytic macroeconomic work in third world countries. Once the modelling skills underlying this volume have been learnt, all that is required to get started analytically in another country context is to develop a consistent set of base year data. How this can be done is therefore also carefully explained in a step-by-step manner in this study. The programmes necessary to allow the reader to implement and start experimenting with the two models on a PC are included in appendix form, and a copy on a disk for immediate use can also be obtained by contacting either of the authors.

Second, we have over the past decade been actively involved in teaching and researching in the area of development economics. This field of enquiry has undergone significant changes in terms of general approaches and strategic outlooks. Many important new insights have been gained, including the realization that an enabling macroeconomic environment and striking a workable balance between the roles of the public and private sector are of essential importance in the development process. Thus we hope, on the one side, that this study will provide the reader with a better grasp of some of the most important building blocks of sound macroeconomic management in a third world setting.

On the other side, we also aspire to illustrate that lucid macroeconomic analysis can in actual practice be used to underpin prodevelopmental oriented approaches to overcoming poverty and inequality. This is contrary to what one is often led to believe in the public debate. Hence, it is recommended that economists and other social scientists be concerned about addressing jointly the momentous problems of the real world rather than about securing the hegemony of one or another scientific approach. Moreover, many basic issues and dilemmas of development remain unresolved. Studying South Africa as we do in this text offers a unique opportunity to challenge one's understanding of general development theory and practice in a concrete country context.

Third, we have for years worked to promote change in southern Africa and infuse research and debate about the future of this embattled region, which deteriorated for so long under apartheid's destructive sway. Hence, one of the most exciting developments on the African continent during the first half of the 1990s has in our view been the political transition in South Africa. One of Africa's poets, who was also President of Angola, once wrote about an African train:

> A train
> climbing from a difficult African vale
> creaking and creaking
> slow and absurd

It shrills and shrills

he who has strived has not lost
but has not yet won

Agostinho Neto

This picture is very illustrative of the South African situation. A lot of battling has been going on. Yet it is seldom easy to reshape old designs, and one can therefore certainly add that the development struggle is still to be won in South Africa. People continue to suffer the consequences of the ill-designed policies and practices of an unjust political, social and economic regime. Hence, trying to (a) develop a quantified analytic input to the ongoing policy dialogue in South Africa and (b) demonstrate that there is indeed room for decisive action by the new government, in cooperation with the private commercial and non-commercial sectors just seemed to us a natural thing to do.

ACKNOWLEDGEMENTS

This volume would never have come into existence had it not been for the help and intellectual stimulation we have received from a number of friends and colleagues. We would, in particular, like to acknowledge that Professors Lance Taylor from the New School of Social Research in New York and Laurence Harris at the School of Oriental and African Studies (SOAS), University of London, played a most useful catalytic role in the initial stages of our work.

We are also grateful for encouragement and suggestions by Professor Graham Pyatt at the Institute of Social Studies (ISS), the Hague, Professor John Toye at the Institute of Development Studies (IDS), University of Sussex, Professor Jørn Rattsø at the Department of Economics, University of Trondheim, and Professor Brian Kahn at the Department of Economics, University of Cape Town. Similar thanks are due to the following Senior Lecturers: Stephen Gelb at the Institute of Social and Economic Research, University of Durban-Westville, Rob Davies at the Department of Economics, University of Zimbabwe, and Bertil Odén, Economist at the Scandinavian Institute of African Studies, Uppsala.

Professor Gerry Helleiner at the Department of Economics, University of Toronto, Professor Benno Ndulu, Executive Director of the African Economic Research Consortium (AERC), and Professor Alan Matthews at the Department of Economics, University of Dublin, as well as Tony Addison and Jeff Round, Lecturer and Reader at the Department of Economics, University of Warwick, also inspired us in a most helpful and friendly manner to proceed with this volume.

Senior Lecturer Trudi Hartzenberg at the Department of Economics, University of Cape Town, assisted in an effective manner in data searching, as did Dirk Ernst N. van Seventer, Policy Analyst at the Centre for Policy and Information, the Development Bank of Southern Africa. Finally, contributions by Willem Naude, Research Associate at the Centre for the Study of African Economies (CSAE) at the University of Oxford during the very initial phase of conceptualizing this study are also recognized.

The modelling frameworks and medium-term scenarios for South Africa presented in this study have been put forward in a number of seminars and conferences over the past couple of years. We wish to express our gratitude for observations and suggestions by participants in these events. They helped in sharpening our analytical approach and made us appreciate more fully the complex economic, political and social situation of South Africa.

We have also been supported wholeheartedly by the respective institutions to which we are attached. Daily inspiration and backing from colleagues and students have contributed to making this research task feasible. Moreover, financial assistance from Danida, which made it possible for us to undertake a number of trips to South Africa over the past couple of years, is highly appreciated. As already noted it is our hope that this study will be of use to the aid practitioner as well as a more academic audience.

Finally, we are most appreciative of the sustained encouragement and effective support provided throughout by Economics Editor Alan Jarvis, his Assistant Ms Ceri McNicol and other Routledge staff.

It is our hope that all of those mentioned, to whom we are in debt, will agree that the quality of this volume has improved due to their interest and involvement. Nevertheless, responsibility for any remaining errors of fact or judgement is ours.

Finn Tarp and Peter Brixen
Copenhagen, January 1996

ABBREVIATIONS

ANC	African National Congress
BRP	Budget Reprioritization Programme
CEAS	Central Economic Advisory Service
DBSA	Development Bank of Southern Africa
FP	Financial Programming
GAMS	General Algebraic Modeling System
GDP	Gross Domestic Product
GDI	Gross Domestic Income
GNP	Gross National Product
GNU	Government of National Unity
IMF	International Monetary Fund
M3	Monetary Aggregate
MERG	Macroeconomic Research Group
NEM	Normative Economic Model
NP	Nationalist Party
RDP	Reconstruction and Development Programme
RMSM	Revised Minimum Standard Model
ROW	Rest of World
SADC	Southern Africa Development Community
SAM	Social Accounting Matrix
SARB	South African Reserve Bank

1

INTRODUCTION

The balance between the use of market forces and instruments of economic planning by the government in furthering the development process in third world countries has moved decisively in the direction of the former approach during the past 15–20 years. Yet the conditions under which unfettered market forces can provide for an optimal allocation of resources are exigent. This is the case when reference is made to a particular point in time, but even more so when alternative development paths for the future are considered. Furthermore, it is generally accepted that governments must assume responsibility for macroeconomic management and stability. Hence, governments continue to confront a series of routine and strategic planning issues, related, for example, to the need for systematic fiscal management and expenditure budgeting, on the one side, and the design of medium and longer-term production, investment and trade policies, on the other.

It is a basic theme of this study that formal macroeconomic models can play an important role in helping governments concerned with economic management and development planning. Economics is certainly not all that matters, when strategies for the future are analysed and designed in developing countries. Economic and non-economic factors are continuously interacting, at times reinforcing and at times contradicting each other. Nevertheless, economic analysis and modelling can *inter alia* help in (a) testing the internal consistency among established goals and policy instruments, (b) assessing trade-offs in light of underlying assumptions and value premises, and (c) defining a research agenda for the collection of further information on relations and mechanisms, which have so far been poorly understood. It can, moreover, be added that quantified modelling has taken a giant step forward due to the technological progress inherent in the computer revolution of the last 15 years. How such advances can be put into use in teaching and applied country economic work is another major concern of this volume.

The topic of the optimal size of the public sector is a difficult and complex one, as witnessed by the intense debate on development issues during the 1980s and early 1990s (Toye, 1993). Nevertheless, an attempt is made throughout this book to distinguish between this theme and questions related to the desirability of macroeconomic stability as measured by standard indicators such as the budget deficit, the inflation rate and the balance of payments. Public sectors can certainly over-expand, and in the past have frequently done so, causing economic instability. Yet, whether public expansion is possible without crowding out private activity and causing macroeconomic problems is an empirical question, which needs to be analysed rather than assumed. If space is, in reality, available, or can be created through government and private sector activity, it had better be used actively, provided of course that government is indeed committed to furthering the development process. The economic, social and political opportunity costs of not doing so may turn out to be very high in countries plagued by poverty and inequality. This thesis is particularly relevant to South Africa, which is the country case we are examining. As background, South Africa's economic and social characteristics are reviewed in Chapter 2, which also sets out in some detail the competing strategic policy frameworks, which influence policy making.

It is an explicit aim of this study to provide a fully quantified macroeconomic input to the policy dialogue on the future prospects for the South African economy, including *inter alia* the important tasks of constructing a medium-term expenditure framework. Accordingly, the particular focus maintained in the research presented is macroeconomic, although the importance of sector and micro level policies is duly recognized. What we have done is to construct three fully quantified and documented six-year medium-term scenarios in Chapters 6 and 7. It is believed that they capture essential differences between the many possible directions which the South African economy may take, and they can each be seen as representative of a much larger sub-set of specific development paths. The need for developing such projections has been alluded to on many occasions by both South African policy makers and scholars, and outside agencies such as the

International Monetary Fund (IMF) and the World Bank have also directed attention to the importance of this area of analysis in the context of policy formulation in South Africa.

While the South African case is in focus in Chapters 2, 6 and 7, the organization of the data and the methodologies followed are easily replicated in other country contexts. Moreover, the scenarios generated have not been constructed on the basis of entirely new theoretical constructs. The approach taken in the choice of modelling frameworks is the pragmatic one, that while aggregate models and quantified projections are indispensable, the theoretical frameworks do not have to be overly complicated.

In deciding which modelling frameworks to use, account was also taken of the fact that the South African government has to deal with a range of influential international agencies, including in particular the World Bank and the IMF. The two Bretton Woods institutions, which have a direct impact through the disbursement of their own financial resources as well as indirect power in affecting private and bilateral capital flows, use a variety of analytical tools in their policy-advisory work. Nonetheless, the so-called Financial Programming (FP) framework of the IMF and the Revised Minimum Standard Model (RMSM) of the World Bank have been important and widely used economy-wide tools in country economic analysis. Furthermore, they illustrate the type of economic reasoning and fundamental perceptions of macroeconomic causality upon which policy recommendations and conditionalities of the two institutions are often based. To master the analytical constructs mentioned is therefore an important precondition for making sure that the policy dialogue gets on a sounder footing than is often reported to have been the case elsewhere in Africa during the 1980s (Mosley *et al.*, 1991).

Hence, despite their critical theoretical shortcomings, which are reviewed in detail in Tarp (1993a), there appears to be plenty of reason to become well acquainted with the FP and RMSM frameworks – even more so, because the two models can actually be used as macroeconomic accounting frameworks in a more flexible manner than often assumed. Finally, they certainly do meet the practical requirement of being relatively simple theoretical constructs. Yet, surprisingly little documentation is actually available in published sources on the IMF and World Bank models, and the same goes even more so for guidelines on how best to implement and use them in specific country cases. In addition, the FP approach and the RMSM are seldom – if ever – implemented simultaneously in a consistent manner even if this is, in principle, fairly easy to do.

To help fill the above gaps in a functional and reproducible manner, so that additional experiments and updating as well as training can be performed with relative ease and effectiveness, is another set of objectives of this volume. It therefore contains three methodological chapters in addition to the chapters dealing more directly with South Africa. Chapter 4 describes and discusses the modelling frameworks used, and the particular modifications made in order to ensure that relevant, compatible and consistent medium-term scenarios could be constructed are also explained. Three types of data were required for the simulation exercises, including a complete data set for a base year. Chapter 3 documents and reviews how these data were generated, and how they fit into a standard national accounting framework. Chapter 5, on the other hand, contains a number of policy experiments, which are performed in order to investigate the main economic mechanisms of the two models.

The detailed base run, which is subsequently developed in Chapter 6, is based on the assumption that it is justified to be moderately optimistic about the economic future of South Africa. The modelling frameworks presented in Chapter 4 are used to ensure consistency among the economic variables considered and the various qualitative assessments made. Since the base run represents what appears as a realistic prognosis, it is used as a benchmark in Chapter 7, where two alternative scenarios are developed. They are based respectively on a more optimistic and a more pessimistic assessment of future perspectives, and demonstrate how two different sets of changes in exogenous variables and parameters can affect the values of the endogenous variables.

Finally both the Financial Programming framework and the Revised Minimum Standard Model were programmed and solved using the General Algebraic Modeling System (GAMS) (Brooke *et al.*, 1988). Appendix A contains the two GAMS programes used to generate the base run and the scenarios, as well as some methodological background. Appendices B, C and D provide detailed statistical tables on the base run and the optimistic and pessimistic scenarios, respectively.

2

GENERAL COUNTRY BACKGROUND

MACROECONOMIC FEATURES AND TRENDS

Based on average income measures, South Africa is a relatively rich country with a Gross National Product (GNP) per capita of close to US$ 3,000 (World Bank, 1995, p. 163). Thus, South Africa belongs to the World Bank category of upper-middle-income countries. Furthermore, South Africa is indeed a regional 'giant' with a GNP which is about three times as big as that of the Southern Africa Development Community (SADC) countries together. Nevertheless, if the average annual income of the black South Africans in the former so-called homelands is used as a measure, South Africa would be categorized among the poorest of the low-income countries. Moreover, while the GNP is large by African standards, total GNP is after all only equal to about 11 per cent of, for example, the GNP of the United Kingdom.

In terms of sectoral contributions to Gross Domestic Product (GDP), industry (including mining and quarrying) accounted for 39 per cent in 1993 according to World Bank data. Services such as finance, insurance, real estate and business services, public administration and defence as well as trade, etc. added up to a total of 56 per cent. Agriculture, forestry and fisheries made a relatively small contribution of around 5 per cent to GDP, but mining and agriculture are much more important to the economy than GDP figures suggest. These two sectors dominate the country's exports and provide essential inputs for manufacturing. Close to 60 per cent of agricultural output is, for example, delivered to secondary industries for processing, and agriculture is also a major employment generator.

Exports of goods and non-factor services account for around one quarter of GNP, and gold is by far the most important export commodity, accounting in 1991 for almost one quarter of all exports. Other mineral products, base metals and chemicals amounted to more than 30 per cent, leaving about one-third for other commodities, including for example food, drink and tobacco as well as textiles. Machinery has been and remains the key import, followed by transport equipment and chemicals. Thus, the South African economy is open as well as highly dependent on fluctuating primary sector exports, and imported capital goods for the domestic industry are essential for the level of activity.

Traditionally, South Africa attracted substantial capital inflows, and international debt rose rapidly between 1970 and 1985. Yet, after 1985 the imposition of international financial sanctions forced the apartheid regime to run current account surpluses to finance external debt repayment and private capital outflows. Consequently, debt started falling to a historic low in the early 1990s.

The South African economy was dynamic during the 1950s and 1960s with annual growth rates in excess of 5 per cent. However, from 1973–4 stagnation and decline became characteristic. The growth rate started falling and by the end of the 1980s it was less than 2 per cent a year, and much more volatile than previously. In 1990 per capita output had actually fallen to only 85 per cent of the level reached in 1975, and GDP continued its downward trend until 1993. Per capita income in 1994 was therefore about the same as in the mid-1960s.

Moreover, during the 1970s and 1980s the composition of expenditure changed towards greater private consumption and less fixed investment. Hence, while fixed investment grew by 8–9 per cent a year during the 1960s, the increase was limited to only 2.2 per cent a year from 1972 to 1979, and during the 1980s investment fell by 1.5 per cent on an annual basis. Private consumption, on the other hand, maintained an annual rate of increase of 3 per cent during the 1980s. Thus, the capital stock became smaller and 'older', and consumption grew more than GDP, so the basis for future growth was gradually undermined.

All employment and labour statistics in South Africa must be interpreted with caution, but it is evident that South Africa is in the middle of a deepening and potentially explosive labour market crisis. The number of formal sector employees has stagnated since the mid-1970s, and while 80 per cent of new entrants on the labour market found formal sector employment at the end of the 1960s, the number is now less than 10 per cent (COSATU, 1992). The only formal sub-sectors in which employment increased from 1980 to 1988 were central government, local administration and homelands, and financial services. Thus, the build up of apartheid's administrative control structures created more jobs, but this increase was cancelled out by less employment in other sectors, and total employment continued to fall steadily from 1989 to 1994 (SARB, September 1995). It is difficult to provide more precise estimates of unemployment, as it is unclear how many people have found at least part time employment in the informal sector. Yet, according to official statistics, 43 per cent of the economically active work force were either unemployed or occupied in the informal sector in 1994 as compared to 19 per cent in 1970 (SARB, September 1995). This obviously underlines the need not only for growth, but also for sector and micro level policies to increase labour absorption.

Public sector budgets have been in deficit ever since 1970. The increase in the number of public employees referred to above is one aspect hereof, but to this should be added increasing debt service obligations as well as military expenditures. The latter have fallen more recently, but nevertheless rose from 2 per cent of GDP in 1970 to 4 per cent during the 1980s. This, *inter alia*, led to a particularly sharp cut back in public investment. Hence, public expenditures, geared towards the realization of the national and international political and military objectives of the apartheid regime, contributed to undermining the basis for future growth and development. The levels of public expenditure and the tax burden are not by themselves worrisome, but the uncontrolled growth in the public sector and a public sector deficit, which grew rapidly to 8.9 per cent of GDP in 1992–3, certainly contributed to the relatively high inflation (Gelb, 1991). South Africa joined much of the rest of the world in experiencing a jump in the inflation rate from 4 per cent to around 15 per cent a year during the period 1960–73. Yet, contrary to what happened elsewhere, it remained at this level until very recently.

SOCIO-ECONOMIC CHARACTERISTICS

It is not only the macroeconomic situation and trends which have caused concern in South Africa (COSATU, 1992). Poverty is widespread, and South Africa has one of the most unequal distributions of income in the world with a gini-coefficient of around

0.65 (Eckert, 1991). Furthermore, the high-income group is relatively large compared to other developing countries (i.e. 20–25 per cent as compared to normally only a few per cent). Thus, much less is left for the poorest, and the number of absolute poor increased from around 15 million in 1980 to over 17 million in 1990 (Tarp, 1993b). Poverty is, in addition, overwhelmingly concentrated among African people and is both more widespread and more severe in rural areas.

It is generally held that inter-racial income inequalities, which are particularly pronounced in South Africa, were reduced as a consequence of deregulations in the labour market over the past decade. However, intra-racial inequalities grew, according to some sources, especially among Africans. It would appear that while modest income gains have been achieved among the middle 60 per cent of the black income scale, the top 20 per cent have experienced very rapid gains while the poorest 20 per cent have had no, or even negative, income growth. Thus, the poorest groups among the blacks have been marginalized, and widening income gaps between formal and informal workers constitute a growing distributional dilemma.

Income inequalities are partly a legacy of race-determined intervention in wage-formation, and the fact that many jobs have been exclusively reserved for whites. To this is added, however, the extremely unequal distribution of income generating assets. Thus, the 'gini-coefficient' for agricultural land ownership is over 0.80, and the white share of property income around 75 per cent. Also the extreme degree of concentration in the manufacturing industry is relevant here. Four private conglomerates (Anglo-American, Rembrandt, South African Mutual and Sanlam) control more than 80 per cent of the companies listed on the Johannesburg Stock Exchange, which is the financial and commercial power centre of the country.

Discriminatory spending on health, education, pensions, housing, infrastructure and other social services was yet another of the apartheid characteristics. Annual per capita expenditure on health for whites was almost double that for blacks in 1990, and despite legal changes many medical facilities remain in practice segregated. Similarly, black education was grossly neglected, damaging the future of black economic advancement as well as the overall growth potential of the country. Adequate housing is a basic human need and is crucial to socio-economic development, the improvement of the quality of life and the prevention of disease. Nevertheless, the distribution of basic infrastructure was also based on racial criteria in South Africa under apartheid. Estimates of the shortage of housing vary, depending on whether informal structures are conceived as housing or not, but whichever measure is used, the backlog is enormous.

Moreover, blacks in South Africa have very inadequate access to water and sanitation. In rural areas only 53 per cent of the population have a safe and accessible water supply, and only 14 per cent of rural people have access to adequate sanitation. In urban areas the situation is somewhat better, but it is notable that more than one-third (of the whole of the urban population) have only minimal sewerage facilities. Furthermore, while South Africa generates 60 per cent of Africa's total electricity production, 70 per cent of black South African households have no access to electricity.

The social imbalances between urban and rural areas have become even more evident after the abolition of racially based legislation and the lifting of influx control. Pushed by poverty and opportunity people have flooded into the major metropolitan areas. Estimates of the numbers involved vary, but people have moved into cities which have been deliberately underdeveloped for decades on the grounds that black people belonged in homelands. Squatter settlements have therefore mushroomed, leading to an overburdening of the social and economic infrastructure. The conditions have been characterized as abhorrent and explosive as well as extremely dangerous, in particular since the majority of the population of South Africa depends on the urban-based formal economy for their livelihood.

To this can be added the fact that the South African population as a whole is growing rapidly at an annual rate of around 2.6 per cent. Yet, there are large differences between the various racial groups. Hence, the composition of the population is shifting. These demographic observations have important policy implications, in particular since the white population pyramid is rectangular in shape, whereas the structure of the African population is broad-based with a high proportion of children under the age of 15.

The striking racial imbalances in the demographic picture are also evident in the health and educational status of the population, reflecting the discriminatory spending patterns referred to above.

The infant mortality rate per thousand live births was around 66 in 1990. This is exceptionally high. Furthermore, this figure is an average that does not reflect racial and regional differences. The infant mortality rate for blacks and coloureds is actually about five times as high as for whites, and rural coloureds and Africans have infant mortality rates which are two to three times higher than for those living in urban areas. Infant mortality rates as high as 130 per thousand were reported in some areas in the 1980s. This is equivalent to the level in Ethiopia in 1990. Furthermore, whites can expect to live about 14 years longer than blacks. Life expectancy for white males and females are respectively 68 and 76 years, whereas the corresponding indicators for black men and women are 55 and 61.

There are complex political, social and economic reasons behind these depressing indicators, but it is evident that the policy of apartheid pursued by the white minority has played a major role. Other aspects include an ill-conceived economic strategy and unfavourable international economic conditions. Further comments on this are made in the following section.

LEGACIES OF APARTHEID IN PERSPECTIVE

International economic sanctions have been identified by some observers as the reason for the decline of the South African economy during the 1980s and early 1990s. This is a misconception. Stagnation had already set in at the beginning of the 1970s, and the sanctions, imposed in 1985–6, can at most be said to have contributed to a process already underway. Inward-looking, import-substituting industrialization coupled with the exploitation of cheap black labour was at the core of the economic plan of the apartheid regime. It was, at the same time, the intention that South Africa would become a political and economic power house in a constellation of states in Southern Africa. Strategic rather than economic considerations therefore played a major role, and inefficiencies, generated by unviable project selection and a host of arbitrary apartheid laws and price controls, hindered an appropriate allocation of economic resources.

Moreover, despite the import-substituting strategy followed since the 1920s, South Africa remains a very open economy. Imports have remained around one quarter of the GDP, and they are essential for the level of economic activity. South Africa is heavily dependent on western technology as a direct consequence of the pattern of demand, which is closely linked to the unequal distribution of incomes and wealth. Exports, on the other hand, are based on primary products to which little value is at present being added domestically.

In sum, apartheid was not only a political system in which a majority of the population had no legal right to vote, it was also an economic and social order, organized to benefit the white minority. Absurd legislation and social as well as political institutions and policies constrained the movement of people and economic resources, dislocated the economic system and created inequalities of enormous dimensions. These contributed to political instability as well as to an inappropriate pattern of economic development. By 1973–4, the previous growth strategy had become unsustainable. Production and prices of gold, which formed the backbone of the import-substitution strategy, began falling; and at the same time South Africa initiated a destructive policy in the region. Instead of concentrating on developing the economy, the apartheid regime (mis)used resources to sabotage and undermine neighbouring states – and in fact South Africa itself. Hence, apartheid became an economic catastrophe.

It follows that the Government of National Unity (GNU) in 1994 took over an economy suffering from important structural weaknesses including

(a) a typical developing country economic structure, highly dependent on a variable international environment;
(b) an industrial sector, which is not, in general, competitive by international standards;
(c) a worn capital stock, which is technologically neither suited to making use of the large reserve of unemployed, low-skilled labour force nor geared to produce the goods, which the black majority of the population need;
(d) a battered agricultural sector, which is in deep crisis;
(e) an inefficient public administration;
(f) a lack of skilled labour due to the low human investment in the black majority; and
(g) an overwhelming concentration of economic power and capital.

Thus, it should come as no surprise that the socio-economic situation *on the ground* in South Africa is characterized by

(a) political division, mistrust and violence;
(b) absence of legitimate delivery mechanisms with capacity, resulting in little outreach to the poorest of the poor, who continue to find it difficult to get even their legal entitlements in terms of social services, etc.;
(c) competition at all levels for the control of resources and the development process itself with resulting duplication, lack of coordination and wastage of resources;
(d) weak local government and fragmentation of authorities at local, regional and national levels; and
(e) very high expectations that the political transition will result in a tangible material and social uplift.

POLICY FRAMEWORKS

Much of the attention of the outside world and the major domestic players in South Africa has over the past decade focused on the need for bringing an end to violence and reaching an acceptable political compact. However, after the take-over of power in 1994 by the GNU, the pressing economic and social issues have quickly moved to the very top of the policy agenda. The political settlement cannot by itself bring about lasting peace and development, and what is required for the historically oppressed majority is not only a right to equal opportunity, but also a right to an equal start in a different social environment. Looking back, it is furthermore clear that 'the' multi-faceted process of thrashing out the elements of a workable growth and development strategy for the future of South Africa in fact started gaining momentum soon after the release of Nelson Mandela from the Pollsmoore prison in 1990.

It is also evident that one fundamental result of the continuing policy dialogue has been that it is by now widely accepted that the key economic issues to be addressed by the new government revolve around the possibilities for making the two objectives of growth and redistribution compatible. Thus, the government must, on the one hand, give priority attention to redistribution of income and wealth and a reduction of unemployment to ensure social stability and progress. On the other hand, redistribution without growth and structural reform cannot ensure a sufficient increase in the purchasing power of the poor. Another common understanding, which has emerged, is that South Africa will in future have a mixed economy, in which market forces play an important role in the allocation of productive resources and income.

Despite general agreement about the above policy principles, consensus is far from complete. There are, in other words, competing analytical approaches as to how changes to past economic policies and the basic structure of the economy are to be implemented in practice. The initial opening talks between the African National Congress (ANC) and the Nationalist Party (NP) on the country's economic options focused on a narrow rhetoric of privatization versus nationalization, and questions related to the extremely high degree of industrial concentration certainly remain unresolved. More recently, it would appear that the macroeconomic development debate has crystallized into two broad lines of thought (Gibson and van Seventer, 1995a). The two basic policy frameworks, which are also known in the international development debate elsewhere, focus respectively on orthodox fiscal discipline in combination with market-oriented policies together with a leaner government, on the one side, and broader based development policies, where less concern is attached to size of government *per se*, on the other side.

The Nationalist Party and institutions such as the South African Reserve Bank (SARB) are clearly in favour of giving priority attention to macroeconomic fiscal and monetary discipline as well as constraining the role of government. This is justified by references to what are perceived as basic lessons from the past 25 years of policy making, often set out as follows:

a) There is no durable trade-off between inflation, on the one hand, and output growth and employment, on the other;
b) the costs of inflation in terms of lost output and job opportunities are much more severe than ever thought before; and
c) knowledge of the behavioural patterns of economic agents is so insufficient that it is difficult to predict with any significant degree of certainty the outcome of government policy interventions.

Inherent in the last of these observations is obviously an attack on Keynesian inspired macroeconomic policy, which formed part of the original building blocks of development economics as traditionally conceived. However, this assault on government's ability to achieve stability in output and economic growth is coupled with a set of ambitious recommendations as far as the wider role of the government in economic development is concerned, which are different in nature from the issues related to more short-run macroeconomic management.

Thus, it is argued that the essential elements of a successful development strategy must include it being led by the private sector with a strong outward orientation and a dynamic export sector, fully integrated into the world economy. Moreover, government's role, in this strategic vision, is limited to providing the legal, social and physical infrastructure within the constraints of affordability, and fiscal and monetary policies are merely perceived as instruments dedicated to achieving and maintaining macroeconomic stability. Structural reforms in a variety of areas to reduce the relative importance of government in the economy are therefore also called for, and it is argued that even if inequality may initially increase, the benefits of growth will eventually 'trickle down' to the poorer segments of society.

The ANC and collaborating partners within the framework of the mass democratic movement, on the other side, have over the years taken a much more interventionistic and development-oriented position. Thus, the ANC aspires, according to its Policy Guidelines for a Future Democratic South Africa (ANC, 1992), to set the country on a sustainable and socially acceptable growth path, involving a revised set of economic and social policies and institutions. Hence, focus is not narrowly on economic growth. The need for economic progress is recognized, but is seen as an integrated component of what is perceived as a more complete vision of the future, which also includes the creation of a democratic state at national, regional and local levels.

The 'developmental state' is, in other words, assigned a key role in building and implementing a new national development strategy. Moreover, it emerges from ANC policy statements that this is not meant to suppress the crucial role of the private business sector, and the maintenance of a sustainable macroeconomic position remains a key target. Nevertheless, the demand for meeting the basic needs of the South African population has been in focus, and the state is assigned a prominent role. Hence, the ANC perspective appears based on the assumption that growth, equity and sustainability can reinforce each other, and that redistribution is a precondition for social and political stability and progress.

The official government strategy to address the social and economic backlogs is embodied in the Reconstruction and Development Programme (RDP) originally formulated by the ANC

(1994). The RDP was designed as a coherent vision for fundamental transformation of South African society. Emphasis is put on six guiding principles set out in the so-called RDP White Paper according to which the RDP must

a) be an integrated and sustainable programme;
b) be a people-driven and people-centred process;
c) promote peace and security for all;
d) promote nation-building;
e) meet basic needs and link reconstruction and development; and
f) democratize the South African society.

(Republic of South Africa, 1995, pp. 8–9)

The White Paper has been the subject of considerable debate, and Nattrass (1994) has characterized the document as a shopping list of principles with no clear prices or priorities. She also laments the absence of hard-nosed statistical projections and consideration of trade-offs, and it is indeed correct that the RDP makes few concrete statements about fiscal and monetary policy. As such it appears concerned in particular with the overall developmental vision of the new government in addition to putting forward a number of ambitious programmes. These included, initially, a series of presidential lead projects directed at furthering rural development, urban reconstruction and housing, capacity building, the promotion of health, and a range of public works initiatives. They have a distinct basic needs flavour, which is in contrast to the 'trickle down' philosophy referred to above.

At the same time, however, it transpires from a variety of sources that the government is firmly committed to a policy of macroeconomic discipline in order to promote an enabling economic environment. Goals such as low inflation are often cited, and repeated references are made in public and academic debates to the dangers of what has been termed Latin American populism (Dornbusch and Edwards, 1991). Moreover, government non-interest recurrent expenditure is supposed to remain constant in real terms, and the government is explicitly aiming at a reduction from the present level of 21 per cent to 17 per cent in the ratio of general government consumption expenditure to GDP. In addition, only a modest increase in capital expenditure from its present level of 2 per cent of GDP is envisaged during the second half of the 1990s (Department of Finance, 1995, p. 2.4), and a reduction in the fiscal deficit is foreseen. Yet no increases in the overall tax burden are intended, and it is a stated aim that external debt should not be used to any large extent as a means of financing the national budget deficit.

When considering the wide ranging targets of the RDP and the vision of an active government, on the one side, and the very stern macroeconomic targets just mentioned, on the other, a difficult dilemma, which reflects the inherent and fundamental conflicts in South African society, becomes conspicuous. The GNU has repeatedly stated that the RDP is not intended as an addition to existing public spending programmes, and that resources must be found by redirecting expenditures from elsewhere in order to make the RDP and the fiscal target compatible. Yet it is difficult to see how this can be done in practice. The room for redirecting public expense will in all likelihood be very constrained, given, in particular, the job guarantees issued to existing civil servants, combined with the need for making the expenditure side of the government budget more equal in racial terms (Nolan, 1995, p. 167). To this can be added the demand for public expenditure on measures to improve the supply side of the economy, including both research and technology development and the critical upgrading of human skills.

Hence, it is far from evident that the above fiscal targets, which would constrain government activity unduly as demonstrated in this study, are appropriate and should be given priority over more development-oriented needs in the present situation. Expanded public outlays on education and health are in reality critical investments to build up social capital and boost the supply side of the economy through much needed human capacity development. Pent-up expectations among the disfavoured majority of the population are also a warning that an increase in recurrent expense may well be required to ensure social stability, which is, in turn, a precondition for growth. Similarly, the ruling out of permanent increases in the overall tax burden with a view to maintaining private sector incentives and confidence is questionable. Redistributive demands are impressive, so it would probably be more sensible to recognize that at least some tax increases may be hard to contain in the medium-term, striving instead towards making sure that a high degree of predictability and transparency is established about what the private sector can expect.

In sum, the development agenda facing South Africa's government is intricate. Stable domestic macro balances and avoiding the private sector being crowded out by government activity will be of critical importance as these difficult domestic policy dilemmas are approached. Yet it has to be realized that government spending on items with an investment nature should not necessarily be fully financed by current taxes, and this is so on efficiency as well as equity grounds. Investment tends to be lumpy, which is an argument for partial debt financing. The equity argument is that the beneficiaries of current investment spending are likely to be future tax payers.

As pointed out in Chapter 1 this volume tries, *inter alia*, to come to grips with the quantitative dimensions within which this balancing act must take place. In this context, the government must also ensure a reasonable degree of balance vis-à-vis the foreign sector. There is a considerable need for increased inflows of capital to finance imports, growth and renovation of the capital stock. Consequently, running current account deficits to ensure this inflow of real resources may make both macroeconomic and social sense. The possibility of capital flight must at the same time be taken into account, and greater foreign direct investment and portfolio inflows will only materialize if the expectations of international investors are influenced in a favourable manner.

The above issues and hazards – as well as the perils of deficient economic management in critical transitional phases of national reconstruction and development – are amply illustrated by the experiences of other countries. Illuminating developing country cases are, for example, reviewed in Dornbusch and Edwards (1991) as well as Taylor (1993). The lessons from these episodes should certainly not be overlooked, in particular since there is in South Africa a definite risk that the pressures on public spending will be difficult to curtail because of the pressing and very real social needs. Nevertheless, restraint alone cannot put South Africa on a higher and sustainable growth path, and it is clear from Chapter 6 that the new government does have at least some room for manoeuvre. It would appear sensible to use this room as actively as possible, while constantly keeping in mind that the space available may both expand and diminish in size, depending on the interplay among external and internal factors. Only in this way will the new South Africa be able to strike a proper balance between the need for redistribution and growth, on the one side, and the specific constraints which form part of the macroeconomic framework, on the other. To manage this task is not easy, however, and there are many areas on which the new government and South African society at large should focus attention. A vivid review of the broader requirements in the area of economic analysis and policy formulation can, for example, be found in IDRC (1991) from which it is clear that sector and micro level policies will have a critical role to play alongside the macro-economic dimensions which are in focus in this book.

3

ACCOUNTING FRAMEWORK AND BASE YEAR DATA

The basis of applied macro models is almost invariably a set of national accounting identities. Their role is to ensure that model solutions satisfy certain equilibrium conditions that hold by definition. For example, the material balance identity states that the supply of goods must be equal to demand, while the balance-of-payments identity implies that the use of foreign exchange matches the amount of foreign exchange available. Although national accounting can be rather tedious, it is a thesis of this study that a consistent accounting framework is a valuable tool when working with applied macro models. First, it provides a natural link to national account data, which will generally be the starting point for exercises attempting to analyse economy-wide policy issues. Second, it imposes a set of constraints, which ensure that policy analysts cannot make predictions that are internally inconsistent, and therefore forces some discipline into discussions of the best choice of economic policies.

A basic national accounting framework and the notation used in this volume are presented in this chapter, and they will reappear in various forms in subsequent chapters where the FP and RMSM frameworks are presented and applied. At the same time, the chapter documents how a base year data set, following the accounting framework, was derived from the South African national accounts. This data set was compiled for several reasons. First, it will be the starting point for the base run and the scenarios constructed in Chapters 6 and 7. Second, some of the data can be used to calibrate certain parameters of the FP and RMSM models, ensuring that the models reproduce actual South African data in the base year. Third, the existence of a complete and consistent data set provides a means by which model checking becomes straightforward, thereby reducing the possibility of specification errors.

The year 1994 was chosen as base year. It is the most recent year for which data were available and the *Quarterly Bulletin*, March 1995, of the South African Reserve Bank (SARB) is the main data source. However, it would be fairly easy to update this data set as new data become available. Although the data set was generated starting from an accounting framework, it was constructed so that it contains data values of all variables entering the FP and RMSM frameworks. In addition to 1994 values of all variables, 1993 values are also included for variables that enter lagged in at least one of the two modelling frameworks.

Besides the base year data set, two other types of data are needed when simulating the two modelling frameworks. First, values of exogenous variables are required for every year of the forecast horizon for which the models are solved. Second, it is necessary to assign values to model parameters. These data will be documented when the base run is presented in Chapter 6.

PRICES AND EXCHANGE RATES

Before turning to the accounting framework, it is convenient to select a set of price normalizations, which will be used to distinguish developments in volumes from those of values. It was thus decided to normalize all prices and the nominal exchange rate to one in 1994, as shown in Table 3.1. The column labelled *Symbol* shows the acronym used for the different variables in this book. On the other hand, the column labelled *Code* refers to the codes

Table 3.1 Prices and exchange rates (1994 = 1)

Variable	*Symbol*	*1993*	*1994*	*Code*
General price index	P	–	1.000	–
Domestic price index	PD	–	1.000	–
World price indices				
Export	XPI	–	1.000	–
Import	MPI	1.024	1.000	6014J, 6014Y
Nominal exchange rate	E	0.907	1.000	5350M

Source: SARB *Quarterly Bulletin* March 1995, Statistical Tables: *Exchange Rates, Gold Price and Trade Financing Rates* and *Expenditure on Gross Domestic Product*

assigned to the data series in SARB *Quarterly Bulletin*, which were used when deriving the figures presented in the table.

Having defined all prices and the exchange rate as one in 1994, the 1993 value of the exchange rate was derived from an index of the annual average of the effective nominal exchange rate given in the *Quarterly Bulletin*. The import price index for 1993 was calculated from the implicit price deflator of imports, which was derived from the national accounts, and the value of the exchange rate given in the table. Since the remaining price indices do not enter lagged in the two models, their 1993 values were not calculated.

MATERIAL BALANCE

A central national accounting identity is the material balance, which concerns the demand and supply of commodities. Using the notation adopted in this study, this familiar equation can be written as:

$$GDP + M = CP + CG + IVP + IVG + X \qquad (3.1)$$

The left-hand side shows that goods can either be produced domestically, GDP, or imported, M. On the other hand, demand consists of private and government consumption, respectively CP and CG, private and government investments, respectively IVP and IVG, and finally exports, X.

Table 3.2 contains values of the different components of the material balance in constant 1994 prices. All 1994 values were taken directly from the SARB *Quarterly Bulletin*. It should be noted, however, that GDP in 1994 includes a residual item of 1.493 billion rand (code 6011J). This residual reflects the fact that more is expended on GDP than is available when calculated from the national product and income accounts. Thus, the figure for GDP at market prices shown in Table 3.2 is higher than the official figure. While the chosen price normalization rule implies that values and quantities are identical in 1994, it creates some problems when generating figures for quantities for 1993 as the SARB *Quarterly Bulletin* presents real data in constant 1990 prices. It was therefore necessary to derive the 1993 figures in the table, but the SARB *Quarterly Bulletin* still provided all the information required.

Private and government consumption as well as export and import values were obtained using the corresponding real 1994 growth rates calculated from the constant 1990 price data given in

Table 3.2 Material balance (constant 1994 billion rand)

Variable	*Symbol*	*1993*	*1994*	*Code*
Consumption	C	338.661	347.669	6007J+6008J
Private	CP	250.617	256.320	6007J
Government	CG	88.044	91.349	6008J
Investment	IV	68.020	78.310	6009J+6010J
Private	IVP	57.840	68.690	6182J+6183J
Government	IVG	10.180	9.620	6181J
Export	X	102.100	102.682	6013J
Import	M	−81.968	−94.415	6014J
GDP	GDP	426.813	434.246	6006J−6011J

Source: SARB *Quarterly Bulletin* March 1995, Statistical Tables: *Expenditure on Gross Domestic Product* and *Gross and Net Domestic Investment by Type of Organisation*

the SARB *Quarterly Bulletin*. Similarly, private and government investments were calculated from current price 1993 investments and an implicit price deflator for total investments (including inventory changes). Thus, it was implicitly assumed that the price of private and government investments changed by the same percentage from 1993 to 1994. From these derived data, a value for real 1993 GDP was calculated. This resulted in a GDP growth rate in 1994 of 2.0 per cent, which is slightly higher than the official rate of 1.7 per cent. It was decided to maintain the official overall real GDP growth rate by adjusting all demand components proportionally downwards. This procedure is, of course, rather crude, but the 1993 values of the variables do not affect the results of model simulations, and they are only included in the data set to get the simulations started.

BALANCE OF PAYMENTS

The balance of payments is at the core of both models applied in this study. This reflects both the role of the Bretton Woods institutions as providers, directly or indirectly, of foreign capital, and the fact that serious external imbalances have frequently haunted most developing countries. The national accounting identity relating the demand and supply of foreign exchange can be stated as:

$$\Delta R = CURBAL + \Delta NFDP + \Delta NFDG \qquad (3.2)$$

All variables are here measured in foreign currency units, and ΔR is the change in international reserves. This is equal to the surplus on current account, *CURBAL*, and changes in the net foreign debt of the private sector and the government, respectively, $\Delta NFDP$ and $\Delta NFDG$. In another version of this identity, the last two terms can be replaced by the surplus on the capital account. It then states that the change in foreign reserves corresponds to the sum of the surpluses on the current and capital accounts. Equation (3.2) provides a complete description of the capital flows that will be considered in this study. This means particularly that potential differences among various types of capital flows, for example foreign direct investments versus short-term portfolio investments, will be largely ignored, although Chapter 6 touches upon this issue. In contrast, the description of the current account is quite detailed. Thus:

$$CURBAL = RESBAL + NETFSY + NTRP + NTRG \quad (3.3)$$

where *NTRP* and *NTRG* represent net transfers from the rest of the world to the domestic private and government sectors, respectively. The resource or trade balance is denoted by *RESBAL* and is defined as the difference between export revenue and import expenditures:

$$RESBAL = XPI\, X - MPI\, M \quad (3.4)$$

where *XPI* and *MPI* are export and import price indices. *NETFSY*, on the other hand, represents net receipts of payments for factor services. They comprise interest payments on the external debt of the private sector and the government, *INFP* and *INFG* respectively, as well as a range of other factor payments that are summarized in the variable *NFP*. In sum, total net factor services from abroad are defined as:

$$NETFSY = NFP - INFP - INFG \quad (3.5)$$

Table 3.3 contains the 1994 current account data of South Africa. Because of the price normalization, rand and foreign currency values as well as quantities are the same. However, the balance-of-payments variables in the models are valued in foreign currency. Imports and exports, and thus the resource balance, follow directly from Table 3.2. Since the SARB *Quarterly Bulletin* includes total interest payments from South Africa to the rest of the world only, an assumption was necessary to allocate them between the government and private sector. It was therefore decided to make the allocation in proportion to the 1993 stocks of net external debt,

Table 3.3 Current account (billion foreign currency units)

Variable	*Symbol*	*1994*	*Code*
Resource balance	RESBAL	8.267	6013J−6014J
Export	XPI*X	102.682	6013J
Import	MPI*M	−94.415	6014J
Net factor services	NETFSY	−10.561	6015J
Interest payments			5064J (Adjusted)
Private	INFP	−2.443	Derived
Government	INFG	−3.888	Derived
Other factor payments	NFP	−4.230	6015J−5064J (Adj.)
Net transfers to			5006J
Private	NTRP	−0.067	−6233J+6243J−6248J
Government	NTRG	0.272	6253J−6258J
Current account	CURBAL	−2.089	6013J

Source: SARB *Quarterly Bulletin* March 1995, Statistical Tables: *Balance of Payments, Services and Transfers, National Income and Production Accounts of South Africa, Current Income and Expenditure of Incorporated Business Enterprises, Personal Income and Expenditure* and *Current Income and Expenditure of General Government*

which will be derived below. This procedure ignores the fact that debt stocks are net of foreign assets, whereas the interest payments are on a gross basis. Yet the foreign asset stocks of both sectors, as shown in the SARB *Quarterly Bulletin*, are small compared to the stocks of liabilities. Moreover, the ratio of assets to liabilities is about the same for both the government and the private sector. Hence, no serious bias is created, and the implicit interest rate on external debt appears reasonable.

Net receipts of other factor payments were calculated as the difference between total net factor payments and interest payments abroad. Finally, net transfers from the rest of the world to the government and the private sector respectively were obtained from data in the SARB *Quarterly Bulletin* on gross transfers to/from abroad.

Table 3.4 contains all data related to the capital account, including the underlying stocks of foreign assets and liabilities. Several problems were encountered in the construction of these data. First, the SARB *Quarterly Bulletin* contains only stock data up to 1993. Second, it is not straightforward to reconcile data on asset stocks with the corresponding flows of assets, which appear in the balance-of-payments accounts. Consequently, several assumptions were required before the figures in Table 3.4 could be completed. It should be mentioned, however, that asset stocks only influence

Table 3.4 Capital account (billion foreign currency units)

Variable	*Symbol*	*Stock*	*Flow*	*Code*
Net foreign debt				
Private	$NFDP_{93}$	17.286	–	5162J+5166J+5170J+5172J−5212J−5216J−5220J−5224J
	$NFDP_{94}$	17.695	–	Derived
	$-\Delta NFDP$		−0.409	Derived
Government	$NFDG_{93}$	27.510	–	5163J−5213J
	$NFDG_{94}$	32.311	–	Derived
	$-\Delta NFDG$		−4.801	5009J+5017J
Foreign reserves	R_{93}	10.982	–	Derived
	R_{94}	14.103	–	5276M
	ΔR		3.121	5020J
Current account	CURBAL		−2.089	5007J

Source: SARB *Quarterly Bulletin* March 1995, Statistical Tables: *Balance of Payments, Foreign Assets and Liabilities of South Africa* and *Gold and Other Foreign Reserves*

the simulations of the FP and RMSM frameworks through their impact on interest payments.

Starting with the net foreign debt of the government, the 1993 value was derived from information on rand values of external assets and liabilities. This figure was then transformed into foreign currency units using the index of the effective nominal exchange rate given in Table 3.1. Subsequently, the 1994 value was obtained by adding the short- and long-term capital flows of the government to the 1993 stock value. These flow data were taken from the balance-of-payments statistics of the SARB *Quarterly Bulletin*. Since the exchange rate was normalized to one in 1994, the rand values of the flows, shown in the SARB *Quarterly Bulletin*, are identical to their value in foreign currency units. The procedure should therefore give a reasonable estimate of the 1994 debt stock.

Next, the 1994 stock of international reserves as well as the change in reserves during 1994 were taken directly from the SARB *Quarterly Bulletin*. The 1993 stock value was then calculated by subtracting the 1994 flow from the 1994 stock, using the exchange rate index to get the 1993 stock value in foreign currency units.

This leaves the stock of private net external debt to be determined, and it is undoubtedly the most problematic of the data in Table 3.4. The following procedure was used. First, the 1993 net debt was calculated from stock data in the SARB *Quarterly Bulletin* and transformed into foreign currency units using the exchange rate index from Table 3.1. Direct investments as well as financial assets and liabilities of all nongovernment sectors were included in the definition of private sector external debt. However, it was decided to leave out the short-term liabilities and assets of the monetary sector, as they are assumed to be captured by the foreign reserve variable. Next, the 1994 flow was obtained as a residual using the balance-of-payments identity (equation (3.2)). Consequently, the change in private sector net foreign debt has the right value under the assumption that all other items in Table 3.4 were calculated correctly. Finally, the 1994 stock of private net foreign debt was obtained as the sum of the 1993 stock and the 1994 flow.

The main problem in relation to these external debt data relates to unrecorded assets held by the private sector abroad. They are notoriously hard to assess, but informal estimates suggest that the private sector had net foreign assets worth 5.6 billion rand in 1990, as compared to net liabilities of around 15 billion rand in the official statistics. Independent of the actual size of the foreign assets, their existence will affect capital flows. As the private sector capital flows were calculated residually, they include *inter alia* the unrecorded foreign assets flows, contained in the balance-of-payments statistics. This implies that the 1994 debt figure used in this volume will conform neither with the recorded net foreign debt nor with the *true* net external debt of the private sector. However, since the impact of stock values will be small in model simulations, it was decided not to pursue this issue further. It should, however, be kept in mind, whenever data on the net foreign debt of the private sector are interpreted.

MONEY MARKET

Having considered the markets for goods and foreign exchange, the third market is a highly aggregated financial market. It will be represented in the form of a market for a single domestic financial asset called money. Implicitly, all financial institutions are aggregated into what is frequently referred to as a monetary survey, which intermediates between savers and borrowers by accepting financial liabilities, such as bank deposits, and extending credit to the private sector as well as the government. International reserves are also recorded as assets of the monetary survey. It is assumed by

Table 3.5 Money supply (billion rand)

Variable	*Symbol*	*1993*	*1994*	*Code*
Domestic credit	DC	201.015	230.047	Derived
Private	DCP	186.060	214.560	Derived
Government	DCG	14.955	15.487	1367M (Adjusted)
Foreign reserves	E*R	9.963	14.103	5276M
Money supply	MS	210.978	244.150	1374M

Source: SARB *Quarterly Bulletin* March 1995, Statistical Tables: *Monetary Aggregates*, *Monetary Analysis* and *Gold and Other Foreign Reserves*

way of definition that the liabilities of the monetary survey match the value of assets exactly. In the FP framework, an equilibrium condition ensures correspondence between money demand and supply, but since there is just one kind of money demand, only the supply of money is considered here. The following equation defines the supply of money, MS:

$$MS = DCP + DCG + E\ R \tag{3.6}$$

Thus, the liability called money supply is matched on the asset side of the balance sheet of the monetary survey by credit extended to the private sector and the government, DCP and DCG respectively, and the stock of foreign reserves, valued in domestic currency units through multiplication by the exchange rate index, E.

Table 3.5 contains the values of the money supply variables. Data for the total money supply and government credit were adopted from the SARB *Quarterly Bulletin*. The former variable is defined as the M3 money aggregate, while the latter is defined as net credit extended by the monetary sector to the government. However, the 1993 stock of government credit was adjusted upwards by 7.5 billion rand to account for a technical change in the relationship between the general government and SARB, cf. *Quarterly Bulletin* March 1995, p. 16.

International reserves were discussed previously, and the only feature to note here is that their 1993 value can be obtained by multiplying the exchange rate index in Table 3.1 by the 1993 value of international reserves in foreign currency units in Table 3.4. Given the values of money supply, foreign reserves and government credit, the credit extended to the private sector as well as the value of total credit were derived residually.

GOVERNMENT ACCOUNTS

The national accounting identities considered so far can be interpreted as market equilibrium conditions, while the remaining accounting framework relates to the income, expenditure and finance of the public sector. In this book, the public sector is defined as general government, excluding in particular public enterprises. The borrowing requirement of government, *BRG*, is defined as:

$$BRG = CG + IVG + INDG + INFG + GT - TG - NTRG \tag{3.7}$$

The expenditures of the government consist of consumption, *CG*, investment, *IVG*, interest payments on domestic debt, *INDG*, interest payments on foreign debt, *INFG*, and finally other expenditures, *GT*. On the other hand, two kinds of revenue are distinguished: government revenue, *TG*, and net transfers from the rest of the world, *NTRG*. Due to the price normalization, prices and the exchange rate can be ignored at this stage, but it should be recalled that government consumption and investment are defined as quantity variables elsewhere, while interest payments on the external debt as well as net transfers from abroad are measured in foreign currency units.

Government revenue and expenditures are shown in Table 3.6. Revenue is the sum of property income, including provision for

Table 3.6 Government budget (billion rand)

Variable	*Symbol*	*1994*	*Code*
Revenue	TG	118.055	6184J+6250J+6004J+ 6251J+6232J−6005J
Transfers from abroad	NTRG	0.272	6253J−6258J
Consumption	CG	−91.349	6008J
Investment	IVG	−9.620	6181J
Interest payments			6255J
Domestic debt	INDG	−21.193	Derived
Foreign debt	INFG	−3.888	Derived
Other expenditures	GT	−15.421	6257J−6252J
Budget surplus	−BRG	−23.144	6202J+6184J−6181J

Source: SARB *Quarterly Bulletin* March 1995, Statistical Tables: *Gross and Net Domestic Investment by Type of Organisation* and *Current Income and Expenditure of General Government*

Table 3.7 Government finance (billion rand)

Variable	*Symbol*	*1994*	*Code*
New domestic credit	ΔDCG	0.532	1367M (Adjusted)
Net new borrowing			
Domestic	ΔNDDG	17.811	Derived
Foreign	ΔNFDG	4.801	5163J−5213J
Borrowing requirement	BRG	23.144	−6202J−6184J+6181J

Source: SARB *Quarterly Bulletin* March 1995, Statistical Tables: *Monetary Analysis, Foreign Liabilities and Assets of South Africa, Gross and Net Domestic Investment by Type of Organisation* and *Current Income and Expenditure of General Government*

depreciation, indirect taxes net of subsidies, direct taxes and current transfers from incorporated business enterprises. Net transfers from the rest of the world amount to the difference between transfers received and transfers paid. Consumption is current expenditure of public authorities, whereas the investment figure is gross capital formation, i.e. including the change of inventories. The calculation of interest payments on the net external debt was discussed above, while interest payments on the domestic debt were calculated as the difference between total and foreign interest payments. Finally, other expenditures consist of net transfers to the household sector.

The other side of the borrowing requirement of the government is financing. Three types of government finance are distinguished. External borrowing and credit from domestic financial institutions were discussed previously, while the third source of government finance is net domestic debt, *NDDG*, covering private sector claims on government. Consequently, the borrowing requirement can also be written in terms of how it is financed:

$$BRG = \Delta DCG + \Delta NDDG + \Delta NFDG \qquad (3.8)$$

Table 3.7 contains data on the flows of government finance. Since the borrowing requirement and changes in external debt and domestic credit can be derived from previous tables, it follows that the change in domestic debt can be calculated residually as indicated in the table. The stocks associated with domestic debt are discussed in the next section.

Table 3.8 Other data

Variable	*Symbol*	*1993*	*1994*	*Code*
Government domestic debt	NDDG	151.379	169.190	Derived
Interest rates				
Domestic	IRD	–	14.0	Assumed
Foreign	IRF	–	14.1	Derived
Gross domestic savings	GDS	–	86.577	Derived

OTHER VARIABLES

Table 3.8 contains a few other variables that are required in the implementation of the FP and RMSM frameworks. The first is the domestic debt of the government. It was estimated indirectly from the interest payments, derived in Table 3.6, and an assumed value for the average interest rate on domestic debt, *IRD*. As shown in Table 3.8, the interest rate was set to be 14 per cent. Assuming that interest payments depend on the debt stock at the end of the previous year, the 1993 value of government domestic debt was assigned the value shown in the table. Subsequently, it was possible to calculate the 1994 debt stock by adding new government borrowing as shown in Table 3.7. This method of generating the debt stocks is admittedly quite crude, yet it proved difficult to obtain more satisfactory measures of the domestic debt of the government from the SARB *Quarterly Bulletin*. One problem is that it is hard to reconcile the financial accounts of the different components of the public sector with those of the general government as defined in the income and expenditure part of the national accounts. It would therefore in any case only have been possible to get an estimate of the domestic debt, and the indirect estimation procedure was therefore chosen for the present study.

The remaining variables in Table 3.8 are the foreign interest rate and a figure for gross domestic savings. The former was derived by dividing the 1994 foreign interest payments of the government (private sector) by the 1993 external debt stock of the government (private sector). Gross domestic saving was also derived from information contained in previous tables, as it can be calculated as either the sum of total investments and the trade balance surplus or the difference between GDP and total consumption.

DISAGGREGATED GDP AND EXPORT DATA

The final data are disaggregated GDP and export data, which will enter the RMSM model. The notation is shown in two equations:

$$GDP = \sum_i GDPS_i \tag{3.9}$$

where $GDPS_i$ is the value in market prices of output in sector i, and

$$X = \sum_j XS_j \tag{3.10}$$

where XS_j is the market value of exports of category j. Four sectors are distinguished in domestic production, agriculture, mining, manufacturing and other sectors. There are also four export categories, agriculture, gold, basic metals and minerals and, finally, other exports.

The disaggregated GDP figures were derived from the SARB *Quarterly Bulletin*, which contains data on gross domestic product by kind of economic activity in current as well as constant 1990 prices. First, the figures for 1993 were transformed into 1994 prices in accordance with the procedures discussed previously. However, these data are only provided at factor costs, while market prices are used in this study. Adjustments were also required to account for the residual, which arises because GDP estimated from the production side is smaller than when estimated from the expenditure side. A preliminary social accounting matrix (SAM) for 1993 from the Development Bank of Southern Africa (DBSA) was used when making the adjustments, as it contains sectoral output values at both factor costs and market prices. The resulting values for sectoral output are shown in Table 3.9.

The preliminary 1993 SAM was also used when deriving the

Table 3.9 Sectoral GDP (constant 1994 billion rand)

Variable	*Symbol*	*1993*	*1994*	*Code*
Agriculture	AGR	17.405	18.865	6031J Adjusted
Mining	MIN	35.943	34.908	6032J Adjusted
Manufacturing	MAN	92.368	94.282	6034J Adjusted
Other sectors	OTH	281.097	286.191	6035J−6037J Adj.
GDP	GDP	426.813	434.246	6003J+6011J

Source: SARB *Quarterly Bulletin* March 1995, Statistical Tables: *Gross Domestic Product by Kind of Activity* and *Expenditure on Gross Domestic Product*; DSBA: preliminary 1993 SAM

Table 3.10 Export by category (constant 1994 billion rand)

Variable	*Symbol*	1993	1994	*Code*
Agriculture	AGR	3.366	6.292	
Gold	GOL	25.462	22.661	5001J
Base metals and minerals	MET	36.064	33.110	
Other export	OTH	37.208	40.619	
Total export	X	102.100	102.682	6013J

Source: SARB *Quarterly Bulletin* March 1995, Statistical Tables: *Balance of Payments* and *Expenditure on Gross Domestic Product*; DSBA: Preliminary 1993 SAM; Central Statistical Service: Foreign Trade Statistics, Statistical Release P6161

disaggregated export data, since the SARB *Quarterly Bulletin* only distinguishes gold and non-gold exports. Having calculated the 1993 values of gold and non-gold exports in constant 1994 prices from the SARB *Quarterly Bulletin*, non-gold exports were allocated on the three remaining categories in proportions derived from the 1993 SAM. For 1994, the value of gold exports was obtained directly from the SARB *Quarterly Bulletin*. On the other hand, non-gold exports were distributed among the three categories based on foreign trade statistics published by the Central Statistical Service as shown in Table 3.10, which contains the disaggregated export data.

CONCLUSION

Having presented all base year data, a familiar national accounting identity will be derived in order to complete the chapter. The next step is to consider the income, expenditures and savings of the private sector, which can be derived from information in the previous section. Hence, define private sector income, YP, as:

$$YP = GDP + GT + INDG + NFP + NTRG \qquad (3.11)$$

which states that private sector income comprises GDP, transfers and interest payments from the government as well as other factor payments and transfers from the rest of the world. On the other side, private consumption, tax payments and interest payments on foreign debt are the components of private sector expenditures, EP, as shown in the following equation:

$$EP = CP + TG + INFP \qquad (3.12)$$

Since all terms on the right-hand sides of both (3.11) and (3.12) are included in the above tables, the values of both private sector income and expenditures can easily be obtained. It is therefore also possible to derive the value of private sector savings, SP:

$$SP = YP - EP \tag{3.13}$$

The last equation of the private sector relates to its capital account. It follows from the above that the private sector receives credit from domestic financial institutions and borrows from abroad, while its net acquisition of financial assets comprises government debt and money. Since private investments represent acquisitions of real assets, the following capital balance equation must be satisfied in equilibrium:

$$SP + \Delta DCP + \Delta NFDP = IVP + \Delta NDDG + \Delta MD \tag{3.14}$$

A similar capital balance can be derived for the government from equations (3.7) and (3.8), if government savings are defined as the difference between investments and the borrowing requirement:

$$SG + \Delta DCG + \Delta NDFDG + \Delta NFDG = IVG \tag{3.15}$$

It is now possible to combine the capital balances of the private and government sectors, equations (3.14) and (3.15), with the balance-of-payments identity, equation (3.2). In this step, all financial claims between the two domestic institutions and the rest of the world disappear, leaving the terms in the following equation:

$$\begin{aligned} & SP + SG + \Delta DCP + \Delta DCG + \Delta R \\ & = IVP + IVG + CURBAL + \Delta MD \end{aligned} \tag{3.16}$$

This expression can be simplified further by transforming the money supply function, equation (3.6), into first differences, and imposing equilibrium in the money market, i.e. the change in supply is equal to the change in demand. The result is the savings-investment identity, known from standard national accounting:

$$SP + SG - CURBAL = IVP + IVG \tag{3.17}$$

Thus, given the definitions of private sector income, expenditures and capital transactions above, the accounting framework presented in this chapter encompasses the condition that domestic savings and the current account deficit equal domestic investments. Although this should come as no surprise at this stage, the accounting equations presented in this section become important in discussions of the FP and RMSM frameworks in the next chapter.

4

MODELLING FRAMEWORKS

The macroeconomic perspectives of the South African economy are analysed in this volume using two modelling frameworks associated with, respectively, the International Monetary Fund (IMF) and the World Bank. Although both frameworks are relatively simple, they do illustrate the fundamental perceptions of macroeconomic causality that are implicit in the economic policy advice given by the two Bretton Woods institutions. Thus, while the framework of the IMF, known as Financial Programming (FP), puts emphasis on monetary factors in short-term economic stabilization, the Revised Minimum Standard Model (RMSM) of the World Bank is primarily focused on medium to long-term GDP growth and other real variables. Besides assessing the macroeconomic perspectives of the South African economy, this study is also aimed at reviewing these modelling tools through various applications.

Since the models are applied jointly in the South African context, a few modifications were made to their standard representations in order to ensure that compatible and consistent medium-term scenarios could be constructed. These modifications are described below, but it is emphasized that they do not change the general spirit and overall properties of the models.

THE FINANCIAL PROGRAMMING APPROACH OF THE IMF

The policy analysis framework of the IMF, commonly known as financial programming, has in reality not been a mathematically specified and consolidated macroeconomic model *per se*. Instead, it has been based largely on an oral tradition comprising a variety of analytical methods. Thus, Robichek (1985) describes the various steps in financial programming, while Swiderski (1992) provides a set of illustrative programming exercises in an actual application. However, recent studies (e.g. IMF, 1987 and Khan *et al.*, 1990) have formalized the approach in terms of a simple macro model in the tradition of Polak (1957). The model, as applied in this study of South Africa, broadly follows the outlines of financial programming in Khan *et al.* (1990) and Tarp (1993a).

In line with the IMF mandate to finance temporary balance-of-payments disequilibria and ensure a stable world economy, the model focuses on financial variables and the monetary side of the economy. Sufficient international reserves as well as low inflation are perceived as central conditions in order to create a sustainable external position of a given country. These two variables are therefore the main immediate targets, which the IMF wishes to influence. In the Meade–Tinbergen tradition, two instruments are needed to influence two targets, and the IMF has traditionally identified the nominal exchange rate and the volume of domestic credit as the two most suitable. Since it is generally assumed, at least implicitly, that the private sector uses credit more productively than the government, a limit is often set on the expansion of domestic government credit, forcing it to reduce expenditures. A theoretical foundation for these linkages is provided by the monetary approach to the balance of payments (e.g. Frenkel and Johnson, 1976 and IMF, 1977). The links between domestic credit and the nominal exchange rate, on the one hand, and the balance of payments and inflation, on the other, are made explicit in the equations described below.

The FP framework consists of 16 equations in the specification used here, and they are shown in Box 4.1. The notation of variables follows that introduced in Chapter 3, as is evident from the lists of variables and parameters referred to in the box.

Real GDP is treated as an exogenous variable, whereas nominal GDP is defined in equation (2) as the product of real GDP and the price level. The latter variable is calculated as a weighted average of the domestic price level and the domestic currency price of imported goods, cf. equation (1).

The money market is described by four equations. First, money demand is specified in the traditions of the quantity theory of money demand and the Cambridge equation. Thus, the demand for money, equation (3), is determined as a fixed proportion of nominal GDP, where the proportionality factor is the inverse of

Box 4.1 Financial Programming Framework

A Prices and monetary sector

(1) $P_t = (1 - \theta)\, PD_t + \theta\, MPI_t$

(2) $GDPN_t = P_t GDP_t$

(3) $MD_t = \frac{1}{\upsilon_t} GDPN_t$

(4) $MS_t - MS_{t-1} = E_t(R_t - R_{t-1}) + (DC_t - DC_{t-1}) + (E_t - E_{t-1})\, R_{t-1}$

(5) $DC_t = DCG_t + DCP_t$

(6) $MS_t = MD_t$

B Government accounts

(7) $INFG_t = IRF_t NFDG_{t-1}$

(8) $INDG_t = IRD_t NDDG_{t-1}$

(9) $BRG_t = P_t(CG_t + IVG_t) + GT_t + INDG_t + E_t INFG_t - TG_t - E_t NTRG_t$

(10) $BRG_t = (DCG_t - DCG_{t-1}) + (NDDG_t - NDDG_{t-1}) + E_t(NFDG_t - NFDG_{t-1})$

C. Balance of payments

(11) $\log M_t = \alpha 0_t + \alpha 1_t \log GDP_t + \alpha 2_t \log \frac{E_t MPI_t}{PD_t}$

(12) $RESBAL_t = XPI_t X_t - MPI_t M_t$

(13) $INFP_t = IRF_t NFDP_{t-1}$

(14) $NETFSY_t = NFP_t - INFG_t - INFP_t$

(15) $CURBAL_t = RESBAL_t + NETFSY_t + NTRG_t + NTRP_t$

(16) $R_t - R_{t-1} = CURBAL_t + (NFDG_t - NFDG_{t-1}) + (NFDP_t - NFDP_{t-1})$

Variables:

BRG	Government borrowing requirement
CG	Government consumption – constant 1994 prices
CURBAL	Current account surplus
DC	Total domestic credit
DCG	Government domestic credit
DCP	Private sector domestic credit
E	Nominal exchange rate – 1994 = 1.000
GDP	Real GDP – constant 1994 prices
GDPN	GDP – current prices
GT	Other government expenditures
INDG	Government interest payments on domestic debt
INFG	Government interest payments on foreign debt
INFP	Private sector interest payments on foreign debt
IRD	Domestic interest rate

Box 4.1 continued

IRF	Foreign interest rate
IVG	Government investment – constant 1994 prices
M	Imports – constant 1994 prices
MD	Money demand
MPI	Import price index – 1994 = 1.000
MS	Money supply
NETFSY	Net factor services from abroad – foreign currency
NDDG	Government domestic debt
NFDG	Government foreign debt – foreign currency
NFDP	Private sector foreign debt – foreign currency
NFP	Other net factor services from abroad – foreign currency
NTRG	Net transfers to government from abroad – foreign currency
NTRP	Net transfers to private sector from abroad – foreign currency
P	General price index – 1994 = 1.000
PD	Domestic price index – 1994 = 1.000
R	International reserves – foreign currency
RESBAL	Trade balance – foreign currency
TG	Government revenue
X	Exports – constant 1994 prices
XPI	Export price index – 1994 = 1.000

Parameters

$\alpha 0$	Constant in import function
$\alpha 1$	GDP elasticity of imports
$\alpha 2$	Real exchange rate elasticity of imports
θ	Weight in price index
υ	Velocity of money circulation

the velocity of money circulation. Since money is the only liability of the financial sector, it is, as discussed in Chapter 3, by definition equal to the total asset value in the balance sheet of the sector. They consist of domestic credit and international reserves as shown by the money supply function, equation (4), which is specified in first differences. Consequently, the change in money supply equals the change in international reserves, valued at the nominal exchange rate in the current period, and the change in credit extended to domestic sectors. Moreover, a third term appears on the right-hand side of the equation. It accounts for valuation changes in the international reserves due to variations in the exchange rate.

It can be argued that capital gains should not affect the money supply, but instead be treated as an increase in the accumulated savings of the financial system. This seems to be the correct specification if capital gains (losses) are not realized, but only appear in the net worth accounting of the Central Bank and other holders of international reserves. If capital gains, by contrast, are realized through sale and purchase of foreign currency, it will influence the money supply and should be included in its specification. For moderate exchange rate changes, however, this term has only limited impact on the total change in the money supply.

Equation (5) is a simple identity stating that total domestic credit consists of credit granted to the private and the government sectors. The description of the money market is then completed by an equilibrium condition, equation (6), which implies that money demand always equals money supply.

Turning next to the government, most components of the expenditures and revenues of this sector are specified as exogenous variables. Yet interest payments on government domestic and foreign debt are determined in equations (7) and (8) by interest rates in the current period and debt stocks, which have been lagged by one period. Equation (9) defines the borrowing requirement of the government as the difference between expenditure and income. The expenditure types distinguished in this book are consumption, investments, and interest payments on domestic and foreign debt as well as other expenditures. Since government consumption and investments are specified as real variables, current values are obtained by multiplying with the general price index. Similarly, the rand value of foreign interest payments is calculated by multiplying with the exchange rate. Two types of income appear in the equation, total domestic income and net transfers received from the rest of the world.

The government can satisfy its borrowing requirement through foreign borrowing, by borrowing from domestic capital markets and by increasing its domestic credit from domestic monetary institutions. Accordingly, the budget constraint of the government can be written as in equation (10). Domestic debt finance is frequently not an option for governments in the developing world. In South Africa, however, this source of finance is substantial, and its inclusion is therefore a necessary extension of the framework when used in the present context.

The six remaining equations of the FP framework relate to the balance of payments. Thus, equation (11) determines the import quantity as a function of real GDP and the real exchange rate, which is defined as the domestic price of import divided by the price of domestic output. The function is specified in natural logarithms, which implies that the coefficients of the two explanatory variables are elasticities. Equation (12) defines the trade or resource balance as the difference between export and import, both valued at their foreign currency price. Corresponding to the interest payments of the government, equation (13) specifies the external interest payments of the private sector as a function of the international interest rate and its net foreign liabilities. Net factor income from abroad is defined in equation (14) as interest payments on government and private sector external debt and net other factor payments received from the rest of the world. All these variables are specified in foreign currency values. Next, the current account surplus is equal to the sum of the trade balance, net factor income and net transfers received by the public and private sectors from abroad, cf. equation (15). Finally, the balance-of-payments identity is imposed on the system in equation (16). The change in international reserves thus equals the current account surplus plus net new foreign borrowing by the government and private sectors, respectively.

Considered as an applied macroeconomic model, the FP framework is simple. It contains only two behavioural equations, the money demand and import functions, and two equilibrium conditions relating to the money market and the balance of payments. The remaining 12 equations are either national accounting identities or relations that hold by definition. Consequently, it is fairly easy to describe the structure of the framework for a given choice of endogenous and exogenous variables. The partitioning of variables into endogenous and exogenous is required because the model contains more variables than equations, and is referred to as the closure of the model. Since the two models applied in this volume include few relationships among the various variables, it is necessary to specify a relatively large number as exogenous, and the actual choice will have a significant impact on model results, as discussed in Chapter 5. Nevertheless, the standard model closure of the FP framework is to specify domestic prices and international reserves as exogenous targets, and the exchange rate and government domestic credit as endogenously determined instruments.

Given a target for the international reserves and fixed values for government and private sector foreign capital flows, the exchange rate adjusts, first, to ensure balance of external payments through variation in the import level. Second, given the target for the price level and the change in domestic credit to the private sector, domestic credit to the government is determined residually in the money market. This results in a constraint on the size of the budget deficit, since changes in both the domestic and foreign debt of the government are set exogenously. Finally, this restricts the level of government consumption in the set-up used here.

It should be noted, however, that other components of the government budget could take the adjustment. For example, the government may wish to maintain a planned level of consumption and therefore decide to change its revenue in response to changes in conditions on the domestic credit markets. Yet it is fully in the spirit of financial programming to emphasize expenditure cuts rather than revenue increases. At least, this is how the policy prescriptions of the IMF are normally perceived.

A final comment related to this example of policy analysis using the FP framework is that the model closure leads to the calculation of the appropriate values of the policy instruments, given values for the target variables. Alternatively, the framework can be used to calculate the outcome in terms of target values, taking the policy instruments as exogenous variables. This type of analysis is frequently applied in standard macroeconomic textbooks, which, for example, investigate how increased taxes influence the level of output.

If the FP framework in Box 4.1 is compared to the accounting framework, presented in Chapter 3, the most striking features are that the material balance identity is not included in the FP framework and the absence of most aspects of private sector behaviour. This implies particularly that it is only possible to infer total absorption of the private sector, but not the allocation between consumption and investments. One concern often raised in this relation is that the exogenous assumption about GDP growth can potentially be inconsistent with the underlying investment behaviour. Although this issue may not appear very important in the short-run stabilization perspective normally adopted by the IMF, it is crucial for the medium-term growth outcome, which should also be central in any advice on economic policy.

Given the relatively simple structure of the FP framework and the important role played by the IMF in the stabilization efforts of numerous developing countries, it is not surprising that the modelling framework has been scrutinized critically in several studies (e.g. Taylor, 1988 and Edwards 1989). One issue is the dichotomy between the real and financial sectors, which implies that GDP growth will not be affected by the credit and exchange rate policies suggested by the FP framework. Exports are not, for example, influenced by change in the exchange rate, and credit to the private sector can be changed in real terms without affecting the level of investments and, subsequently, economic growth. Another set of problems relates to the portfolio behaviour of the private sector. Recalling the capital balance of the private sector, equation (3.14) in Chapter 3, both the external borrowing and the acquisition of domestic government debt are specified as exogenous variables in the FP framework. Yet there are no mechanisms in the model to ensure that the private sector would actually behave in this way. Generally, it should be expected that portfolio behaviour is determined by variables such as the level of inflation and interest rates and influenced by intertemporal considerations, including expectations and uncertainty. It is therefore not clear that the implicit assumptions concerning private sector behaviour will be consistent with a prescribed set of economic policies. There are other reservations related to the FP framework, but since they also apply to the RMSM, a review is postponed to the concluding section of this chapter.

THE REVISED MINIMUM STANDARD MODEL OF THE WORLD BANK

Contrary to FP programming framework, the Revised Minimum Standard Model (RMSM) of the World Bank emphasizes the real sector and economic growth. Consequently, it is occasionally referred to as a growth programming framework (Tarp 1993a). The RMSM is in the tradition of two-gap models, which focus on estimating the required levels of investments, imports and external borrowing, given that a target for real GDP growth is to be satisfied (Chenery and Strout, 1966). It is, however, important to be aware of the scope of analyses the RMSM can be used for. The model does not, for example, prescribe the economic policies that can generate a given GDP growth rate. Instead, it shows that if an economy is to grow at the predetermined rate, then constraints are imposed on certain variables. This interpretation also makes clear why the RMSM is to be considered more as an accounting framework than as a full-scale applied economic model, which can lead to clear policy prescriptions.

This section describes the RMSM as it was implemented in this study. The specification is based on Addison (1989), but modifications were required to obtain the above-mentioned correspondence with the FP approach. In particular, the balance-of-payments block was adopted directly from the FP framework. The World Bank version includes a more detailed description of capital flows, but it was chosen to opt for a simpler framework here as the focus will be more on overall balance problems than on the exact sources of external finance. It should also be mentioned that work has been undertaken in the World Bank with the aim of extending the RMSM. One result is the so-called RMSM-X (Everaert *et al.,* 1990). One important difference between the RMSM and RMSM-X is that the latter introduces exchange rate sensitivity into import demand. This effect was also included in this study, whereas more recent attempts in World Bank modelling such as mark-up pricing in the structuralist tradition were not included. The same accounts for the various contributions to the three-gap literature, such as Taylor (1989), Bacha (1990) and Ndulu (1990).

The RMSM specification can be found in Box 4.2, which also contains lists of parameters and variables. The model consists of 23 equations that can be divided into three blocks: (a) the real sector, (b) terms-of-trade effects on income aggregates, and (c) the balance of payments. These three blocks will be outlined below, and the section will be completed with some remarks on the choice of model closures.

Equation (1) determines real GDP as the sum of value added in the various production sectors. Four sectors are, as pointed out in Chapter 3, distinguished here, namely agriculture, mining, manufacturing and other sectors. Sectoral GDP is determined by exogenously specified growth rates in equation (2). Exports are similarly specified in equations (3) and (4). However, the disaggregation is different from that of GDP with the following four types of export being identified: agriculture, gold, basic metal and minerals and other exports.

Total gross investments are determined in equation (5), which shows that the ratio of investments to GDP depends upon a constant and the GDP growth rate in the current period. This specification was derived from an assumption of a constant capital–output ratio and an identity that links the capital stock, gross investment, the lagged capital stock and a constant rate of physical depreciation. It is, moreover, straightforward to show that the

Box 4.2 Revised Minimum Standard Model

A Real sector

(1) $GDP_t = \sum_i GDPS_{i,t}$

(2) $GDPS_{i,t} = (1 + \sigma_{i,t})\ GDPS_{i,t-1}$

(3) $X_t = \sum_j XS_{j,t}$

(4) $XS_{j,t} = (1 + \gamma_{j,t})\ XS_{j,t-1}$

(5) $\dfrac{IV_t}{GDP_t} = \kappa 0_t + \kappa 1_t \dfrac{GDP_t - GDP_{t-1}}{GDP_t}$

(6) $\log M_t = \alpha 0_t + \alpha 1_t \log GDP_t + \alpha 2_t \log \dfrac{E_t MPI_t}{PD_t}$

(7) $C_t = CP_t + CG_t$

(8) $IV_t = IVP_t + IVG_t$

(9) $P_t CP_t = (1 - \beta_t)\ (P_t GDY_t - TG_t + GT_t)$

(10) $C_t = GDP_t - IV_t - X_t + M_t$

B. Income effects from terms-of-trade changes

(11) $XTTADJ_t = \dfrac{XPI_t}{MPI_t} X_t$

(12) $TTADJ_t = XTTADJ_t - X_t$

(13) $GDY_t = GDP_t + TTADJ_t$

(14) $GDS_t = GDY_t - C_t$

(15) $RG_t = M_t - XTTADJ_t$

C Balance of payments

(16) $RESBAL_t = XPI_t X_t - MPI_t M_t$

(17) $INFG_t = IRF_t\ NFDG_{t-1}$

(18) $INFP_t = IRF_t\ NFDP_{t-1}$

(19) $NETFSY_t = NFP_t - INFG_t - INFP_t$

(20) $CURBAL_t = RESBAL_t + NETFSY_t + NTRG_t + NTRP_t$

(21) $R_t - R_{t-1} = CURBAL_t + (NFDG_t - NFDG_{t-1}) + (NFDP_t - NFDP_{t-1})$

(22) $R_t - R_{t-1} = \dfrac{MPI_t\ M_t - MPI_{t-1}\ M_{t-1}}{\delta_t}$

(23) $P_t = (1 - \theta)\ PD_t + \theta\ E_t\ MPI_t$

Box 4.2 continued

Variables:

C	Total consumption – constant 1994 prices
CG	Government consumption – constant 1994 prices
CP	Private sector consumption – constant 1994 prices
CURBAL	Current account surplus
E	Nominal exchange rate – 1994 = 1.000
GDP	Real GDP – constant 1994 prices
$GDPS_i$	Sectoral GDP – constant 1994 prices
GDS	Gross domestic saving – constant 1994 prices
GDY	Gross domestic income – constant 1994 prices
GT	Other government expenditures
INFG	Government interest payments on foreign debt
INFP	Private sector interest payments on foreign debt
IRF	Foreign interest rate
IV	Total investment – constant 1994 prices
IVG	Government investment – constant 1994 prices
IVP	Private sector investment – constant 1994 prices
M	Imports – constant 1994 prices
MPI	Import price index – 1994 = 1.000
NETFSY	Net factor services from abroad – foreign currency
NFDG	Government foreign debt – foreign currency
NFDP	Private sector foreign debt – foreign currency
NFP	Other net factor services from abroad – foreign currency
NTRG	Net transfers to government from abroad – foreign currency
NTRP	Net transfers to private sector from abroad – foreign currency
P	General price index – 1994 = 1.000
PD	Domestic price index – 1994 = 1.000
R	International reserves – foreign currency
RESBAL	Trade balance – foreign currency
RG	Resource gap – foreign currency
TG	Government revenue
TTADJ	Terms of trade adjustment
X	Exports – constant 1994 prices
XPI	Export price index – 1994 = 1.000
XS_j	Exports by commodity – constant 1994 prices
XTTADJ	Terms of trade adjusted exports

Parameters:

$\alpha 0$	Constant in import function
$\alpha 1$	GDP elasticity of imports
$\alpha 2$	Real exchange rate elasticity of imports
β	Private sector saving propensity
δ	Ratio of international reserve to import changes
γ	Export growth rates by category
$\kappa 0$	Constant in investment function
$\kappa 1$	Capital–output ratio
σ_i	Sectoral GDP growth rates
θ	Weight in price index

coefficient on GDP growth corresponds to the capital–output ratio, whereas the constant is approximately equal to the product of the physical depreciation rate and the capital–output ratio. Yet it should be noted that the capital–output ratio used here relates output changes to net investments. It is therefore in the base run assigned a lower value as compared to studies where it describes a linkage between output changes and gross investments. This functional form differs from that in Addison (1989), but was chosen because it proved convenient to work with in model simulations.

The aggregate import function in equation (6) is identical to the one used in the financial programming framework. It was decided to use the same specification because it simplified the construction of consistent scenarios based on both the RMSM and FP frameworks. However, this implies that only aggregate imports appear in the model. In the standard RMSM, on the other hand, import is disaggregated by domestic use, i.e. final consumption, intermediate demand and investments. Consequently, the issue of which import types that need to be compressed in a situation with limited availability of foreign currency cannot be addressed formally in this study. Another advantage of this simplification is that the concerns about 'guestimates' of the different elasticities, necessary to apply the model with import disaggregation, disappear.

Equations (7) and (8) take care of the disaggregation of total consumption and total investment between the public and private sectors. Equation (9), determining private sector consumption, is not included in Addison (1989), but appears in other representations of the RMSM (e.g. Khan *et al.*, 1990). The functional form is very simple, specifying nominal consumption as a fixed proportion of nominal disposable income, which is defined as nominal gross domestic income less public sector domestic revenue, net of government transfers to the private sector. Since government revenue and transfers are nominal variables and the real exchange rate enters the import function, it is necessary to introduce both the general and the domestic price levels into the RMSM model. The former is determined in equation (23) as a weighted average of the exogenous domestic price level and the domestic price of imported commodities as in the FP framework. The general price level is used in equation (9), assuming that the deflators for gross domestic income and private consumption are identical. Finally, equation (10) is the material balance national accounting identity, which in the standard closure of the RMSM determines the level of total real consumption.

The role of equations (11)–(15) is to calculate various national accounting aggregates that take care of income effects arising from changes in the terms of trade. Thus, the foreign currency value of export is deflated by the import price index in equation (11), while the difference between this figure and the export quantity is calculated in equation (12). Next, gross national income is calculated in equation (13) as the sum of the gross national product and the terms-of-trade adjustment. Finally, gross domestic saving and the external resource gap are calculated in equation (14) and (15), respectively. Without terms-of-trade changes, the resource gap equals the trade balance deficit in real terms.

The standard RMSM model (e.g. Addison 1989) contains a fairly detailed balance-of-payments block, focusing on the external financing gap. However, for the purpose of this study it was, as already noted, decided to adopt the balance-of-payments equations exactly as they appear in the financial programming framework. The motivation for this choice is that it makes comparisons between the two models more straightforward and that considerable resources would have been required to forecast the different types of exogenous capital flows. Nevertheless, one equation of the standard RMSM was maintained. It appears as equation (22) and lets the change in foreign reserves be endogenous in the RMSM, depending upon the change in the foreign currency value of imports.

The partitioning of RMSM variables into endogenous and exogenous variables is fairly straightforward with a few exceptions. First, the external sector can be closed by exogenizing either the exchange rate or the external borrowing of the government. It is in the spirit of the RMSM, however, to exogenize the exchange rate, since this variable does not appear at all in the standard version of the model. In Chapter 5, experiment results will be presented for both model closures.

The second closure issue concerns domestic consumption and investment. With respect to the former, this problem was solved by the inclusion of a private consumption function, which makes it necessary to have government consumption as an endogenous variable. Finally, it seems reasonable to exogenize government investment, leaving private investments to be determined residually, as this corresponds to the closure implicit in the financial programming framework.

With this closure, the functioning of the RMSM is easily described. An exogenous exchange rate implies that the balance-of-payments identity must be satisfied through variations in capital flows, and this is mostly thought of as government borrowing abroad. The first question raised by the RMSM is therefore: is the necessary external finance available, so the external gap can be closed? Next, the material balance provides with the chosen closure the feasible level of government consumption. Since this can be interpreted as a constraint on the deficit of the public sector, the fundamental question asked here is if there is sufficient domestic savings to match the required level of investments. This is the domestic gap.

The RMSM has not been subjected to the same degree of critique as the FP framework, probably because its use does not lead to explicit policy prescriptions, as discussed in, for example, Mills and Nallari (1992, pp. 99–118). This can, on the other hand, be considered a main weakness of the model. It may not be very useful to know the levels of investments and capital inflows needed to obtain the targeted growth rate, if they cannot be realized by applying reasonably realistic and feasible economic policies. One frequently mentioned problem of the RMSM does not feature in the version presented here. Thus, while government consumption is taken as the residually determined variable of the material balance above, this role is often played by private consumption in applications of the RMSM. In this set-up, it is implicitly assumed that there exist mechanisms ensuring consistency between private sector savings and the required level of investments. Stated slightly differently, additional foreign capital inflows are assumed to be used for investments, and not more private consumption.

Compared with the accounting framework of Chapter 3, the RMSM ignores completely the domestic financial markets, including the potential link from government deficits to inflation that was central in the FP framework. In fact, a solution for the level of government consumption can imply a large budget deficit, which can only be financed through additional money creation, resulting in inflationary pressures, or through unrealistic reductions in private sector credit, which in turn may render the required level of private investments impossible.

DISCUSSION

Before turning to a discussion of the FP and RMSM frameworks, the complementarity of the two models is worth noting. Thus, the FP framework does not incorporate the material balance, which is central in the RMSM, while it includes the monetary sector, which is absent from the RMSM. It might therefore be considered a logical and easily made improvement to combine them into a single model, and this was done by Khan *et al.* (1990). The combined model will thus comprise the central monetary and material balance national accounting identities and the key linkages between the monetary and real side of an economy. However, the merged version of the FP and RMSM frameworks does not in any case address most of the critique mentioned above as well as below, since important economic behaviour and institutional information remain unspecified. Moreover, the marriage between the FP and RMSM is in many ways an uneasy one. In particular, the FP model was originally conceived as a simple representation of the analytics underlying the financial programming of the IMF, and not as an applied macro model *per se*. It has therefore been argued that it does not make much sense to merge the FP and RMSM models (Polak, 1990). Nonetheless, these reservations against the FP framework as an applied model do not change the fact that it appears to describe actual IMF policy advice adequately, although admittedly in a rather simplified way.

Nevertheless, this study relied in reality on a combined version of the FP framework and the RMSM when the base run and scenarios, which will be presented in Chapters 6 and 7, were constructed. Although a formal integration was not undertaken, an iterative procedure during which all variables and parameters were effectively treated as endogenous was used. This ensured that the base run and the scenarios adhere to all national accounting identities, outlined in Chapter 3, and are consistent in the sense that variables appearing in both models have the same values. By treating all variables and parameters as endogenous, many of the problems discussed above are avoided. Thus, the specified behavioural equations are only used as guiding points of reference, which can be changed accordingly, while omitted relationships among variables are taken into account by relying on information outside the two frameworks.

Besides the critical remarks mentioned already, the FP and RMSM frameworks have come under attack for a number of other reasons, which can be classified roughly into two categories. Although both modelling frameworks are, as already discussed, little more than consistent accounting frameworks, the FP framework having two and the RMSM three behavioural equations, they are essentially one-sector macro models. Therefore, the first set of critique questions whether they are good macro models. However, it can also be discussed whether aggregate macro models are appropriate tools for analysing the economic problems facing third world countries, and this question leads to the second set of issues dealt with in the literature.

Starting by considering the underlying macroeconomic theory, there are no supply-side specifications in the FP, while the RMSM specifies only one link from investments to GDP. Consequently, both models ignore important factors that can potentially influence output, including the degree of capacity utilization. Monetary variables are among those factors as there is plenty of evidence that lack of investment and working capital finance, as well as very high real interest rates, have had substantial negative effects on production in many developing countries. Similarly, there are several examples of situations where output has been suppressed because imports of necessary raw materials and capital goods were crowded out by imports of consumption goods, when foreign capital was in short supply. However, it must be noted here that some versions of the RMSM address this problem by distinguishing among different types of imports and letting consumption goods be the variable determined residually.

A more recently recognized problem of the theoretical foundation of the FP and RMSM frameworks relates to the capital account of the balance of payments. Thus, both models take private capital inflows as exogenous, while the external borrowing by government is perceived more as a policy variable than as being determined by market forces. Although these may be appropriate assumptions in the context of poor African countries, they become questionable if the country in question has relatively well-developed domestic financial markets and a liberalized capital account. In these circumstances, it is crucial to account for the endogeneity of capital flows and to distinguish between the various types of private capital flows when assessing the sustainability of the overall balance-of-payments situation. The experience of Mexico in 1995 illustrates this point clearly, and is also highly relevant for the South African policy debate.

As far as macroeconomic theory is concerned, it is evident from the sources mentioned that the theoretical foundations of the FP and RMSM frameworks are relatively old, both being based on contributions from the 1950s. Yet economic theory has progressed substantially since then, and Edwards (1989) lists a wide range of recent developments that could be incorporated in the specifications especially of the FP framework. These include issues related to the intertemporal nature of portfolio choices, including the capital account transactions, the role of time consistency and pre-commitments in economic policy and, finally, the notion of rational expectations. Although the list could easily be extended, it is at this stage sufficient to note that neither the FP framework nor the RMSM are very advanced as far as aggregate macro models are concerned.

The second type of argument frequently used against the FP and RMSM frameworks focuses on the one-sector structure of the model, and will as such apply to all aggregate macro models applied to issues of economic development. By specifying just one market clearing condition for the goods market, i.e. the material balance equation, the importance of differential sectoral responses to price signals, for example, the exchange rate, are ignored. Similarly, it is implicitly assumed that imports and domestic output as well as exports and domestic supplies to domestic markets are perfect substitutes. By contrast, the fundamental idea behind, for example, the dependent-economy model, is that a satisfactory description of the goods markets must at least recognize the heterogeneity of imported and domestic production as well as the difference between traded and non-traded domestic output. This becomes particularly important in economies where market forces are partly curtailed by price controls and other types of government regulations. Economic policies can under such circumstances lead to very different outcomes from those predicted when assuming perfectly competitive and price-clearing markets. More generally, both the FP and RMSM frameworks are criticized for not taking due account of specific structural and institutional characteristics when applied by the Bretton Woods institutions in country analyses.

Although economic growth and macroeconomic stability are certainly important elements, it must finally be acknowledged that issues such as employment, urban–rural divisions and income distribution, as well as many non-economic factors are just as crucial as measures of the development process and for the well-being of the population. To cover these issues in the analysis, applied macro models are obviously not appropriate tools. Instead, other analytical frameworks such as applied general equilibrium models, for example, are required. In the context of South Africa, this alternative modelling strategy has been pursued by, for example, Naude and Brixen (1992, 1993) and Gibson and van Seventer (1995b). It is beyond the scope of this study to cover these alternative modelling strategies, yet their existence as well as the limitations of the FP and RMSM frameworks should be fully appreciated.

Although both the FP framework and the RMSM can be criticized for being old-fashioned and too simple, their simplicity is also a significant strength. Thus, they require few data, and they are simple to use and understand (Tarp, 1993a, p. 155). In addition, a model that simultaneously took into account all the above-mentioned features would probably be impossible to implement for many developing countries, where lack of data is a serious constraint. Moreover, it is questionable if it would add much to the policy dialogue as the complexity would be likely to give it the status of a black box, where the underlying mechanisms and results would only be understood by a few experts. It is therefore an underlying thesis of this study that different models are required to answer the many questions related to economic development, and even simple models can be useful as long as their limitations are duly acknowledged and taken account of in drawing up policy advice.

It is in this light that the applications of the FP framework and RMSM in this study should be seen. In the following chapters, the frameworks are used in two fundamentally different ways in order to illustrate how they can be both used and abused. In the first application, the models are used as proper macroeconomic models for policy analysis in Chapter 5. This means that the effects of changing an exogenous variable or a parameter are analysed, keeping all other exogenous variables as well as parameters constant. Second, the models are, as already discussed, used primarily as consistency frameworks in the construction of a medium-term base run of the South African economy in Chapter 6 and two alternative scenarios in Chapter 7. In this application, their primary function is to support three perspectives about the medium-term future by ensuring consistency among assumptions and outcomes.

5

MODEL EXPERIMENTS

All macro models can, as discussed in Chapter 4, be applied for two fundamentally different purposes. First, they can be used to generate economic forecasts or scenarios, and Chapters 6 and 7 will show how the FP and RMSM frameworks can usefully be applied for this purpose. This chapter will, on the other hand, illustrate the second type of application, where the two models are put into use in a number of model experiments. The aim of this exercise is to reveal the marginal properties of the two frameworks, which can then be compared both with each other and with results from the general economic literature.

Seven experiments are reviewed in this chapter, and they will provide quite a comprehensive picture of the differences between the two models, their strengths and weaknesses as well as the importance of the choice of model closure. Although not described in detail, seven more experiments were carried out and the central qualitative effects of all 14 experiments are summarized in Table 5.1 at the end of the chapter.

The outcomes of experiments are generally described in terms of deviations from the base run, which will be discussed in Chapter 6. Since both the FP and RMSM frameworks are nonlinear, their marginal properties are not independent of the actual choice of base run values of variables and parameters. Consequently, the numerical results presented in this chapter are conditional on the base run. However, the focus of the chapter is more on the qualitative properties of the two models, and they will generally be independent of the underlying base run. Whenever the base run matters for the results presented below, the relevant features will be outlined briefly.

The issue of the external model closure was introduced in

Chapter 4 in relation to the specifications of the FP and RMSM frameworks. Standard practice in applications of the FP framework is to assume an endogenous exchange rate and exogenous capital flows, reflecting the role of the first variable as a policy instrument. In contrast, the RMSM is normally specified with the opposite closure, i.e. an exogenous exchange rate and endogenous external borrowing by the government. As shown below, these different model closures influence significantly the properties of the two models, which makes it difficult to compare them. It was therefore decided to carry out all experiments on the two models using both closures. To distinguish the different model versions, the following notation is applied below. FP-1 refers to the FP framework with exogenous exchange rate and endogenous government external debt, while FP-2 has endogenous exchange rate and fixed government external debt. Similarly, RMSM-1 and RMSM-2 refer respectively to closures with exogenous and endogenous exchange rates.

EXPERIMENT 1: EXCHANGE RATE DEPRECIATION

This experiment can, of course, only be carried out using the external closure with exogenous exchange rate and endogenous government net foreign debt. Similarly, it is only possible to change the net external debt of the government exogenously under the alternative closure. That experiment is considered in the next section, while the current section reviews the effects of exogenous changes in the exchange rate. Based on these two initial experiments, differences between the two models are analysed, whereas the importance of model closure will become apparent in subsequent experiments.

The nominal exchange rate depreciates by 2.9 per cent annually in the base run, maintaining a constant real exchange rate. In the first experiment the annual rate of depreciation was increased to 3.9 per cent, which implies that the nominal exchange rate has increased by 6.2 per cent, compared to its base run value, in the sixth and final year of the time horizon under consideration.

Given the relative simplicity of the RMSM and FP frameworks, their causality structures can be described in diagrams. Figure 5.1 shows how the frameworks work in the exchange rate experiment, while subsequent figures will highlight how the causality structures depend on model closure as well as the experiment. The acronyms used in the figure correspond to the variable names introduced in Chapters 3 and 4. Solid lines are used to indicate the quantitatively most important channels of transmission, whereas the less important linkages are shown as dotted lines.

Beginning with the RMSM, one central chain of effects is that the depreciation of the nominal exchange rate leads to falling imports in response to a depreciating real exchange rate. Since fewer commodities are imported, less external finance is required to maintain the balance of payments, so external borrowing by the government is reduced. Second, the lower quantities of imports also lead to a smaller total supply of commodities. Consequently, real government consumption has to be adjusted downwards to maintain the material balance. This improves the government budget or, equivalently, decreases its borrowing requirement.

Although the borrowing requirement of the government does not appear explicitly as a variable in the RMSM model, cf Box 4.2, it was decided to refer to it in this chapter as it summarizes a range of different effects. A comparison of the government budget equation in the FP model and the variables in the RMSM model will show that the latter contains all but one variable necessary to calculate the budget deficit. The exception is interest payments on the domestic debt of the government. In order to calculate the borrowing requirement of the government in the RMSM, it was therefore assumed that these interest payments remain at their base run values throughout the simulation horizon.

Turning to Figure 5.1(a) again, five smaller stories unfold besides the main chain of effects already mentioned. First, lower imports are associated with a fall in the required amount of international reserves, further reducing the need for the government to borrow abroad. Second, a reduced government external debt leads to lower interest payments with a lag of one period, which constitutes an additional improvement in public sector finances. Third, the borrowing requirement of the government is measured in nominal terms. It is therefore influenced directly by changes in the exchange rate since interest payments on foreign debt and net receipts of transfers from abroad are fixed in foreign currency values. The size of this effect depends on the net value of the foreign transactions of the government. Yet since interest payments always exceed net transfers in this study, the depreciation implies a worsening of the government budget in the present context.

(a) RMSM–1

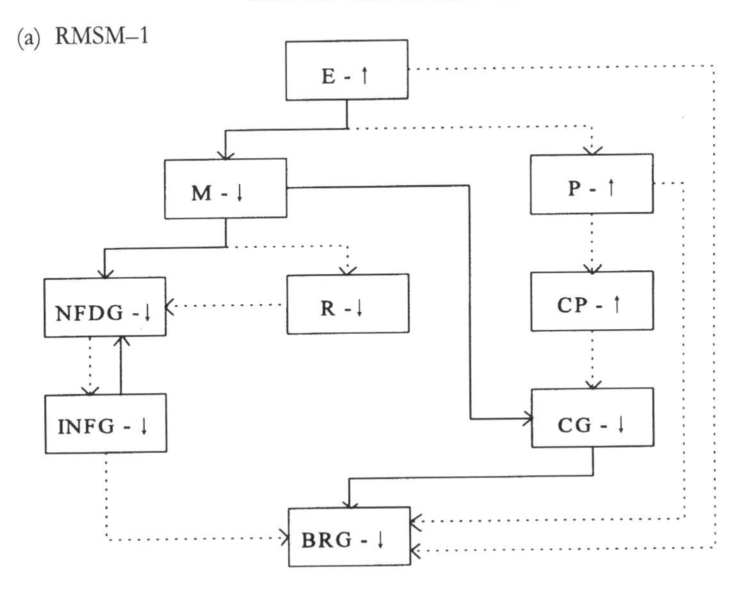

(b) FP–1

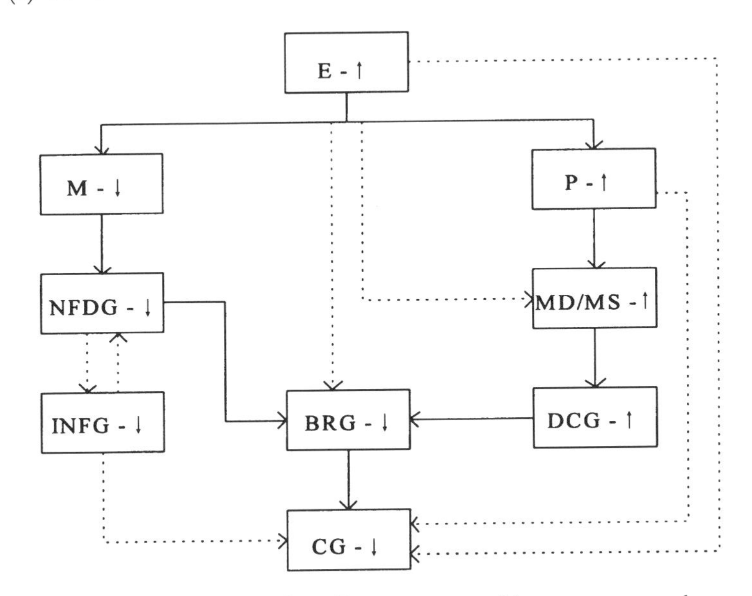

Figure 5.1 Experiment 1: Causality structures with exogenous exchange rate

The last two smaller effects work through the increase in the general price level that results from a currency depreciation as the rand price of imports increases. The fourth effect is that the higher price level increases real private consumption. This mechanism is caused by the nominal rigidity in the tax system implied by domestic tax revenues and other government transfers to the private sector being fixed in nominal terms. Hence, increasing prices raise the real disposable income and, consequently, the consumption of the private sector, thereby reducing government consumption even more than is required due to the fall in imports. The fifth and final effect is that the price level affects the government budget directly in the RMSM, as the costs of both consumption and investment increase as the price level goes up. It can be seen in Figure 5.1(a) that the borrowing requirement is influenced through four channels, working in opposite directions. Yet the reduction in the financing requirement, implied by falling real consumption and interest payments, outweighs by far the worsening that follows from the depreciated exchange rate and higher price level. In sum, the borrowing requirement is reduced by 31.8 per cent as compared to the base run in the last year, and the deficit of the government has fallen from 4.3 per cent of GDP to 2.9 per cent. This completes the picture of the qualitative effects of an exchange rate depreciation. Further observations on the absolute size of these effects are made below, while the effects of the experiment within the financial programming framework are described next.

A depreciation of the exchange rate has two immediate effects in the FP framework, which also occurred in the RMSM. Imports fall and the general price level goes up. The lower imports are as before countered by falling government borrowing from abroad, but the effect on the government budget now works directly through the finance constraint causing reduced government consumption. The second effect on government finance goes through the money market. Thus, the increase in the price level leads to higher money demand, so money supply has to adjust. Part of the required adjustment follows directly from the exchange rate depreciation, which has increased the rand value of foreign reserves. However, this only corresponds to a share of the increased money demand, and the remaining increase in money supply is obtained through increased government credit. This effect is contrary to the one working through the balance of payments, and this is also true for the third channel that affects the borrowing requirement of the government. Thus, the depreciation increases the rand value of the foreign borrowing by the government. Yet, as indicated in Figure 5.1(b), the dominating effect is the previously identified fall in the external borrowing of the government. Finally, real government consumption also falls. This mainly happens because of the reduced value of the available financing, but both the exchange rate depreciation and the higher domestic price level pull in the same direction, while the lower debt service on foreign debt reduces the need to cut government consumption slightly.

Comparing the results of the experiment in the RMSM and FP frameworks, it follows from the discussion above that most of the qualitative effects are the same. Government external borrowing, imports and real government consumption decrease, while the general price level goes up, and both models lead to a smaller public sector borrowing requirement. There are, however, differences in both the size of the effects and the channels through which they occur.

In Figure 5.2, the time paths of the government external debt following the exchange rate depreciation are shown, measured as percentage changes from base run levels. Although the external debt is falling continuously in both models, it has by year six fallen by around 31 per cent in the RMSM, but only by around 27 per cent in the FP framework. Returning to Figure 5.1, the explanation of this deviation is that the fall in imports, which takes place in both models, leads to a fall in the required international reserve accumulation in the RMSM, but not in the FP model.

Despite this effect of differences in model specifications, it should probably not be over emphasized. Although international reserves are specified exogenously as a target variable in the FP framework, it would not represent a fundamental break with the approach to specify it as a target in terms of import values as in the RMSM. Similarly, the international reserves could be treated as an exogenous variable in the RMSM model as discussed in Chapter 4.

A more significant deviation is the difference between the two model approaches when it comes to the explanation of the fall in real government consumption. Figure 5.3 reveals that government consumption declines almost equally in both models and is down by 6 per cent in the sixth year. Yet in the RMSM, this reduction is caused by the fall in imports and the constraint imposed by the material balance, whereas it is a consequence of reduced government deficit finance in the FP framework. The similarity of the net

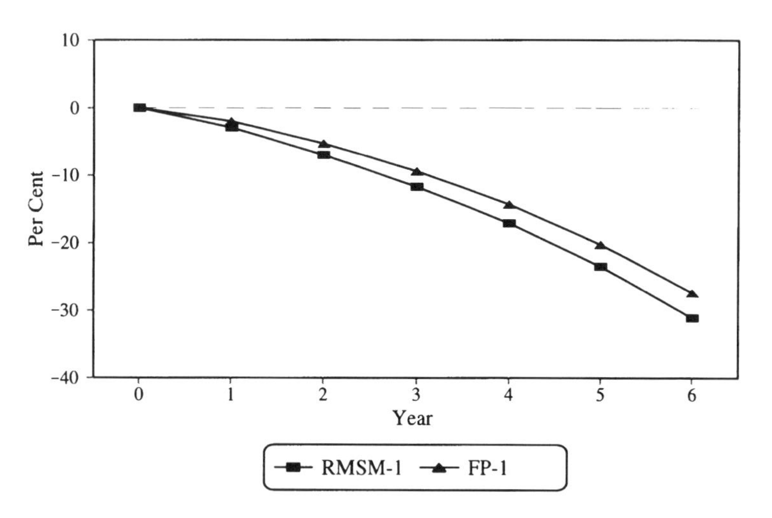

Figure 5.2 Experiment 1: Government foreign debt (deviation from base run)

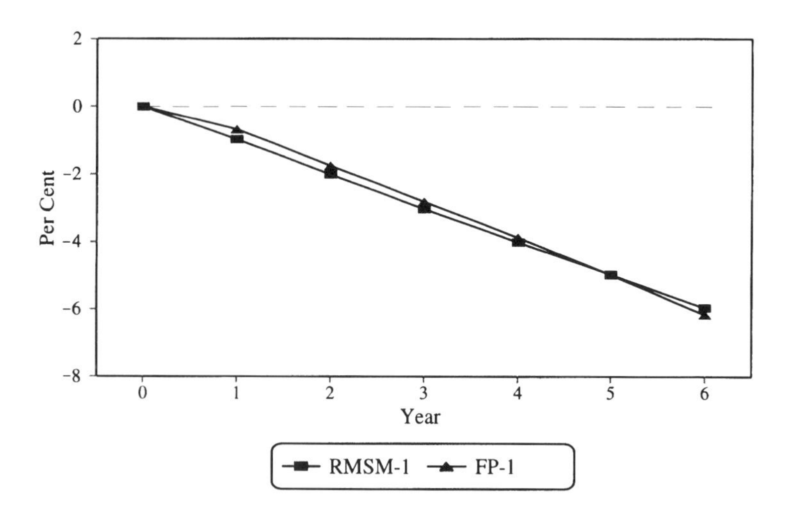

Figure 5.3 Experiment 1: Real government consumption (deviation from base run)

results is due to the fact that the dominating effect in both models works through the balance of payments. Thus, the reduction in real government consumption is caused mainly by the fall in imports in the RMSM, whereas it is the subsequent fall in government external borrowing that plays the dominating role in the FP.

This completes the description of the first experiment. Real government consumption was in focus, and this indicator generally reflects almost identical changes in the budget deficit. Since all other components of the government budget are effectively fixed in nominal or real terms, consumption must bear the main burden of adjustment within both models. However, the government could alternatively choose different patterns of adjustments such as, for example, changing its investments, transfer payments to the private sector or the revenue it raises from taxes. Although government consumption is used here as a measure of the overall state of the government budget, the exact use of available resources and the structure of the public budget will depend upon political decisions not discussed in this chapter.

EXPERIMENT 2: GOVERNMENT EXTERNAL BORROWING

In the alternative external model closure of the RMSM and FP frameworks, the exchange rate is endogenous while the net foreign debt of the government is fixed. This experiment will therefore analyse model responses to changes in net foreign debt of the government using this closure. In practice, the foreign currency value of the debt was fixed so its annual growth rate is approximately five percentage points higher than in the base run. Figure 5.4 shows causality diagrams for the two models in this experiment.

Comparing the causality diagrams for the two models with the corresponding diagrams in Figure 5.1, there are several similarities, although the changes of all variables have the opposite sign due to the experiment design. In the RMSM, increased external borrowing by the government requires an appreciation of the exchange rate in order to reestablish the balance of payments through increased imports and reserve accumulation. The dominating consequences of the increased imports are a rise in real government consumption and a deterioration of the public budget. Real government consumption increases also in the FP framework in this experiment,

(a) RMSM–2

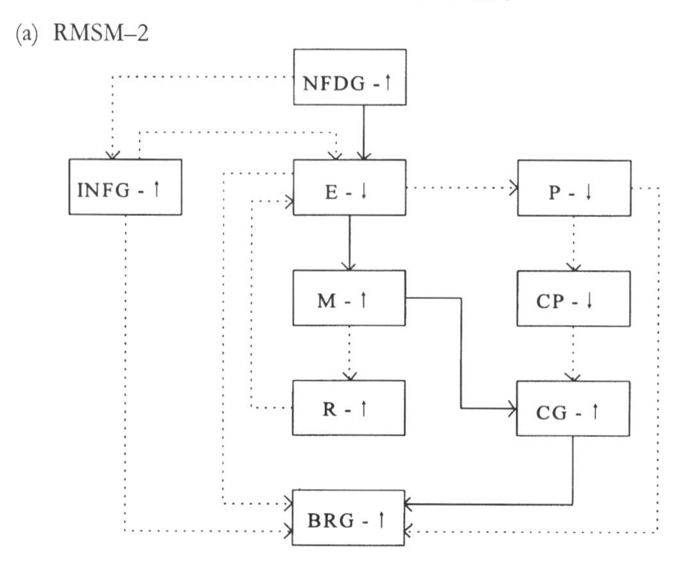

(b) FP–2

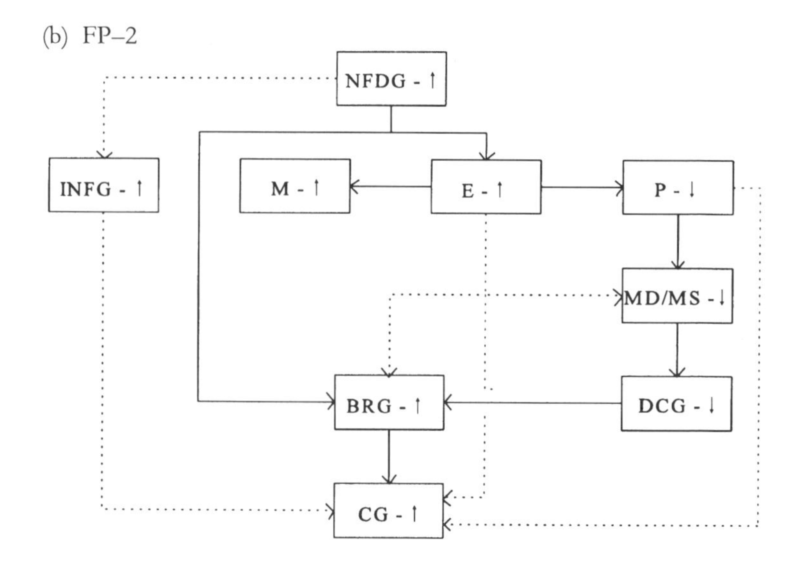

Figure 5.4 Experiment 2: Causality structures with exogenous government foreign debt

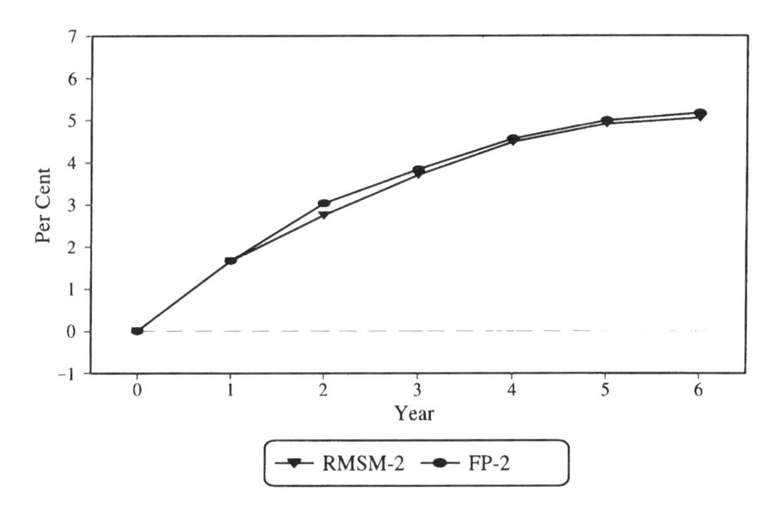

Figure 5.5 Experiment 2: Real government consumption (deviation from base run)

but the linkage is more direct as the increased borrowing in itself enables the expansion of government consumption.

Figure 5.5 shows for both models the changes in real government consumption relative to its base run levels, and the similarity between the two curves is notable. Also the gradual increase in government consumption as compared to the base run stands out. This is, however, an outcome caused by the base run profile of government external debt and the experiment design in combination. The net foreign debt of the government is increasing in the base run, which implies that increases in its growth rate result in the absolute annual changes getting larger over time. Moreover, since government consumption in both models depends on government borrowing, i.e. the flow equivalent of debt, this variable must also gradually increase more as compared to the base run as time progresses.

Whereas the remaining effects of the experiment follow directly from the descriptions of Experiment 1, the difference between the RMSM and FP frameworks in their specification of international reserves is illustrated in Figure 5.6. As mentioned above, the changes in reserves depend on import changes in the RMSM, while the stock of reserves is exogenous in the FP framework. Both results are included in the figure together with the reserve to import ratio from the base run. First, it can be noted that

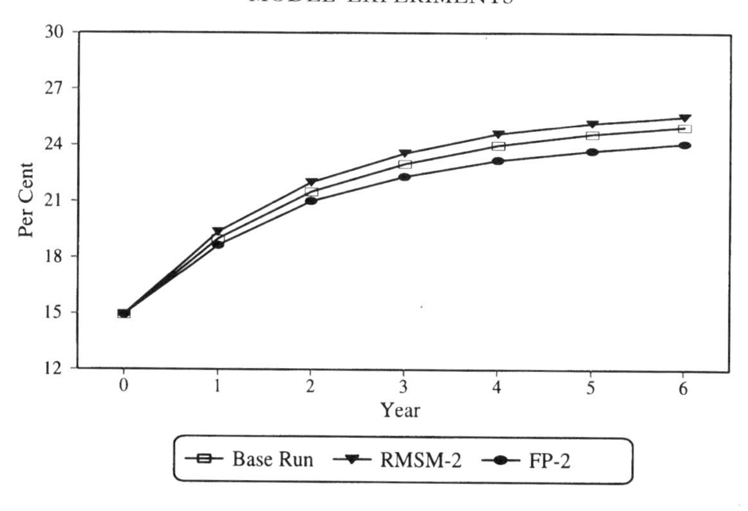

Figure 5.6 Experiment 2: International reserves (per cent of import value)

international reserves are accumulated quite rapidly in the first three years of the base run in order to reach a targeted level of 25 per cent of the import value, corresponding to three months' worth of imports. Second, the figure shows that the reserve to import ratio exceeds its base run level in the RMSM, and this result is once more caused by a combination of model specification and the profile of base run data. Since the RMSM links the change in reserves to the change in import value, the fast accumulation of reserves in the beginning of the period implies that an extra unit of imports is followed by extra reserves, which exceed the 25 per cent level. In fact, the choice of parameter values in the base run implies a marginal reserve accumulation amounting to almost 50 per cent of the import increase in the first year. Although a rather technical feature, it does affect the results here as well as in the following. The third feature revealed by Figure 5.6 is that the fixed international reserves in the FP framework imply a falling ratio of reserves to import values when the latter increases.

EXPERIMENT 3: FOREIGN RESERVES

Whereas the two experiments described so far were specific to the chosen model closure, the remaining experiments are carried out in the RMSM as well as the FP framework using both closures. In the first of these experiments, the effects of higher international reserves are analysed. Focus will in particular be on the importance of the choice of external closure, but other differences in the specifications of the RMSM and FP frameworks will also be highlighted.

The international reserve is a target variable in the financial programming framework, so it is straightforward to implement the experiment as an increase of 10 per cent in the target value for all years of the forecast horizon. This experiment design implies that most of the necessary adjustment takes place in the first year, where reserves are accumulated to reach the new required level, cf Figure 5.7. In the RMSM, the experiment implementation is different since the international reserve is an endogenous variable, linked to the foreign currency value of imports. Hence, it was decided to specify the experiment as a first year decrease in the ratio of import change to reserve change. The new value of the ratio was selected such that the reserves would be 10 per cent higher as compared to the base run value, given unchanged imports. If all variables maintained their base run values during the forecast horizon, this experiment would approximate the FP equivalent. Yet changes occur during the period, and

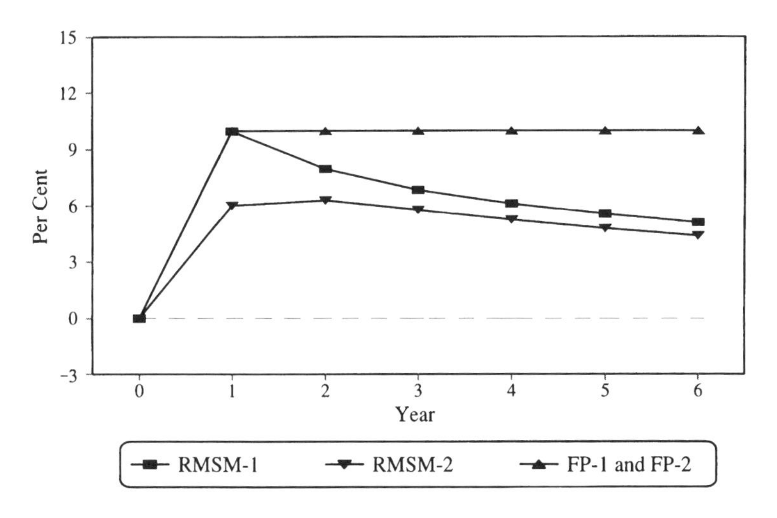

Figure 5.7 Experiment 3: Foreign reserves (deviation from base run)

the implied changes in international reserves are shown in Figure 5.7 for all four versions of the experiment.

Whereas the experiment in the FP framework results in international reserves that are in every year 10 per cent higher than their base run value, increases are in general smaller in the RMSM. In RMSM-1, where the exchange rate is exogenous, this is, however, caused by experiment design rather than by differences in model specification. Since there are increasing international reserves in the base run as the import value increases over time, the annual reserve accumulation required to maintain a constant ratio of reserves to import value also grows over time. Yet the required reserve accumulations are unchanged in this experiment, except in the first year, and they will consequently be smaller relative to the stock in the experiment than in the base run. The percentage increase in the stock of international reserves will therefore decline over time as reflected by the profile of the RMSM-1 curve in the figure. Finally, the figure shows that international reserves in all years increase by less than 10 per cent as compared to their base run level in the RMSM-2 version of the experiment. The reasons for this will become clear in the following.

Returning now to a more thorough description of experiment outcomes in the various model versions, they are particularly simple in RMSM-1 where the exchange rate is kept fixed and external borrowing by the government is endogenous. Hence, the need to accumulate reserves is met by increased government borrowing, cf Figure 5.8, and in the first year, the additional borrowing precisely matches the change in international reserves. Increased government debt does, however, lead to higher interest payments in the following years, thus further expanding external borrowing. Nevertheless, the figure shows that the resulting external debt of the government converges to its base run level from the second year. This profile of the change in government external debt is caused by the base run developments of imports and foreign debt, and the actual path taken should be interpreted carefully. Apart from the changes in net government foreign debt and interest payments, the only other affected variable is the government budget deficit, which grows due to higher debt service.

Using the alternative closure with fixed government external borrowing and an endogenous exchange rate, the effects of the higher reserve requirement become more interesting, since additions to the international reserves cannot be offset by similar

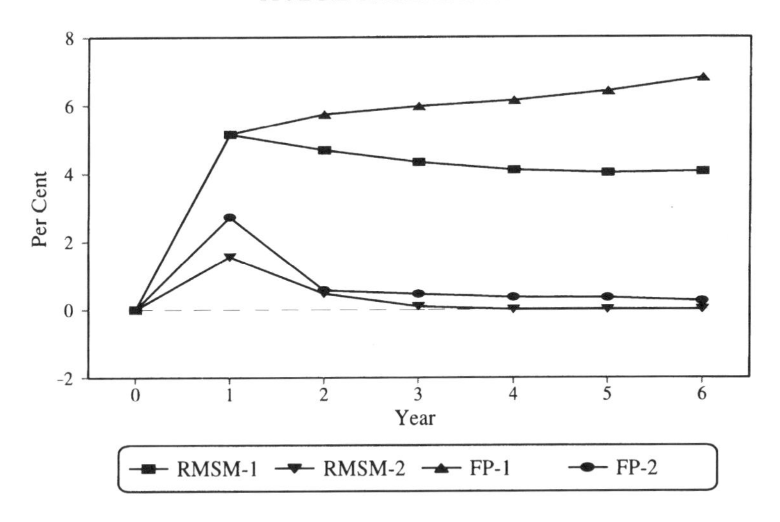

Figure 5.8 Experiment 3: Exchange rate and government foreign debt (deviation from base run)

Note: For RMSM-1 and FP-1, the figure shows the percentage deviations of government net foreign debt, whereas it is the percentage changes in the exchange rate shown for RMSM-2 and FP-2.

increases in government borrowing. Instead the exchange rate depreciates, as shown in Figure 5.8, in order to maintain the balance of payments through a reduction in imports. The fall in imports has two additional effects. First, it reduces the required international reserves by less than the initial increase, so the net effect becomes an increase of around 6 per cent in the first year, cf Figure 5.7. Second, lower imports imply that fewer commodities are available for domestic absorption, so government consumption has to go down. This process is reinforced by a small expansion in private consumption caused by increased nominal GDP, which follows from the exchange rate depreciation and subsequent general price level increase. The total effect of the experiment on real government consumption is a decline of 1.6 per cent in the first year as shown in Figure 5.9. The effects described so far relate mainly to the first year of the forecast horizon, but from the second year onwards the economy gradually converges to its base run path. Accordingly, the changes of all real variables are virtually zero from year four as can be seen in Figures 5.8 and 5.9,

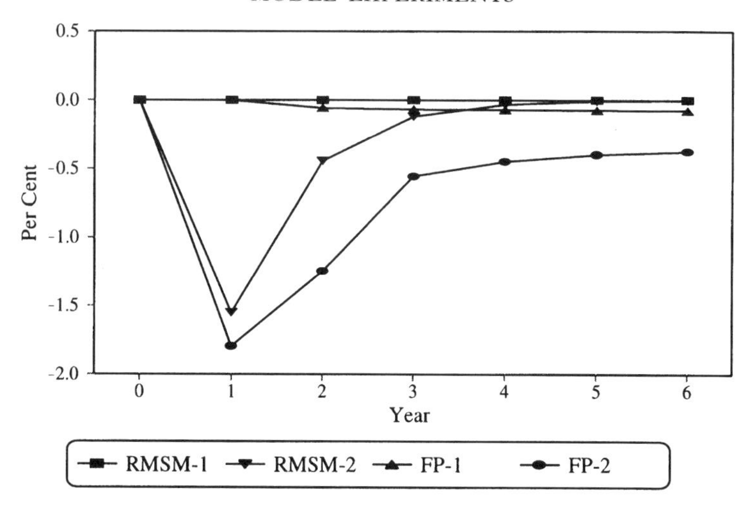

Figure 5.9 Experiment 3: Real government consumption (deviation from base run)

and only the international reserves continue to deviate from their base run level, cf Figure 5.7.

The effects of higher international reserve requirements are small in the FP framework when the exchange rate is exogenous, as was the case in the RMSM. Thus, increases in international reserves are offset by more government external borrowing. This does not, however, lead to increased government consumption as the higher international reserves need to be countered by a similar reduction in government credit in order to maintain money supply at the level dictated by money demand. Although this in principle should neutralize any effect on government consumption, Figure 5.9 shows a small drop in real government consumption. This is caused by the term in the money supply equation that takes care of the changed rand valuation of international reserves. Since the stock of reserves has grown and the exchange rate depreciates in the base run, further reductions in government credit and consequently in consumption are necessary. It was argued in Chapter 4 that this term in the money supply function can be omitted if it is assumed that capital gains are not realized by the holders of international reserves. Figure 5.9 confirms also the point made in Chapter 4 that the importance of the valuation term is modest in the context of this study.

The last version of the experiment is made using the FP framework in its standard set-up with endogenous exchange rate and fixed government external borrowing. One effect of increasing international reserves is once again a decrease in government credit through the money supply equation. However, under the present closure, additional reserves cannot be accumulated by more government external borrowing. Instead the necessary current account improvement is obtained by an exchange rate depreciation and lower imports, just as in the RMSM-2. As shown in Figure 5.8, the required depreciation is larger in the FP framework than in the RMSM because there is no linkage between international reserves and imports. The second important effect in this experiment is the contraction of government credit occurring for the same reason as in FP-1. Increased international reserves cause a reduction in domestic credit to maintain the money supply at the level of money demand. This variable expands slightly, however, as the exchange rate depreciation implies a modest increase in the general price level. This effect, as well as the higher rand value of foreign borrowing by the government, has the opposite effect on the nominal budget deficit. However, both effects are small, and a budget improvement is therefore necessary, leading to a compression of real government consumption in the first year, cf Figure 5.9.

The most interesting feature apparent in Figure 5.9 is probably how the change in real government consumption depends more on the choice of model closure than on the choice of model. When the exchange rate is exogenous, hardly any change is required in government consumption in either model, while an endogenous exchange rate framework leads to an initial fall in response to the increased foreign reserves in both the RMSM and FP. Moreover, the basic profiles of the responses are similar.

EXPERIMENT 4: DOMESTIC INFLATION

Like international reserves, the domestic inflation rate is a standard target in the FP framework, and in Experiment 4 the annual inflation rate was increased from its base run level of 6 per cent to 8 per cent. Figure 5.10 reveals that the choice of model closure has again a significant impact on the result. Real government consumption expands in both the FP and RMSM frameworks, when the exchange rate is maintained at its base run level, whereas

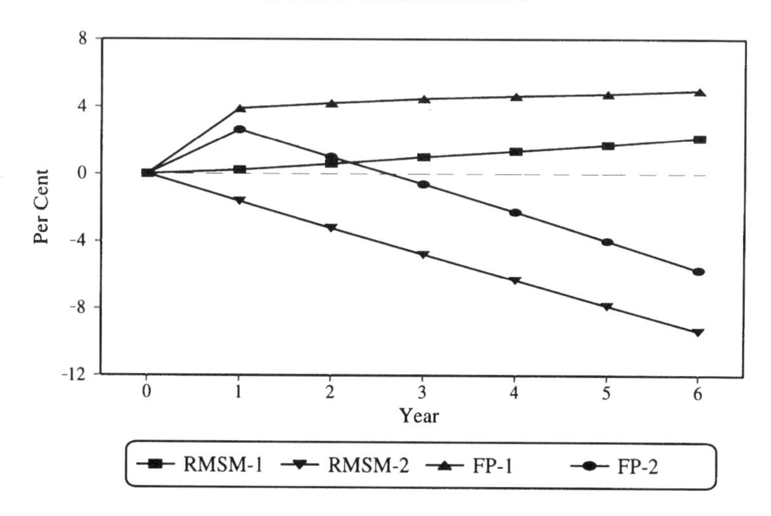

Figure 5.10 Experiment 4: Real government consumption (deviation from base run)

an endogenous exchange rate leads to falling government consumption in both models. Focus will first be put on the two cases with fixed exchange rates.

The first chain of effects of the increased inflation rate is almost identical in both models. Higher inflation implies deteriorating competitiveness and consequently more imported goods. By the sixth year, imports exceed their base run level by 8.5 per cent in both models. Higher imports require more external financing, and the public external debt has gone up by 53.7 per cent in the final year when the FP framework is used, and by 61.1 per cent in the RMSM. The difference is caused by the endogenous international reserves in the RMSM.

Besides this common effect, each model has one additional major line of effects. In the RMSM, this is that the private sector consumes more as higher domestic prices imply increased real disposable income because taxes, net of transfers from the government, are fixed in nominal terms. The larger supply of commodities resulting from increased imports is thus divided between private and government consumption, and in the sixth year the former has increased by 3.0 per cent and the latter by 2.1 per cent, cf Figure 5.10. Real government consumption also goes up in the FP framework, but the explanation is different, as it is the increased external borrowing of the public sector that directly enables it to expand consumption. Yet another effect is at work through the money market. Higher inflation increases the demand for money and consequently the ability of the monetary system to extend credit to the government. This source of deficit finance accounts for 1.2 per cent of GDP in the sixth year as compared to nothing in the base run. Similarly, the new external borrowing of the government is up to 4.3 per cent of GDP from 1.8 per cent. However, while the deficit finance obtained abroad increases gradually to this level, most of the adjustment in domestic credit finance occurs in the first year. This difference is reflected in Figure 5.10 where the curve for the FP framework, FP-1, jumps by almost four percentage points in the first year, while the increase is much slower afterwards. On the other hand, the RMSM-1 curve exhibits a gradual rise over the entire time horizon.

Turning now to the closure with endogenous exchange rate, Figure 5.10 shows that real government consumption declines in the medium-term in both models. Also the balance-of-payments effects of the experiment are the same. Thus, increased domestic inflation causes a matching depreciation of the exchange rate, leaving all components of the balance of payments unaltered in foreign currency values. In the RMSM, the only real effect is therefore that private consumption expands in response to higher real disposable income, which crowds out real government consumption. This effect cumulates progressively over time, and government consumption has fallen by 9.4 per cent in the sixth year. In the medium-term government consumption also falls in the financial programming framework, but initially it jumps to a level that is 2.6 per cent higher than in the base run. The explanation of this feature is as before found in the domestic money market, which responds instantaneously to the increased inflation level by enabling more credit to be extended to the government. However, the shift in the inflation level is transformed into a cumulative increase in the price level, so the government is forced to reduce its real consumption since the base run level cannot be sustained by the available increase in finance.

Focus has until now been on real consumption as far as the government is concerned. Although this is an important variable in any policy discussion, so is the government borrowing requirement, which together with the current account are key indicators of macroeconomic balance problems. In terms of the two models

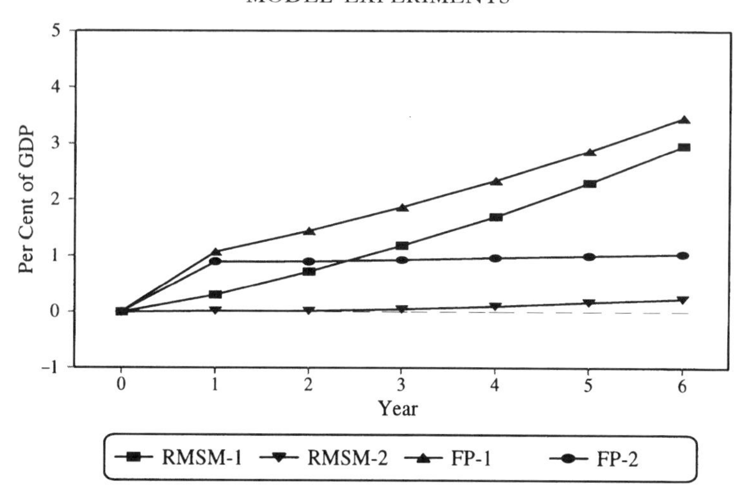

Figure 5.11 Experiment 4: Government borrowing requirement (deviation from base run)

applied in this study, Figure 5.11 clearly illustrates that government consumption is only one part of the story. Thus, the budget deficit measured in per cent of GDP deteriorates in all four versions of this experiment, despite the fall in real government consumption that occurred in both models when the exchange rate was assumed to be endogenous, i.e. RMSM-2 and FP-2.

Although the qualitative effects depend on whether government consumption or the budget deficit is considered, there are still notable similarities between Figures 5.10 and 5.11. First, the budget deficit increases more in the fixed exchange rate regime, which was also the closure that resulted in increased real government consumption. Second, the jump in government consumption which appeared in the first year of both financial programming experiments is mirrored in the budget deficit. Comparing all four versions of the experiment, the worst outcomes are obtained in the FP framework, which yields larger increases in the budget deficit as well as a higher level of government consumption than the corresponding RMSM versions of the experiment. This difference is due to the different reactions of the private sector to higher inflation in the two frameworks. In the RMSM the private sector expands consumption, thereby constraining the rise in government consumption. By contrast, in the FP framework it expands money demand, allowing more credit to be extended to the government sector. While this difference in specifications does influence the effects of all experiments in this chapter, it is especially important when the inflation rate is increased directly. In the other experiments, the general price level only changes in response to variations in the exchange rate, because the domestic price is maintained at its base run level. These price changes tend moreover to be relatively small and dominated by other linkages in the two frameworks. This observation implies that a fall in government consumption will generally lead to an improvement of the budget deficit.

EXPERIMENT 5: GDP GROWTH

The differences between the modelling approach taken in the RMSM and FP frameworks are clearly illustrated in this experiment, where the annual real GDP growth rate is increased by one percentage point in all years. Thus, real GDP is increased by 6 per cent in the sixth year as compared to the base run. In the RMSM, this was achieved by a uniform increase in the sectoral growth rates.

Figure 5.12 contains the causality structures of the two models in this experiment, when the exchange rate is exogenous. The figure immediately reveals that the story needed to explain the effects of higher growth is far more complicated in the RMSM than in the FP framework.

Higher GDP growth initially has three effects in the RMSM. Since an increase in real GDP corresponds to a rise in real income more imports are demanded, and private consumption increases. Moreover, the increase in GDP can only be realized through increased investments, which means more private investment as government capital formation is fixed in real terms. It is notable that the initial change in GDP and these three effects work in opposite directions as far as government consumption is concerned. In sum, total supply is increased, both through more domestic production and higher imports, and this leads to a higher level of real government consumption. This effect is countered, however, by the expansion in private sector absorption.

The net effect is that government consumption falls in the first year compared to its base run level, because the required change in investments occurs mainly as a shift in the investment level in the

(a) RMSM–1

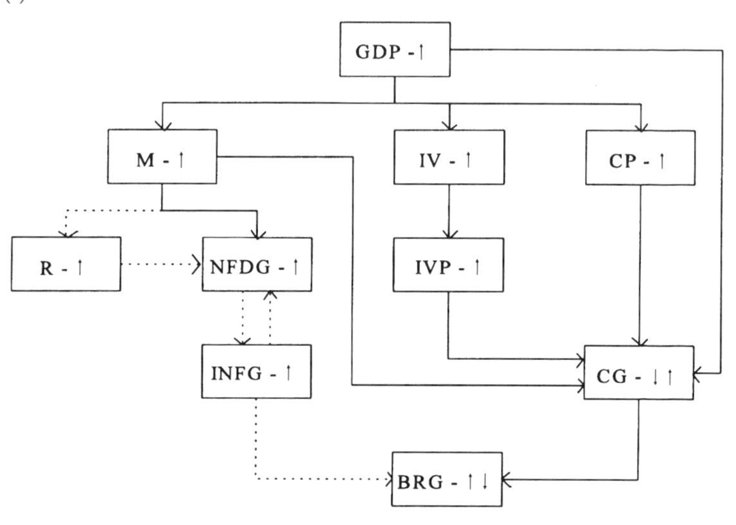

(b) FP–1

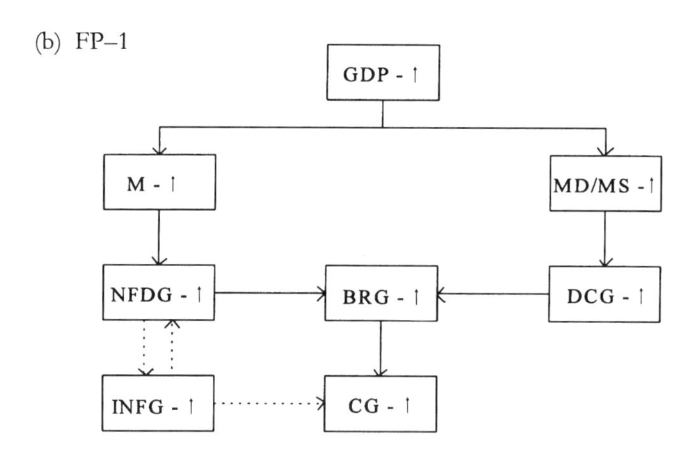

Figure 5.12 Experiment 5: Causality structures with exogenous exchange rate

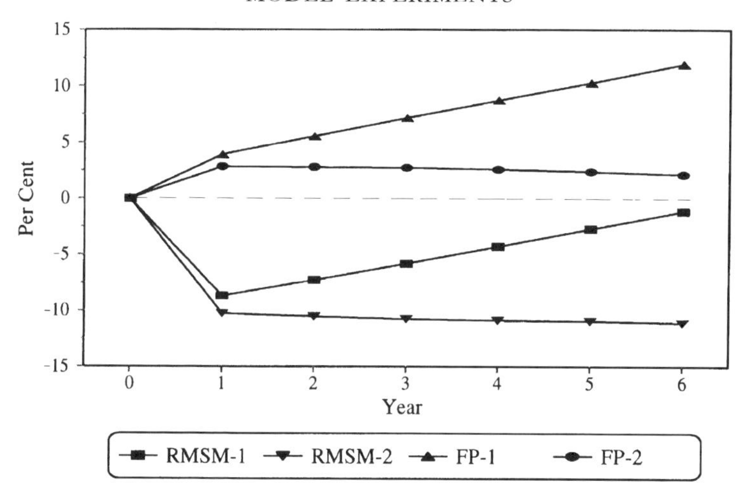

Figure 5.13 Experiment 5: Real government consumption (deviation from base run)

first year of the projection period. Therefore, the effects from increased domestic supply start to work from year two, and real government consumption has almost returned to its base run level in the final year, cf Figure 5.13. This qualitative shift in the change of government consumption is also found in the budget deficit, which improves in terms of GDP in each of the first five years, but is higher in the sixth year. Finally, the growth experiment also results in the by now familiar effect working through the balance of payments. Higher imports and the associated increase in international reserves are financed by more government borrowing, which leads to additional interest payments.

Turning to the FP framework, the first effect of higher GDP growth is an expansion of the demand for money. This enables the government to extract more domestic credit without changing the rate of inflation. Second, more import follows from the increased GDP, and since it is financed through government borrowing, this further increases the amount of finance available for the government. Consequently, government consumption increases in all years. Although the gap between the curves for the two models appears to be converging slowly, the FP framework results in a substantially higher level of government consumption. Since GDP and imports increase by the same amount, and as real government investments are identical in the two models, absorption by the private sector must be compressed more in the FP framework than in the RMSM. Consequently, if the investment hypothesis of the RMSM is accepted, private consumption will implicitly be lower in the FP framework than in the RMSM.

Figure 5.13 shows that the medium-term effect on government consumption of higher growth changes substantially when the external closure is altered, and the foreign debt of government is maintained at its base run level. The relative change of government consumption is almost the same from the second year onwards, and this is so both in the RMSM and the FP framework. This can be compared with the result under the fixed exchange rate regime, where government consumption increased more in real terms as time progressed. The explanation for this difference follows directly from the causality diagrams in Figure 5.12, since the increase in domestic commodity supply is not supported by more imports when the net foreign borrowing of the government is fixed. Instead, the required adjustment of the balance of payments is obtained through a depreciation of the exchange rate. Apart from this major difference in the results under the alternative closures, the remaining effects, illustrated in Figure 5.12, are generally the same, although some additional effects arise when the exchange rate depreciates and the price level changes. They will not, however, be described further, because they appeared in a similar way in the previous experiments and are relatively small.

Although not obvious from the discussion so far, this experiment implicitly reveals an important feature of the RMSM through the initial negative relationship between GDP and government consumption. If the RMSM instead had been closed in a Keynesian fashion with exogenous government consumption and GDP as an endogenous variable, an exogenous increase in government consumption, or any other component of autonomous demand, would lead to a fall in GDP. This result is, of course, opposite to the outcome in macro models based on Keynesian macroeconomics, but complies with growth models in the tradition of Harrod-Domar, Solow and others. The difference in model results depends on the difference in the marginal saving and investment responses to increases in output. Thus, if the marginal savings rate exceeds the marginal investment rate, then there would be a positive relationship between autonomous spending and GDP, and *vice versa*. It can therefore be concluded that the RMSM as a growth programming framework exhibits some of the features normally associated with economic growth theory.

EXPERIMENT 6: EXPORT QUANTITY VERSUS EXPORT PRICE

The differences between the two models as well as between the two external closures have been discussed in detail in relation to the previous experiments, so the sixth and last experiment has a different layout. What will be done is to compare the outcomes of changes in the export quantity and the price of exports, respectively. Yet, both experiments will only be analysed using the RMSM with endogenous exchange rate. The effects of the alternative experiment versions, which can be seen in Table 5.1, follow directly from the discussions above and in this section.

The experiment with increased export quantity (RMSM-2) was implemented as a one percentage point addition to the annual growth rate of all export categories, whereas the export price experiment (RMSM-1) consisted of a one percentage point increase in the annual growth of the export price index. Therefore, the two experiments resulted in approximately the same expansion of export revenue, valued in foreign currency. This implies that the balance-of-payments effects of the two experiments are almost identical, and the increased export revenue leads to an appreciation of the exchange rate and an increase in imports, which in the sixth year are approximately 5.5 per cent larger than in the base run.

The interesting features concern, therefore, the domestic variables, and the changes in private and government consumption are shown in Figure 5.14 and 5.15, respectively. Beginning with the rise in export quantity, total domestic supply is almost unchanged in the experiment as exports and imports are increased by the same amount. However, the exchange rate appreciation feeds into falling domestic prices, which through the consumption function causes a decrease in real private consumption, cf Figure 5.14, leaving more goods for government consumption. Figure 5.15 reveals at the same time that the modest decline in domestic supply occurring in the beginning of the period dominates this effect, causing real government consumption to go down as well. As time passes, the fall in private consumption becomes larger, and government consumption increases compared with its base run level.

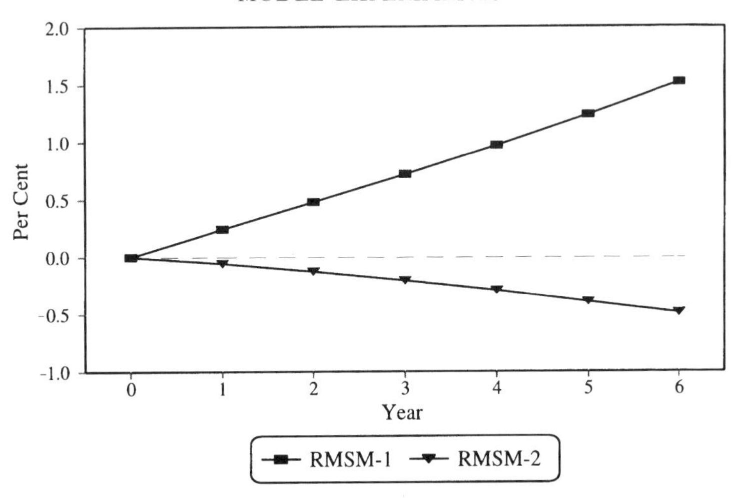

Figure 5.14 Experiment 6: Real private consumption (deviation from base run)

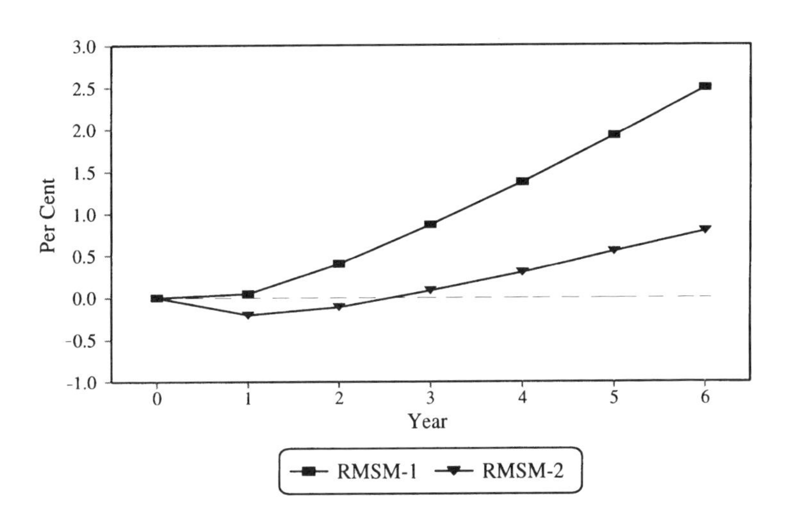

Figure 5.15 Experiment 6: Real government consumption (deviation from base run)

Turning to the export price experiment, the key difference relative to the increased export quantity is that the increase in imports translates into more domestic supply, enabling simultaneous increases in government and private consumption. Since government consumption is determined residually, it needs to be explained why private consumption goes up, contrary to what happened in the export quantity experiment. First, private consumption is once more affected negatively by the fall in domestic prices, occurring because of the exchange rate appreciation. However, there is now an additional effect working in the opposite direction, namely increased gross domestic income induced by improved terms-of-trade resulting from higher export prices. This effect dominates the effect originating from the fall in prices, and private consumption increases, cf Figure 5.14. There is, however, still room for an expansion of government consumption, as is evident from Figure 5.15.

CONCLUSION

The aim of this chapter was to demonstrate how the FP and RMSM frameworks work in terms of economic transmission mechanisms. Although other experiments could have been investigated, most would have effects that are qualitatively identical to those described above in one or more experiments. Table 5.1 summarizes the central effects of experiments reviewed in this chapter as well as of some additional experiments. These experiments were chosen with the construction of two alternative scenarios in mind. Thus, most exogenous variables and parameters for which experiments were carried out appear among the changing assumptions used to generate the optimistic and pessimistic scenarios presented in Chapter 7.

The experiments show, first, that the results depend crucially on the choice of model closure. Several qualitative effects have different signs under the alternative closures. Hence, it is important to be aware that the FP framework is normally presented with endogenous exchange rate, while the standard version of the RMSM assumes an exogenous exchange rate. Second, the models generally yield similar qualitative results, but the channels are different, and the quantitative effects often deviate substantially. It can also be emphasized once more that both modelling frameworks, as illustrated by the causality diagrams, are very simple. This

Table 5.1 Central qualitative effects of experiments

	Net government external debt	*Nominal exchange rate*	*General price level*	*Private consumption*	*Government consumption*	*Government budget*	*Current account*
	(Foreign currency)			*(Constant rand)*	*(Constant rand)*	*(Per cent of GDP)*	*(Per cent of GDP)*
1 Exchange rate depreciation							
RMSM-1	−		+	+	−	+	+
FP-1	−		+		−	+	+
2 Increased net government foreign debt							
RMSM-1		−	−	−	+	−	−
FP-1		−	−		+	−	−
3 Increased foreign reserves							
RMSM-1	+		0	0	0	−	−
RMSM-2		+/0	+/0	+/0	−/0	+	+/0
FP-1	+		0		−	−	0
FP-2		+	+		−	+	+
4 Increased domestic inflation							
RMSM-1	+		+	+	+	−	−
RMSM-2		+	+	+	−	−	0
FP-1	+		+		+	−	−
FP-2		+	+		+/−	−	0

5 Increased GDP growth							
RMSM-1	+		0	+	−/+	+/−	−
RMSM-2		+	+	+	−	+	−
FP-1	+		0		+	−	−
FP-2		+	+		+	−	−
6 Increased export growth							
RMSM-1	−		0	0	−	+	+
RMSM-2		−	−	−	−/+	+	+
FP-1	−		0		−	+	+
FP-2		−	−		−/+	+	+
7 Increased export price							
RMSM-1	−		0	+	−	+	+
RMSM-2		−	−	+	+	+/−	+
FP-1	−		0		−	+	+
FP-2		−	−		−/+	+	+

Table 5.1 continued

	Net government external debt	*Nominal exchange rate*	*General price level*	*Private consumption*	*Government consumption*	*Government budget*	*Current account*
	(Foreign currency)			*(Constant rand)*	*(Constant rand)*	*(Per cent of GDP)*	*(Per cent of GDP)*
8 Increased public investments							
RMSM-1	0		0	0	0	–	0
RMSM-2		0	0	0	0	–	0
FP-1	0		0		–	0	0
FP-2		0	0		–	0	0
9 Increased tax revenue							
RMSM-1	0		0	–	+	+	0
RMSM-2		0	0	–	+	+	0
FP-1	0		0		+	0	0
FP-2		0	0		+	0	0
10 Increased private foreign debt							
RMSM-1	–		0	0	0	+	0
RMSM-2		–	–	–	+	–	–
FP-1	–		0		–	+	0
FP-2		–	–		–/+	+	–

11 Increased private credit							
FP-1	0		0		−	+	0
FP-2		0	0		−	+	0
12 Increased money velocity							
FP-1	0		0		−	+	0
FP-2		0	0		−	+	0
13 Inc. constant in investment							
RMSM-1	0		0	0	−	+	0
RMSM-2		0	0	0	−	+	0
14 Increased savings propensity							
RMSM-1	0		0	−	+	−	0
RMSM-2		0	0	−	+	−	0

Notes: + indicates increases, which particularly means larger government budget and current account surpluses
− indicates decreases
+/− indicates increase initially followed by decreases, and similarly for other combinations
0 indicates no change
blank when variable non-existent or exogenous in the applied model set-up

implies necessarily that many important economic linkages are absent. This relates not only to the relatively limited sets of variables, appearing in each of the two models, but also to the relationships lacking among variables that are actually present. Chapter 4 reviewed the most crucial omissions, but the experiments in this chapter have demonstrated that neither the FP framework nor the RMSM are very suitable for applied policy analysis. It would, for example, be hard to justify the quantitative results of the exchange rate experiment as even an approximation to what would happen if South Africa was to devalue the rand. Nonetheless, the experiments provide illustrations of some of the central economic transmission mechanisms that should be taken into consideration by any policy-maker. Moreover, the combined structure of the FP and RMSM frameworks can be used for constructing consistent scenarios, as demonstrated in the following two chapters.

6

BASE RUN

BACKGROUND

Restraint cannot by itself restructure the economy of South Africa and ensure social stability in the transition phase. Nevertheless, it is equally correct, as pointed out in Chapter 2, that unless the much needed redistribution and satisfaction of basic human needs go hand in hand with renewed growth, the necessary increase in the purchasing power of the African population cannot take place. The base run put forward in this chapter therefore involves a shift to a new growth path. Hence, it is assumed that South Africa will be able to pursue a successful growth strategy. Higher growth requires as a critical precondition a substantial increase in existing physical capital as well as investments in human resource development. Consequently, domestic savings–investment balances are bound to come under pressure in the medium-term, in particular since the government must play an active role in the transition and restructuring process. South Africa will therefore have to rely on foreign savings. Nevertheless, the base run demonstrates that such a result is not in contradiction with the goal of keeping macro-economic balances in check provided the underlying moderately optimistic assumptions are fulfilled.

The base run was composed from projections generated within the FP and RMSM frameworks. Yet it is highlighted that these two pillars of the joint base run were developed in an iterative and consistent manner. Hence, all variables which appear in both models have the same value in the two original projections, although some minor differences occur due to rounding. Moreover, values of the exogenous variables were selected in a way which leads to reasonable projections in the medium-term. Yet as

Table 6.1 Parameter values in base run

Parameter	*Symbol*	*Year 0*	*Year 1*	*Year 2*	*Year 3*	*Year 4*	*Year 5*	*Year 6*
Investment – constant	$\kappa 0$	0.142	0.124	0.135	0.140	0.142	0.142	0.142
Capital–output ratio	$\kappa 1$	2.25	2.25	2.25	2.25	2.25	2.25	2.25
Import – constant	$\alpha 0$	−2.74	−2.69	−2.66	−2.64	−2.64	−2.64	−2.64
Import – GDP elas.	$\alpha 1$	1.20	1.20	1.20	1.20	1.20	1.20	1.20
Import – RER elas.	$\alpha 2$	−0.73	−0.73	−0.73	−0.73	−0.73	−0.73	−0.73
Savings propensity	β	0.227	0.230	0.233	0.236	0.240	0.243	0.245
Reserve–import ratio	δ	3.36	2.01	2.23	2.49	2.66	3.05	3.28
Weight in price index	θ	0.20	0.20	0.20	0.20	0.20	0.20	0.20
Velocity of money	ν	1.78	1.78	1.78	1.78	1.78	1.78	1.78

some of the chosen values would imply rather large changes as compared with the base year, they were phased in gradually over the time horizon studied.

Only summary results are presented in this chapter, but detailed results are available in the tables in Appendix B. The base year appears as *Year 0*, and these data are actual historical data, while *Years 1–6* refer to the medium-term six-year forecasting horizon. Reference is made to *Years 1–6* rather than to years 1995–2000 as this book is concerned with the transition to a new growth path rather than focused on short-run fluctuations around medium-term trends. Consequently, the base run data for *Year 1* were, in particular, chosen with a view to incorporating already known developments in 1995 as well as to ensure a smooth transition to medium-term paths. Similarly, the base run values of all model parameters, defined in Chapter 4, are summarized in Table 6.1. They were either based on outside information or calibrated from the base year data described in Chapter 3. Some parameters were, however, adjusted during the forecast horizon of the models to generate a reasonable base run as discussed in detail below.

DEMAND AND SUPPLY

Projecting real output growth is complex in the South African case, for political and economic reasons. Some improvement due to efficiency gains and the return to a more stable political environment can be expected. However, substantial and sustainable growth, which is socially equitable, presupposes as noted above not only an increase in existing physical capital, but also investments in broad based human resource development. By their very nature, such investments have a long gestation period. Thus, even if human capital investments are of strategic importance in the longer term in South Africa, as elsewhere, they are unlikely to yield immediate results. Moreover, while private sector confidence and investments are expected to continue recuperating, political and economic uncertainties are bound to persist for some time to come and will only gradually give way to a more stable environment.

In sum, there seems to be widespread agreement that annual GDP growth of around 3.5 per cent is a likely outcome in the medium-term in South Africa (McGrath and Holden, 1994). Consequently, this rate was relied on in the construction of the base run. It was, in addition, assumed that this GDP growth level is

Table 6.2 Material balance (real annual growth rates)

Variable	*Symbol*	*Year 1*	*Year 2*	*Year 3*	*Year 4*	*Year 5*	*Year 6*
Consumption	C	2.8	3.2	3.1	3.1	3.1	3.1
Private	CP	3.1	2.8	2.6	2.4	2.4	2.7
Government	CG	2.0	4.0	4.5	5.0	5.0	4.0
Investments	IV	15.1	9.0	6.1	4.2	3.5	3.5
Private	IVP	16.8	9.7	6.6	4.3	3.5	3.5
Government	IVG	2.0	2.5	3.0	3.5	3.5	3.5
Exports	X	3.0	4.0	4.5	5.0	5.5	5.5
Imports	M	10.0	7.5	5.6	4.2	4.2	4.2
GDP	GDP	3.5	3.5	3.5	3.5	3.5	3.5

reached in the first year as shown in Table 6.2, which is based on values in constant 1994 rand. The table also provides a summary of the South African material balance as projected in this volume, and the aggregate GDP growth prediction, which forms part of the base run, is consistent with the sectoral real growth rates presented in Table 6.3.

It can be seen from Table 6.3 that the output of the mining sector remains at its base year level, while agriculture was set to grow at a slower rate than overall GDP. Other sectors were estimated to grow in parallel with the aggregate rate. By contrast, a relative expansion of the manufacturing category was assumed. The rationale behind this assessment of sectoral perspectives is two-fold. Existing structural problems are severe in agriculture and mining, and it is expected that they will constrain future growth relatively more than is the case on average. Furthermore, it is generally assumed in this study that growth will have to have a manufacturing base, and that expansion in the other sectors category must be close to average GDP as this sector accounted for two thirds of GDP in the base year.

Table 6.3 Sectoral GDP (real annual growth rates)

Variable	*Symbol*	*Year 1*	*Year 2*	*Year 3*	*Year 4*	*Year 5*	*Year 6*
Agriculture	AGR	2.5	2.5	2.5	2.5	2.5	2.5
Mining	MIN	0.0	0.0	0.0	0.0	0.0	0.0
Manufacturing	MAN	5.0	5.0	5.0	5.0	5.0	5.0
Other sectors	OTH	3.5	3.5	3.5	3.4	3.4	3.4
GDP	GDP	3.5	3.5	3.5	3.5	3.5	3.5

For the above reasons, the first two sectors mentioned are bound to grow at a rate which is lower than is the case in the remainder of the economy. The actual choice of growth rate for the other sectors was calculated on a residual basis in order to ensure consistency with overall growth. Finally, the different sectoral growth rates will modify the sectoral composition of GDP over the period considered, so the distribution in the final year is as follows: agriculture 4.1 per cent, mining 6.5 per cent, manufacturing 23.7 per cent, and other sectors 65.7 per cent.

The elasticities, which appear in the import function as shown in Table 6.1, are both based on estimates presented in Kahn *et al.* (1992). The real exchange rate elasticity was adopted directly, while it was decided for the purpose of this study to increase the GDP elasticity from the estimated value of 1.13 to 1.20. One justification for this adjustment is that the original estimation period includes the years from 1985 when sanctions were in place. It can therefore be argued that involuntary import compression caused a downward bias in the estimate. Moreover, real imports were as shown in Table 6.1 given an additional boost during the first few years of the base run projection through increases in the constant in the import equation. The value of the constant in the base year was calibrated from 1994 data, but the adjustment is sensible in view of the widely recognized and severely pressing rehabilitation needs, and the fact that the existing import protective system is being reformed in accordance with the General Agreement on Tariffs and Trade (GATT) (Hirsch, 1994). In sum, real imports are growing, with 10 per cent in the first year falling gradually to an annual increase of 4.2 per cent. As a share of GDP, imports rise from 21.7 per cent in the base year to 25.0 per cent at the end of the forecasting period.

It cannot be expected that South Africa will be able to replicate the performance of the Newly Industrializing Countries (NICs) in the immediate future. South African industries will have to undergo a major and difficult overhaul to become competitive, and one of the most significant effects of the GATT Agreement on South Africa is that export subsidies are to be phased out, including the General Export Incentive Scheme. Moreover, it is by no means certain that international markets will be buoyant in general, so the process of reviving exports is bound to be gradual at best.

This is underlined by the fact that the importance of structural and demand related problems in the various sectors should – as already alluded to – not be underestimated. While mining is an important source of foreign exchange, it is an extremely vulnerable sector, and technological constraints are becoming increasingly severe, as extraction has to take place deeper down. Agriculture is largely uncompetitive in international markets in a number of major crops, and will not be able to compete without substantial investment and a completely modified system of economic incentives.

Manufactured exports performed well during the 1980s with annual growth rates reaching a level of 10 per cent in some years, and as such, manufactured exports have increased their importance in the South African economy. Yet a major factor behind this development was declining domestic demand and accompanying low rates of capacity utilization. Contrary to this, local demand for manufactured products can be expected to grow significantly during the coming years. Finally, international competition has by no means become less stringent over the past decade.

For these reasons, annual growth in export quantity was assumed to increase gradually from 3 per cent in the first year to 5.5 per cent in the last year of the forecasting period as shown in Table 6.2. This reflects a respectable average rate of increase of 4.6 per cent, and in the base run real exports therefore increase from 23.6 per cent of GDP in the base year to 25.2 per cent at the end of the period.

The procedure followed in disaggregating the overall export performance was similar to the procedure used in disaggregating GDP growth. More specifically, it was assumed in Table 6.4 that agricultural and gold exports grow at rates below average. Basic metals and minerals, however, may grow more or less around average growth if the present policy of adding value to South Africa's natural resource products through further beneficiation (such as in the area of stainless steel) starts giving results. Whether this potential will be realized depends on growth in global primary product demand, and it must be acknowledged that the present situation is not particularly encouraging given the existing sluggish demand and excess capacity. However, a moderately optimistic position is taken here. Finally, calculating the growth rates for other exports on a residual basis, it follows that they must generate a significant contribution. This is consistent with the interpretation that the engine of future exports must be located in manufactured exports, which make up the major part of other exports. This underlines the need to address the structural problems of this sector as a matter of urgency.

Table 6.4 Export (real annual growth rates)

Variable	*Symbol*	*Year 1*	*Year 2*	*Year 3*	*Year 4*	*Year 5*	*Year 6*
Agriculture	AGR	2.0	2.0	2.0	2.0	2.0	2.0
Gold	GOL	0.0	0.0	0.0	0.0	0.0	0.0
Basic metals and minerals	MET	3.0	3.5	4.0	4.5	4.5	4.5
Other	OTH	4.8	6.8	7.5	8.1	9.0	8.9
Total exports	X	3.0	4.0	4.5	5.0	5.5	5.5

It follows from the above observations that the composition of exports will change, so the distribution in the final year of the projection is as follows: agriculture 5.3 per cent, gold 16.9 per cent, basic metals and minerals 31.2 per cent and other exports 46.7 per cent. Thus, other exports are the only category which increases its share over the forecasting period.

As pointed out in Chapter 4, only government investment enters as a variable in the FP model, whereas total investments (i.e. the sum of private and public investment) are determined by the aggregate investment function in the RMSM model. Hence, the use of the latter model requires that the level of investment is consistent with the overall 3.5 per cent annual growth rate referred to above. Accordingly, it was decided to put the capital–output ratio at 2.25 for the whole of the projection as shown in Table 6.1. It is reiterated, however, that the capital–output ratio used in this book relates output changes to net investments, and not gross investments as discussed in Chapter 4. This implies a stable aggregate investment level of 21.8 per cent of GDP from the fourth year onwards. Compared with historical data in Kahn *et al.* (1992), this seems reasonable, though probably somewhat on the low side. The chosen value of the capital–output ratio results in a calibrated constant term of 0.142 in 1994. This implies that investments of 14.2 per cent of GDP are required if GDP is to remain unchanged. The investment level in the base run was in addition adjusted downwards, as is clear from Table 6.1, through variations in the constant in the investment function in the early years of the forecast period to account for excess capacity. Based on the path of government investments, to be further reviewed below, the above choices imply that private investments grow quickly from around 15.8 per cent of GDP in the base year to 19.6 per cent in the fourth year of the forecast period, staying at this level for the remaining three years. Thus private confidence in future developments and willingness to invest is relied on in accordance with the moderately optimistic underpinning of the base run.

As pointed out in Chapter 4, real private consumption is normally determined on a residual basis in growth programming exercises carried out within the RMSM framework. This is possible from the material balance equation since GDP, real imports and exports as well as investment (private and government) follow from the assumptions already made, and since government consumption can be determined from the government finance side using the FP framework. Nevertheless, the version of the RMSM used in this study includes a private consumption function, where private consumption is determined in proportion to disposable private income, i.e. nominal GDP less taxes net of transfers from government. Consequently, the marginal propensity to save was technically set in such a way that consistency is ensured, and it is recalled that all variables were, in fact, treated as endogenous in the review process in line with the methodology outlined in Chapter 4.

Thus, the marginal savings propensity was calculated in each year from the nominal GDP and tax variables from the FP base run, reflecting that private consumption will have to take the major brunt of adjustment when investment and government consumption are given. However, the constant term in the investment function, as already noted, was adjusted downwards in the early years, and this helps ensure a more sensible growth rate in private consumption than would otherwise have been the case. Hence, as shown in Table 6.2, private consumption is expected to grow by 3.1 per cent in real terms in the first year and by around 2.5 per cent in the rest of the period. The resulting movement in the private sector savings propensity corresponds as indicated in Table 6.1 to a steady increase from the calibrated 1994 value of 0.227 to 0.245 in the final year. This reflects that the private sector will respond to assumptions behind the base run by increasing its propensity to save, in contrast to what has been the case over the past decade.

PRICES AND EXCHANGE RATES

In constructing the base run, it was assumed that SARB will manage its foreign reserves in such a way that the real exchange rate remains constant during the whole period under consideration.

It is admittedly difficult to make fully reliable predictions in this area, and keeping the real exchange rate constant implies some modification of policies pursued during the second half of the 1980s. From 1985 until 1988, the desire to ensure that rand prices received by the mining sector were kept stable at a high level dominated. In accordance with the falling international gold price, the rand was allowed to depreciate in nominal terms, which also pushed the real rate below its historical level. A policy where the real exchange rate is kept constant, as in the base run presented here, implies that rand prices received by the mining companies will fluctuate substantially more than in the past, since variations in the gold price vis-à-vis the general world price level tend to be significant.

Nevertheless, a constant real exchange rate would help establish much needed stability for exporters of manufactured goods, making this an attractive reason to pursue a stable real rate of exchange. In addition, since 1988 SARB has shown definite concern about the level of the real rate and intervened to maintain a relatively high degree of stability (Kahn, 1995). Given the independence of SARB, which was maintained after the GNU take-over, a stable rate appears a sensible reference point. Furthermore, this would in any case appear the most useful assumption given the medium-term nature of the present exercise, where short-run exchange rate policy is not in focus, and the lack of in-depth studies of whether the rand is at its long-run equilibrium level or not.

As far as the domestic price level is concerned, it was, as shown in Table 6.5, set to grow by 6 per cent on an annual basis. This is approximately the domestic inflation actually realized in 1995, and is a level which should be easily acceptable to policy makers, when experiences elsewhere are brought to mind. Trying to opt for a lower rate of inflation does not seem warranted as this could affect the real economy adversely, unless more optimistic assumptions than those underlying the base run materialize. It can, in fact, be argued that a higher level might well be manageable. However, it was decided to use the low inflation option in building the base run, so as to demonstrate how much room for manoeuvre this would imply in terms of fiscal and monetary policy, and this is in any case more in line with the distinctly anti-inflationary policy approach pursued by SARB.

Both import and export prices were assumed to grow by 3 per cent on an annual basis. Hence, terms of trade remain constant,

Table 6.5 Prices and exchange rates (1994=100 and per cent annual change)

Variable	*Symbol*	*Year 0*	*Year 1*	*Year 2*	*Year 3*	*Year 4*	*Year 5*	*Year 6*
General price index	P	100	106	112	119	126	134	142
Inflation			6.0	6.0	6.0	6.0	6.0	6.0
Domestic price index	PD	100	106	112	119	126	134	142
Inflation			6.0	6.0	6.0	6.0	6.0	6.0
Export price index	XPI	100	103	106	109	113	116	119
Inflation			3.0	3.0	3.0	3.0	3.0	3.0
Import price index	MPI	100	103	106	109	113	116	119
Inflation			3.0	3.0	3.0	3.0	3.0	3.0
Nominal exchange rate	E	100	103	106	109	112	115	119
Depreciation			2.9	2.9	2.9	2.9	2.9	2.9

and both export and import prices increase to a level which is in the final year of the projection about 20 per cent above the base year price level. Some variation in the terms of trade will no doubt occur in practice over the coming years, but constant terms of trade do appear a useful starting point for the analysis because of the inherent complexities of projecting the relevant price series. A constant real exchange rate and the assumed rates of inflation imply an annual depreciation of the nominal exchange rate of 2.9 per cent, and an annual rate of growth of 6 per cent in the general price level. The former result follows from the definition of the real rate, and the latter from the way in which the overall price level is determined (i.e. as a weighted average of the domestic price level and the domestic currency price of imported goods). It can be noted here that the weight of import prices in the price index as shown in Table 6.1 was set at 0.20 so as to reflect the estimated share of imports in domestic supply. Consequently, the exchange rate rises by approximately 20 per cent during the projection period, and nominal GDP is assumed to grow by 9.7 per cent during the whole forecast.

BALANCE OF PAYMENTS

The surplus on the trade balance disappears in the second year of the base run, yet it reappears in the final year. It can also be noted that export and import values as a share of nominal GDP are equal to the real shares referred to above due to the assumed constancy of the real rate of exchange of the rand. Year-to-year developments are shown in Table 6.6.

Interest payments on the foreign debt of the private sector and government, which are fully endogenized using an imputed nominal foreign rate of interest of 14.1 per cent from Table 3.8, increase from a level of 1.5 per cent of GDP in the base year to 3.7 per cent at the end of the period. In annual growth terms, interest payments grow by around 15 per cent in the first year. Hereafter the build-up of foreign debt implies that annual growth in foreign interest payments increases gradually to 35 per cent in the third year before starting to fall again towards a rate of 25 per cent in the last year.

It was also assumed that other factor payments and net transfers from abroad as shares of GDP remain at their base year levels throughout the period. Given South Africa's high per capita GDP

Table 6.6 Current account (billion rand and share of GDP in per cent)

Variable	*Symbol*	*Year 0*	*Year 1*	*Year 2*	*Year 3*	*Year 4*	*Year 5*	*Year 6*
					Billion rand			
Exports	X	102.7	112.1	123.6	136.9	152.4	170.4	190.6
Imports	M	−94.4	−110.0	−125.4	−140.3	−155.0	−171.2	−189.1
Trade balance	RESBAL	8.3	2.1	−1.8	−3.4	−2.6	−0.8	1.5
Interest payments	INTP+INTG	−6.3	−7.3	−9.8	−13.3	−17.5	−22.4	−27.9
Other factor services	NFP	−4.2	−4.6	−5.1	−5.6	−6.1	−6.7	−7.4
Total factor services	NETFSY	−10.5	−11.9	−14.9	−18.9	−23.6	−29.1	−35.3
Net transfers	NTRP+NTRG	0.2	0.2	0.2	0.3	0.3	0.3	0.4
Current account	CURBAL	−2.1	−9.6	−16.5	−22.0	−26.0	−29.7	−33.4
					Per cent of GDP			
Exports	X	23.6	23.5	23.6	23.9	24.2	24.7	25.2
Imports	M	−21.7	−23.1	−24.0	−24.5	−24.6	−24.8	−25.0
Trade balance	RESBAL	1.9	0.4	−0.4	−0.6	−0.4	−0.1	0.2
Interest payments	INTP+INTG	−1.5	−1.5	−1.9	−2.3	−2.8	−3.2	−3.7
Other factor services	NFP	−1.0	−1.0	−1.0	−1.0	−1.0	−1.0	−1.0
Total factor services	NETFSY	−2.5	−2.5	−2.9	−3.3	−3.8	−4.2	−4.7
Net transfers	NTRP+NTRG	0.1	0.1	0.1	0.1	0.1	0.1	0.1
Current account	CURBAL	−0.5	−2.0	−3.2	−3.8	−4.1	−4.3	−4.4

Note: Due to rounding, the figures do not in all cases add up

most aid flows are expected to be on loan terms, and as such they are included in government net foreign borrowing. Yet it is obvious that if aid transfers on grant terms increase more than expected, the net transfer figure should be adjusted upwards. Similarly, to the extent that loans have, for example, a longer grace period than assumed above, net interest payments will be lower. The overall effect of such modifications is likely to be rather limited, however, given the magnitude of the variables involved. Consequently, the current account is projected to deteriorate steadily from a deficit of 0.5 per cent of GDP in the base year to a deficit of 4.4 per cent of GDP at the end of the period. This should not give rise to particular concern, however, provided a socially just and sustainable growth path is established in the process, and it is highlighted that the deficit is projected to stabilize. In this manner, the need for continued borrowing from international capital markets should eventually disappear.

As far as the capital account is concerned, the level of external debt reached very low levels in the early 1990s due to financial sanctions. With the admission of post-apartheid South Africa to international financial markets, both the government and the private sector again have access to foreign savings. It was therefore assumed, on the one side, that the annual net capital inflow caused by government foreign borrowing increases from 1.1 per cent of GDP in the base year to 2.2 per cent in the middle of the projection. Then the ratio starts falling to 1.8 per cent of GDP towards the end of the time horizon. As regards private capital flows, it can be noted that private direct foreign investment has traditionally played a significant role in the South African economy, and over 130 new foreign investments were already made during the three-year period prior to mid-1993 (ODI, 1994). If the government manages to curtail social unrest and clarify existing uncertainties regarding future economic policy and investment incentives in a convincing manner, the expectations of domestic and foreign investors can no doubt be influenced favourably. Hence, it is possible that direct foreign investments may speed up, while the risk of capital flight is at the same time being minimized. Moreover, South Africa is well placed to benefit from the recent surge in international liquidity in search of profitable emerging markets. Such inflows could provide an injection of foreign resources in the short- to medium-term, although the inherent mobility of such flows must obviously be taken into account at all times.

Table 6.7 Balance of payments (billion rand and share of GDP in per cent)

Variable	*Symbol*	*Year 0*	*Year 1*	*Year 2*	*Year 3*	*Year 4*	*Year 5*	*Year 6*
					Billion rand			
Current account	CURBAL	−2.1	−9.6	−16.5	−22.0	−26.0	−29.7	−33.4
Net new borrowing:								
Government	ΔNFDG	−4.8	−7.2	−10.6	−12.7	−14.0	−13.9	−13.5
Private sector	ΔNFDP	−0.4	−8.8	−11.3	−13.8	−16.0	−19.6	−23.8
Change in reserves	ΔR	3.1	6.4	5.4	4.5	4.0	3.8	3.9
					Per cent of GDP			
Current account	CURBAL	−0.5	−2.0	−3.2	−3.8	−4.1	−4.3	−4.4
Net new borrowing:								
Government	ΔNFDG	−1.1	−1.5	−2.0	−2.2	−2.2	−2.0	−1.8
Private sector	ΔNFDP	−0.1	−1.8	−2.2	−2.4	−2.6	−2.8	−3.1
Change in reserves	ΔR	0.7	1.3	1.0	0.8	0.6	0.6	0.5

Note: Due to rounding, the shares do not in all cases add up

The above capital account items in the models used in this study are captured through changes in the net foreign borrowing by the private sector, which therefore includes all net private flows whether they are debt creating or not. Thus, annual private net capital inflows are expected to increase steadily from hardly anything in the base year to 3.1 per cent of GDP in the final year, reflecting the important role private foreign borrowing will have to play in the medium-term. Table 6.7 provides details on year-to-year fluctuations. In relation to this table, it is emphasized that the capital inflow must be seen in relation to the projected increase in investments. If increased foreign borrowing is siphoned off to finance unproductive consumption, the current account deficits would be undesirable and probably unsustainable.

The change in foreign reserves in the RMSM is determined by the change in the foreign currency value of imports and calibration of the ratio of foreign reserves to imports using 1993 and 1994 data, resulted in the value shown for *Year 0* in Table 6.1. Moreover, since reserves are rather low in the base year, the reserve–import parameter was set rather low in the first year so as to ensure that additional reserves are built-up. Subsequently the reserve–import ratio was gradually adjusted upwards during the forecast horizon in order to ensure a reasonable level of reserve accumulation, leading to a stock of reserves which is equivalent to three months of imports in the last year. Foreign reserves as a share of GDP grow steadily from 3.2 per cent in the beginning to 6.2 per cent at the end of the period.

GOVERNMENT ACCOUNTS

To address the economic and social legacies left behind by apartheid, fiscal policy is going to play a crucial role. To meet basic human needs and achieve the twin goals of economic growth and redistribution, government must aim at reviving investments in physical and social infrastructure and implementing other programmes, which imply a tangible up-lift of the African population. This must, however, be done without compromising the confidence and dynamism of the business sector. Avoiding lagging private investment and capital flight are, as already noted, two of the preconditions which must be fulfilled if South Africa is to break decisively out of the stagflationary, vicious circle.

The centrality of fiscal policy is further underscored by the fact that public debt has grown significantly during the first half of the

1990s. Whereas the government borrowing requirement to GDP ratio was in the order of 1.5 per cent at the beginning of the decade, the ratio had risen to 8.6 per cent of GDP in 1992–3 due to rapidly increasing public sector budget deficits. Thus, it is crucial to be aware of the financial constraints under which the government will operate in the coming years, if the desire to maintain macroeconomic balance and avoid crowding out private sector investment is to be realized. It follows that prospects for the government's sources of deficit finance as well as its incomes and expenditures have to be established.

Given the need to revive investment in physical and social infrastructure, it is tempting to target a considerable increase in this expense. Yet, taking account of widely reported problems with implementing the RDP (*Financial Mail*, April 1995), which are unlikely to disappear quickly, it has to be expected that government will find it difficult to ensure a growth rate of government investments above that of GDP. Accordingly, it was assumed that government investment will remain at its base year level of 2.2 per cent of GDP throughout as shown in Table 6.8. As far as other government expenditures and transfers to government from the rest of the world are concerned, they were also fixed as percentages of GDP (i.e. increasing by 3.5 per cent each year in real terms).

Interest payments on domestic and foreign public debt were linked to the respective debt stocks. The rate of interest on foreign debt has already been discussed above, and the underlying assumption regarding the rate of interest on domestic debt is that the real rate initially increases considerably from 5 to 8 per cent as inflation drops from 9 per cent in the base year to 6 per cent in the first year. This corresponds well with what actually happened in 1995 and reflects the nominal rate of 14 per cent shown in Table 3.8. This assumption is left unchanged in the second year, where the real rate remains at 8 per cent, but it is then assumed that the nominal rate starts tapering off by half a percentage point each year. Thus, the underlying real rate of interest on government domestic debt gradually falls to 6 per cent in the final year, corresponding to a nominal rate of 12 per cent.

The only remaining variable on the expenditure side is government consumption which increases as a share of GDP from 20.7 per cent in the first year to 21.8 per cent in the final year. This may not appear significant, but it does imply an expansion of the public sector by 23.9 per cent in real terms when consumption and

Table 6.8 Government budget (billion rand and share of GDP in per cent)

Variable	*Symbol*	*Year 0*	*Year 1*	*Year 2*	*Year 3*	*Year 4*	*Year 5*	*Year 6*
					Billion rand			
Revenue	TG	118.1	129.6	143.2	158.8	177.4	198.1	219.6
Net transfers from ROW	NTRG	0.3	0.3	0.3	0.4	0.4	0.4	0.5
Consumption	CG	−91.3	−98.8	−108.9	−120.6	−134.2	−149.4	−164.7
Investment	IVG	−9.6	−10.4	−11.3	−12.3	−13.5	−14.9	−16.3
Foreign interest payments	INFG	−3.9	−4.7	−5.9	−7.6	−9.7	−12.0	−14.4
Domestic interest payments	INDG	−21.2	−23.8	−26.2	−27.5	−28.7	−29.7	−30.7
Other expenditures	GT	−15.4	−16.9	−18.6	−20.4	−22.3	−24.5	−26.9
Budget surplus	-BRG	−23.1	−24.7	−27.3	−29.3	−30.7	−31.9	−32.8
					Per cent of GDP			
Revenue	TG	27.2	27.2	27.4	27.7	28.2	28.7	29.0
Net transfers from ROW	NTRG	0.1	0.1	0.1	0.1	0.1	0.1	0.1
Consumption	CG	−21.0	−20.7	−20.8	−21.0	−21.3	−21.6	−21.8
Investment	IVG	−2.2	−2.2	−2.2	−2.2	−2.2	−2.2	−2.2
Foreign interest payments	INFG	−0.9	−1.0	−1.1	−1.3	−1.5	−1.7	−1.9
Domestic interest payments	INDG	−4.9	−5.0	−5.0	−4.8	−4.6	−4.3	−4.0
Other expenditures	GT	−3.6	−3.6	−3.6	−3.6	−3.6	−3.6	−3.6
Budget surplus	-BRG	−5.3	−5.2	−5.2	−5.1	−4.9	−4.6	−4.3

Note: Due to rounding, the figures do not in all cases add up

investment are added. It is, finally, highlighted that the actual composition of government investment and consumption may, of course, vary and the classification will in many cases be rather arbitrary if due account is taken of the productive impact of social expense, registered as current items.

As far as government revenue is concerned, there is in South Africa an indispensable need as well as some scope for increasing taxation as a share of GDP. The Katz Commission has, for example, pointed out that improvements in tax administration and collection could yield a significant amount of additional revenue (Department of Finance, 1995, p. 2.27). Thus, tax revenue is estimated to increase from 27.2 per cent of GDP in the base year to 29.0 per cent in the final year. This implies an annual growth rate, which increases in real terms from 3.6 per cent in the first year to 5.4 per cent in the fourth year. Then the real growth rate falls to 4.6 per cent in the last year, and this is also equal to the average annual growth rate for the whole period. Given that the base run is built around a growing economy, the higher tax rate and government revenue do not undermine real private consumption. Moreover, the assumptions concerning expenditures and revenue result in a deficit, which decreases from 5.3 per cent of GDP in the base year to 4.3 per cent in the last year of the scenario. Although this is higher than the strict targets of the GNU, a deficit of this size, is as documented here, fully compatible with a stable macroeconomic performance. It can also be noted that the government estimates that the budget deficit will fall to 4 per cent of GDP in 1998–9 under the present fiscal stance (Department of Finance, 1995, p. 2.3). However, the definition of the deficit used in this study differs from that of the government. Thus, while the official deficit was 6.3 per cent of GDP in 1994–5, the corresponding 1994 figure used here is 5.3 per cent.

The finance of the government deficit from the rest of the world was referred to above, and the easing up of the external capital constraint is an encouraging aspect of the future development outlook for the South African economy. As far as domestic credit is concerned, this source of finance, contrary to what has been typical in many other developing countries, is not expected to contribute at all to government deficit financing. This would seem an appropriate assumption given the concern in South Africa with the undesirable inflationary consequences of excessive monetization of fiscal deficits. The remaining deficit is therefore as

Table 6.9 Government finance (billion rand and share of GDP in per cent)

Variable	*Symbol*	*Year 0*	*Year 1*	*Year 2*	*Year 3*	*Year 4*	*Year 5*	*Year 6*
					Billion rand			
Domestic credit	ΔDCG	0.5	0.0	0.0	0.0	0.0	0.0	0.0
Domestic borrowing	ΔNDDG	17.8	17.4	16.7	16.5	16.7	18.0	19.3
Foreign borrowing	ΔNFDG	4.8	7.2	10.6	12.7	14.0	13.9	13.4
Borrowing requirement	BRG	23.1	24.7	27.3	29.3	30.7	31.9	32.8
					Per cent of GDP			
Domestic credit	ΔDCG	0.1	0.0	0.0	0.0	0.0	0.0	0.0
Domestic borrowing	ΔNDDG	4.1	3.7	3.2	2.9	2.7	2.6	2.6
Foreign borrowing	ΔNFDG	1.1	1.5	2.0	2.2	2.2	2.0	1.8
Borrowing requirement	BRG	5.3	5.2	5.2	5.1	4.9	4.6	4.3

Note: Due to rounding, the figures do not in all cases add up

shown in Table 6.9 covered by borrowing in domestic financial markets.

This will provide an amount of finance to the government which is equal to 3.7 per cent of GDP in the first year, but then the share falls gradually to a medium-term level of only 2.6 per cent of GDP. The corresponding medium-term annual growth rate of this source of finance is 7.2 per cent, i.e. less than the expected growth rate of nominal GDP of 9.7 per cent, but higher than the annual rate of inflation of 6 per cent. The underlying behavioural assumption would appear reasonable given the moderately optimistic position taken as far as growth and stability are concerned, which makes it sensible to assume that the private sector is willing to increase its stock of government debt in real terms. It is noted, however, that the issue of making sure that the private sector is willing to hold sufficient government stock is a complex one, which is, *inter alia*, in interplay with the interest policy the government decides to opt for.

In sum, total available credit from the three sources identified above (i.e. borrowing from the rest of the world, the banking system and the private sector through the issuance of domestic debt) corresponds with the projected decrease in the government budget deficit from 5.3 per cent in the base year to 4.3 per cent in the last year of the scenario.

ASSET STOCKS

With the assumed constant velocity of money circulation, shown in Table 6.1, which was calibrated from the 1994 data for money demand and nominal GDP, the growth rate of nominal GDP translates directly into money demand. Thus, money demand and supply grow by 9.7 per cent on an annual basis during the whole period. It follows that the money stock as a share of GDP remains constant at the base year level of 56.2 per cent as indicated in Table 6.10.

With regard to domestic credit, the stock of domestic credit extended to the government as a share of GDP drops consistently to 2.0 per cent in the last year as this source of deficit financing is not used. In addition, given the assumptions about international reserves and public sector credit already discussed above, credit extended to the private sector can be determined residually. Hence, private credit grows at rates slightly below those of nominal GDP in the early years. The result is that private credit as a percentage of

Table 6.10 Money supply (billion rand and per cent annual growth)

Variable	*Symbol*	*Year 0*	*Year 1*	*Year 2*	*Year 3*	*Year 4*	*Year 5*	*Year 6*
					Billion rand			
Private sector	DCP	214.6	231.5	251.4	274.6	301.0	330.4	363.0
Government	DCG	15.5	15.5	15.5	15.5	15.5	15.5	15.5
Foreign reserves	E*R	14.1	20.9	27.0	32.3	37.2	42.1	47.3
Money supply	MS	244.2	267.9	293.9	322.4	353.7	388.1	425.7
					Per cent annual growth			
Private sector	DCP		7.9	8.6	9.2	9.6	9.8	9.8
Government	DCG		0.0	0.0	0.0	0.0	0.0	0.0
Foreign reserves	E*R		48.3	28.9	19.7	15.3	13.2	12.2
Money supply	MS		9.7	9.7	9.7	9.7	9.7	9.7

Note: Due to rounding, the figures do not in all cases add up

Table 6.11 Debt stocks (share of GDP in per cent)

Variable	*Symbol*	*Year 0*	*Year 1*	*Year 2*	*Year 3*	*Year 4*	*Year 5*	*Year 6*
Government domestic credit	DCG	3.6	3.3	3.0	2.7	2.5	2.2	2.0
Government domestic debt	NDDG	39.0	39.2	38.9	38.3	37.6	36.9	36.2
Government foreign debt	NFDG	7.4	8.5	10.0	11.6	13.1	14.3	15.2
Total government debt		50.0	51.0	51.9	53.2	53.2	53.4	53.4
Private sector foreign debt	NFDP	4.1	5.7	7.5	9.4	11.4	13.5	15.8

GDP drops a little from 49.4 per cent in the base year to its medium-term level of 47.9 per cent. On the other hand, private credit growth rates are larger than price inflation, so this represents a real increase in private credit of almost 20 per cent in the final year as compared to the base year. Thus, private sector expansion is supported by making additional credit available at an average annual rate of growth in real terms of 3 per cent.

The stock of government borrowing in domestic financial markets grows at an annual rate of 10.3 per cent in the first year after which it falls to a medium-term level of 7.6 per cent. Consequently, the stock of government domestic debt is as shown in Table 6.11 projected to decrease from 39.2 per cent in the first year to 36.2 per cent of GDP in the final year, since the economy grows and inflation decreases the real value of existing government debt.

As far as the stock of foreign debt is concerned, net government foreign debt will increase during the whole period in line with developments in the financing of the government deficit. Overall, the stock of government foreign debt increases as a share of GDP from 7.4 per cent in the base year to 15.2 per cent in the last year as shown in Table 6.11. This reflects an average annual rate of growth of 20.1 per cent in rand terms. All in all, this implies that total government debt as a percentage of GDP increases from 50.0 per cent in the base year to 53.4 per cent. Thus, there are no signs of the government running into a debt trap, in particular since interest payments remain more or less at the base year level of 5.8 per cent of GDP and annual growth rates in the debt show a declining trend from the second year.

Finally, it follows from the assumptions made about the capital account of the balance of payments that the stock of private sector foreign debt increases at an average annual rate of growth in foreign currency terms which amounts to 33.7 per cent. This corresponds to 4.1 per cent of GDP in the base year and to 15.8 per cent in the final year, which can be considered a fairly low ratio.

CONCLUSION

The base run established in this chapter demonstrates that the government of in South Africa is not without room for manoeuvre. Thus, it may well succeed in promoting growth as well as greater equity, if appropriate policy measures are taken. There is macroeconomic space to implement a substantial investment and social rehabilitation programme to the benefit of the disadvantaged group of the population, and this can be done without crowding out the private sector and disturbing macroeconomic balances excessively. There is some excess productive capacity, and the access to international capital markets will also provide a welcome boost to the economy, if used judiciously. South Africa is, after all, potentially a very rich economy due to its impressive natural resource base.

In conclusion, however, it must be stressed that growth will not by itself ensure that the moderately optimistic path put forward in this chapter is socially just and sustainable. The growth strategy of South Africa must, as pointed out by Gibson and van Seventer (1995a) be consistent both in the accounting sense and in regard to the objectives being pursued. Thus, an explicit set of micro level policies designed to promote employment creation and avoid a worsening of the income distribution will be indispensable in combination with the macro policies referred to above.

7

ALTERNATIVE SCENARIOS

INTRODUCTION

The dual needs for redistribution and growth are, as is clear from previous chapters of this study, no longer an issue in South Africa. It is, moreover, apparent that South Africa will in future have a mixed economy, in which market forces play a major role in the allocation of resources in productive activity. Thus, the basic approaches to economic policy have been converging in recent years as compared to the positions taken by the ANC and the Nationalist Party (NP) before the GNU came to power in 1994. Yet the consensus is far from complete.

The Nationalist Party and institutions such as SARB, on the one side, are clearly in favour of an orthodox growth maximizing strategy, in the expectation that the benefits of growth will eventually trickle down to the disadvantaged poor. This was originally illustrated by the specific targets put forward within the framework of the Normative Economic Model (NEM) (CEAS, 1993). More recently, as noted in Chapter 2, this position has also been argued on the basis of the view that there is no durable trade-off between inflation and output growth and unemployment, in combination with opposition to the government taking an active stance as regards policy interventions. The ANC, on the other side, has over the years held a more developmental position as expressed in its Policy Guidelines for a Democratic South Africa (ANC, 1992) and the more recent RDP (ANC, 1994).

The base run established in Chapter 6 demonstrates that even substantial increases in government activity are not in contradiction with the need to promote private sector activity and attain macro balance within the analytical frameworks used in this book.

Hence, escaping the vicious circle of the 1980s may be feasible, and an even stronger revival of economic activity cannot be excluded *a priori.* Yet government expansion can obviously be pushed too far in response to domestic social and political pressures, crowding-out not only private but also public expense of key importance to the growth process. Thus, future prospects depend critically on the underlying assumptions, and it is justified to call as well for prudence in the assessment of future economic policy options. This chapter therefore presents both an optimistic and a more pessimistic assessment of medium-term perspectives. These two alternative scenarios are intended to highlight, in a quantitative manner, the broad macroeconomic confines within which future policy choices will have to be made. As such they can, we hope, serve as useful points of reference, together with the base run, in macroeconomic dialogue, the construction of an appropriate medium-term expenditure framework, and the assessment of the many inherent trade-offs with which policy makers are faced. The two additional projections are asymmetrical in the sense that the changes in the relevant exogenous variables, parameters and policy instruments, summarized in Table 7.1, are not mirror images of each other. They have, instead, been constructed, based on insights from Chapter 5 and information from outside the models, so as to tell two different stories, with features which are distinct from those of the base run. However, the three projections share certain common characteristics in terms of their overall macroeconomic focus, and they were all developed on the basis of the analytical frameworks presented in Chapter 4.

ALTERNATIVE ASSUMPTIONS

Optimistic scenario

In view of the difficult challenges South Africa will face in the coming years, it can certainly be argued that the base run is in many ways less than what might be hoped for from a social and political perspective. In addition, if South Africa could manage to emulate Chilean or East Asian success in terms of growth performance more could be achieved on the socio-economic front. Such an optimistic scenario would no doubt involve an increase in domestic savings and investment, while export demand needs to surge to new heights and supply constraints are overcome in a flexible and expedient manner through appropriate government policies at macro, sector and micro levels. Another dimension might therefore be that additional unused capacity can be found. This would, *ceteris paribus*, lower investment requirements in the short-term to a more manageable level and be consistent with the need to allow private consumption to expand in per capita terms. To underpin such a scenario, a high degree of political stability will be necessary. Thus, the government must act in a competent and convincing manner in the management and restructuring of the country's economic and political affairs, promoting technological progress and employment creation. Nevertheless, the relatively peaceful political transition presently under way in South Africa is an important indication that the above combination of factors may indeed materialize.

Thus, in the construction of the optimistic scenario, it was decided to add an extra 1.5 percentage points to the level of growth in aggregate and sectoral GDP and an additional two percentage points to the aggregate and disaggregated export growth rates. Accordingly, real GDP in the final year of the projection is 9 per cent higher in the optimistic scenario than in the base run. Moreover, the private sector saving propensity was set to increase steadily from 0.227 in the base year to 0.285 towards the end of the forecast in light of positive economic developments. The constant in the investment function was adjusted downwards in the early years to capture additional excess productive capacity and smooth out developments in the investment–consumption balances.

On the side of government, it was assumed that real government investment and other government expenditures (i.e. transfers excluding interest payments) increase in line with GDP at a path which is about 1.5 percentage points above that of the base run so their shares of GDP remain the same; and that government revenue is reduced in nominal terms due to lower inflation, established in what follows. Nevertheless, real taxes were pitched in such a manner that the real rate of growth in government revenue in the optimistic scenario is at a path which is 0.9 percentage points above that of the base run. Hence, while real taxes increase, the actual tax burden, as measured by the government revenue to GDP ratio, drops from 29.0 to 28.0 per cent in the last year.

As far as financing the government deficit, it was built into the optimistic scenario that government refrains from using domestic credit expansion as a source of funding as was the case in the base run. It was, moreover, assumed that the government will reduce its external borrowing so the net government foreign debt in foreign currency terms grows along a path which is 3.6 percentage points below that of the base run. This would be consistent with a desire to limit the exposure to international capital markets, utilizing in this way part of the space opened up by the better growth and export performance.

Regarding credit to the private sector, it was assumed that the South African government will find annual increases in real terms, which are 2.6 per cent above that of the corresponding path in the base run, acceptable. Taking account of the increase in the money stock due to GDP growth and an assumed reduction in the velocity of money circulation of 1 per cent annually, inflation can drop to 3 per cent on an annual basis. The change in money velocity is justified by people gaining improved expectations of the future and lower rates of interest, which imply that they will, in all likelihood, be willing to hold more monetary assets. Moreover, the drop in inflation would be in line with the SARB desires to reduce price increases to an annual rate below that of the base run.

The nominal domestic interest rate is assumed to fall somewhat slower than the rate of inflation, reflecting the fact that the interest rate on existing debt is fixed. Hence, it decreases gradually from the level of 14 per cent in the base year to 9 per cent in the last year of the optimistic scenario, corresponding to a fall from 10 to 6 per cent in the real rate over the time horizon considered. Finally, the accumulation of foreign reserves was set so that the ratio of reserves to imports adjusts as before from two to three months of import coverage. This implies an average annual growth rate, which is 1.8 percentage points above that of the base run.

Pessimistic scenario

The social fabric of South Africa has been threatened for decades. Large groups of the population have felt they had a better chance of survival in conditions of anarchy than in conditions of stability, and to reorient the future course of the economy to the benefit of the discriminated majority is going to be an extremely difficult task. Hence, fundamental problems go deep, as pointed out in Chapter

2, and there is plenty of reason to remain cautious in the assessment of the future prospects of South Africa. Consequently, while the threat of organized unrest has subsided rapidly in the last few years, violence and criminal behaviour could easily erupt and escalate if the depth and aptness of leadership weakens and unsurmountable internal conflicts and management problems occur. This would no doubt inhibit badly needed economic restructuring, limit the inflow of foreign capital and intensify capital flight. In turn, this would constrain import capacity, impairing economic recovery, and depress domestic output and exports. Under such circumstances it would become increasingly difficult for the government to picture the existing high expectations as being in a process of fulfilment. A more pessimistic scenario should not, therefore, be discarded *a priori*.

Such a scenario would from a macroeconomic point of view undoubtedly involve a worsening of savings and investment as well as output and export growth as compared to the base run. Consequently, the savings rate was reduced by one percentage point throughout the projection, and the aggregate and sectoral GDP growth paths were shifted downwards by 1.5 percentage points, implying an accumulated shortfall in the last year of the pessimistic scenario of 8.4 per cent of GDP in constant prices. In addition, the initial excess capacity assumed in both the base run and the optimistic scenario was removed by setting the constant in the investment function at its calibrated base year value based on the view that the use of South African capital does not become more efficient in the pessimistic scenario. The export performance projected is somewhat more positive than that of output growth, but under bleak conditions it will be difficult to avoid a downwards shift of about one percentage point as compared to the base run, due to domestic demand pressures. This is therefore the change used here.

Export prices were set to grow at only 2 per cent annually as compared to 3 per cent in the base run to illustrate the risk of deteriorating terms of trade. The potential negative influence from developments in the world economy might also include the fact that South Africa captures a diminished share of international capital liquidity. Consequently, annual growth in the stock of net foreign debt by the private sector was reduced by an average of 13.4 percentage points as compared to the base run and the optimistic scenario. This implies that the stock of net private foreign debt in the final year amounts to only slightly more than half the debt stock in the other two scenarios. Foreign borrowing by the government was kept unchanged in dollar terms, however, based on the view that government will continue to have some access to international capital markets in the pessimistic scenario.

Nevertheless, with economic performance below the level projected in the base run, government will certainly find it increasingly difficult to finance its activities. It was therefore decided to let government investment and other government expenditures decrease in line with economic performance in terms of growth. Thus, their growth paths are 1.5 percentage points below those of the base run, and their shares of GDP remain the same. Moreover, as issuance of additional domestic debt is unlikely to be a feasible response to the government financing constraints due to the detrimental effects this may have on the interest rate, government will have to rely on domestic credit expansion, in contrast to the situation in the base run and the optimistic scenario. Consequently, growth in real private sector credit will be squeezed in the pessimistic scenario, reflected in annual rates of increase, which are between 1.9 and 7.9 percentage points below those of the base run. Thus, whereas the average annual growth of real private credit amounts to 3 per cent in the base run, real private credit drops on average by 3 per cent per year in the pessimistic scenario.

Turning to government revenue, this variable will decrease in real terms in spite of considerable nominal increases, reflecting accelerating inflation, reaching an annual rate of 14.6 per cent in the final year. It was assumed here that the growth of real government revenue is 2.1 percentage points below that of the base run except in the first year. Accordingly, the shortfall in real government revenue amounts to 9.6 per cent in the last year of the pessimistic projection as compared to the base run. It can also be noted that the increasing rate of inflation is consistent with a velocity of money circulation and a level of foreign reserves, which are assumed to remain at their base run values throughout instead of respectively falling and increasing as in the optimistic scenario.

Finally, the real domestic interest rate was assumed to remain at the first year level of 8 per cent in all years instead of falling gradually to 6 per cent as in the base run and the optimistic scenario. This implies a nominal annual rate that grows from the 14 per cent level in the base year to 22.7 per cent in the final year, when account is taken of inflation.

Table 7.1 Assumptions underlying the base run and the alternative scenarios*

Variable	*Symbol*		*Base run*	*Optimistic*	*Pessimistic*
			Real growth rates in per cent		
GDP	GDP		3.5	+1.5	−1.5
Exports	X		4.6†	+2.0	−1.0
Government investment	IVG		3.1†	+1.5	−1.5
Government revenue	TG		4.6†	+0.9	−2.1†
Other government expenditures	GT		3.5	+1.4	−1.5
Private sector credit	DCP		3.0†	+2.6	−5.8†
			Growth rates in per cent		
Net foreign government debt	NFDG		20.1†	−3.6	0.0
Net foreign private debt	NFDP		33.7†	0.0	−13.4†
Foreign reserves	R		18.9†	+1.8†	0.0
Export price index	XPI		3.0	0.0	−1.0
Money velocity	ν		3.0	−1.0	0.0
				Levels	
Domestic interest rate§	IRD	Year 1:	0.140	−0.010	+0.010
		Year 3:	0.135	−0.030	+0.042
		Year 6:	0.120	−0.030	+0.109
Savings propensity§	β	Year 1:	0.230	+0.010	−0.010
		Year 2:	0.245	+0.039	−0.010
Constant in investment function§	$\kappa 0$	Year 1:	0.124	−0.025	+0.018
		Year 4:	0.142	−0.005	0.000
		Year 6:	0.142	0.000	0.000

Notes: * For the base run, actual values of annual growth rates and levels are shown, while it is the changes of these values that are shown for the optimistic and pessimistic scenarios. All figures are based on domestic currency values except net foreign government debt (NFDG), net foreign private debt (NFDP) and foreign reserves (R), which refer to foreign currency figures

† The annual growth rate varies over the time horizon, and the value represents the average annual growth rate

§ Selected years are listed to illustrate changes over time

Summing-up

In the construction of the alternative scenarios various modifications were made in the relevant exogenous variables, as set out in detail above (including the traditional target variables in the underlying analytical frameworks), parameters and policy instruments as compared to the base run. In Table 7.1, these alterations are summarized together with the base run values of the variables and parameters involved.

It is reiterated that the optimistic and pessimistic scenarios are not mirror images of each other. It can, in particular, be noted from Table 7.1 that foreign capital flows develop in distinct ways, and also the numerical magnitude of the effects involved are different. Finally, it is recalled that all variables were, in fact, treated as endogenous in the review process in line with the comments made in Chapter 4. Consequently, Table 7.1 should also be read in conjunction with the results to be discussed in the next section.

RESULTS

By way of introduction to the results of the alternative scenarios, it can be noted that they could be presented in the same way as the base run in Chapter 6. However, instead of summarizing the data in tabular form, it was decided to make use of a series of illustrative figures in this chapter to capture the relevant characteristics. All the necessary detailed background data are available in Appendices C and D.

They show, first of all, that the terms-of-trade deterioration assumed in constructing the pessimistic scenario corresponds to a share of real GDP, which increases from 0.2 per cent in the first year to 1.5 per cent in the last year of the forecasting period. This is equivalent to 0.9 and 4.2 billion rand respectively in constant base year prices. Thus, whereas there is no difference between real GDP and real GDY in the base run and the optimistic scenario, the growth path of real GDY is below that of real GDP in the pessimistic scenario. The difference amounts to approximately 0.25 of a percentage point. As far as real output growth is concerned, as pointed out in Chapter 6, it is difficult to make projections in the South African case. However, given the assumptions made in the above section, real GDY will develop as shown in Figure 7.1, and it should be mentioned that the optimistic scenario ends up in the sixth year of the projection with a real GDY which is 17.2 per cent higher than the real GDY of the pessimistic scenario.

Despite the increased need for investment to underpin the better growth performance of the optimistic projection, there is room to expand both private and government consumption by 3.5 per cent

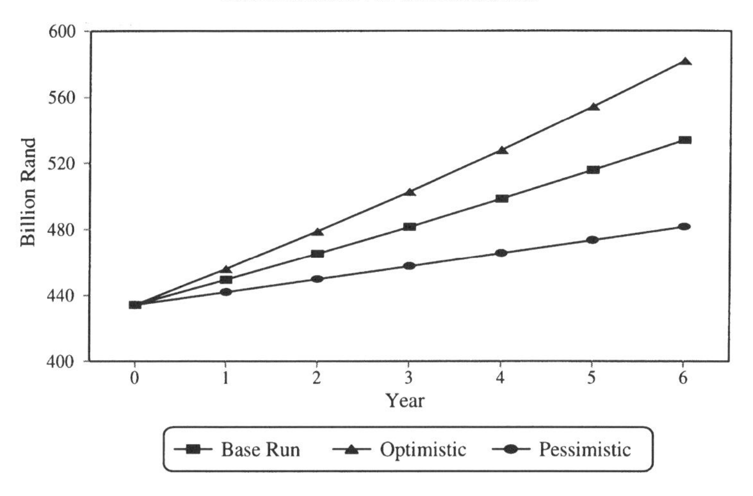

Figure 7.1 Gross domestic income (constant 1994 prices)

and 4.3 per cent respectively per year on average. Real private and government consumption in constant base year prices therefore reach levels in the final year which are 5.0 per cent and 1.5 per cent above their base run values. This corresponds to a difference of 14.2 and 2.4 billion rand in constant prices as shown in Figures 7.2 and 7.3.

Also in the pessimistic scenario, there is initially room for an expansion of government consumption as compared to the base run, and this increase is actually larger than the boost in the optimistic scenario as shown in Figure 7.3. This is caused, however, by the more limited expansion of investment due to the lower growth performance. Hence, from the middle of the projection real government consumption drops below the level of the base run. As a consequence, the level achieved in the final year of the pessimistic scenario is only 17.3 per cent higher than in the base year. This implies practically no increase in per capita terms considering a population increase of around 2.6 per cent a year. This observation is put further into perspective by noting that it can be projected that real private consumption drops by 1.4 per cent per year on average in the pessimistic scenario. Hence, the implied real drop in per capita consumption (government and private) reaches 9.4 per cent by the final year of the projection. Moreover, falls in per capita private consumption set in already in

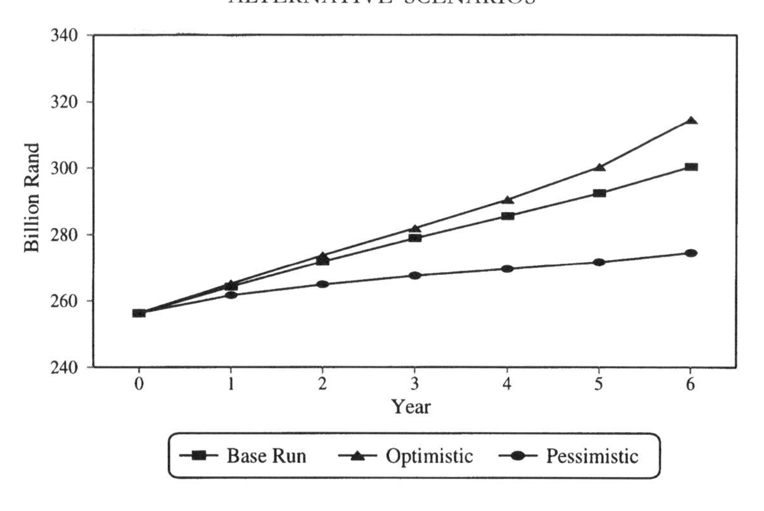

Figure 7.2 Private consumption (constant 1994 prices)

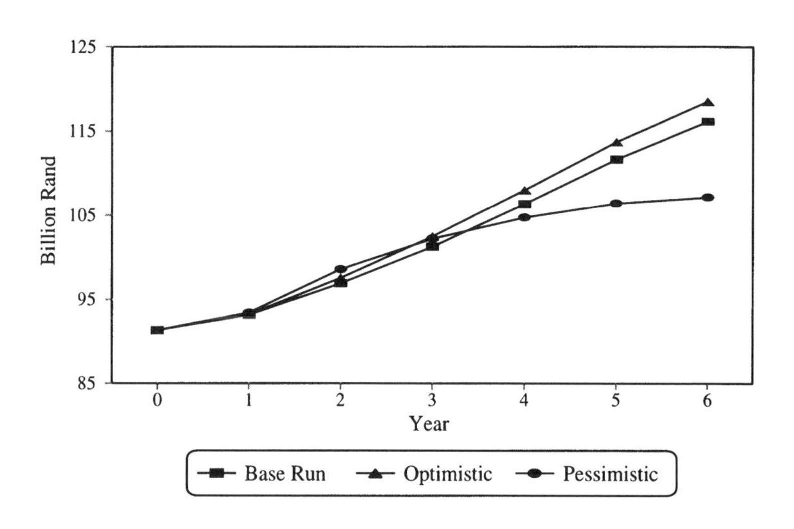

Figure 7.3 Government consumption (constant 1994 prices)

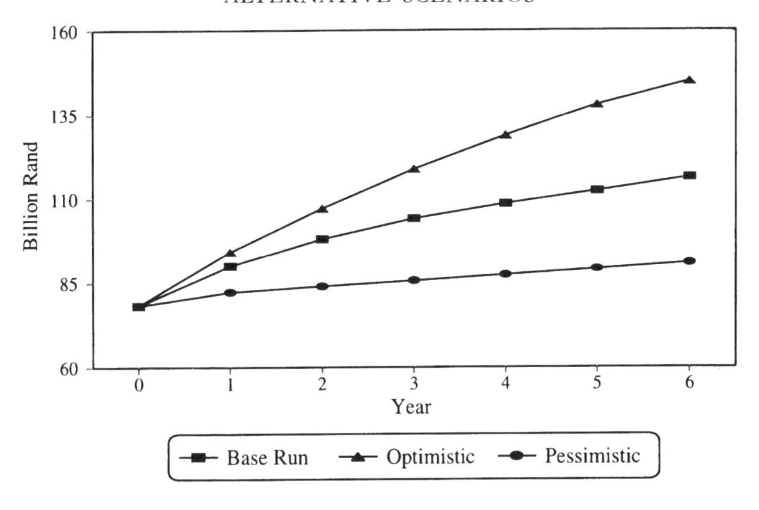

Figure 7.4 Total investments (constant 1994 prices)

the first critical years, and they are larger than the initial expansion in government consumption referred to above.

Total real investment including both private and government investment is, as is clear from Figure 7.4, projected to increase in all of the projections put forward. Yet average growth rates and investment ratios are very different, corresponding largely with the deviations in terms of growth performance. Thus, while investment grows at an average annual rate of 10.8 per cent in the optimistic scenario, the corresponding figures in the base run and the pessimistic scenario are 6.8 per cent and only 2.5 per cent, respectively. Consequently, the optimistic scenario involves a very considerable expansion of real investment, reaching a level which is 24.6 per cent above the base run value in constant base year prices in the last year of the projection. The pessimistic scenario, on the other hand, ends up being 21.8 per cent below the base run level, reflecting, first of all, a serious drop in private investment. The cumulative difference in total real investment over the six-year period between the optimistic and pessimistic scenarios is equal to no less than 233.7 billion rand. This corresponds to 53.8 per cent of total GDP in the base year.

In this context it can also be highlighted that the investment expansion in the base run and the optimistic scenario is particularly pronounced in the first three years, after which investment settles

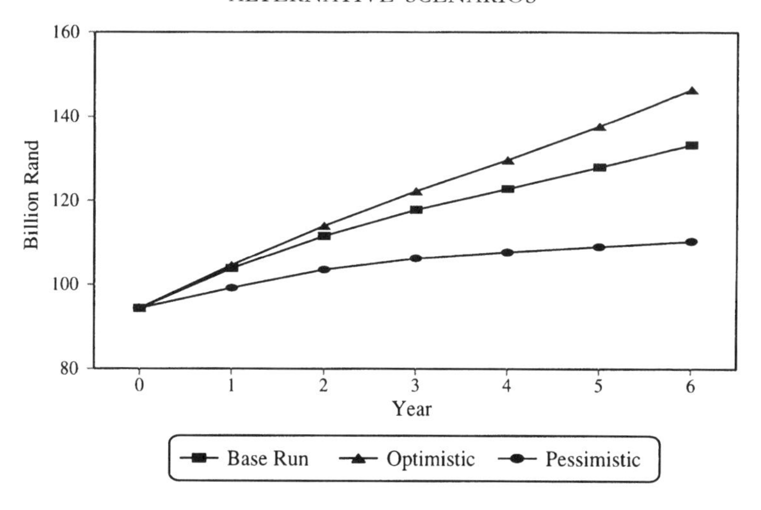

Figure 7.5 Imports (constant 1994 prices)

at a higher level where annual increases are more limited. In the pessimistic scenario, the initial expansion is hardly noticeable, so investment growth is almost constant. Moreover, while the investment ratio in the last year of the base run is 21.8 per cent of GDP, it drops to an obviously insufficient 18.5 per cent in the pessimistic scenario. In the optimistic projection, the investment ratio arrives at 24.9 per cent, well above the base year level of 18 per cent.

As far as real imports are concerned, they grow in all of the three scenarios presented in this study, as shown in Figure 7.5. Nevertheless, whereas the annual average rate of growth is 5.9 per cent in the base run, it amounts to 7.6 per cent and 2.6 per cent in the optimistic and pessimistic scenarios, respectively. In addition, while the difference between the base run and the pessimistic scenario is limited in the first year, the spread in import level between these two paths gradually opens up to 22.9 billion rand in constant prices in the last year. The difference between the optimistic and the pessimistic scenarios ends up amounting to 36.1 billion rand in constant prices. This is almost 40 per cent of total imports in the base year.

Import growth is particularly high in the early years of the optimistic scenario and the base run, but the rate is brought down to a more sustainable level in the third year. Consequently, imports amount to around 25 per cent of GDP in the last year of

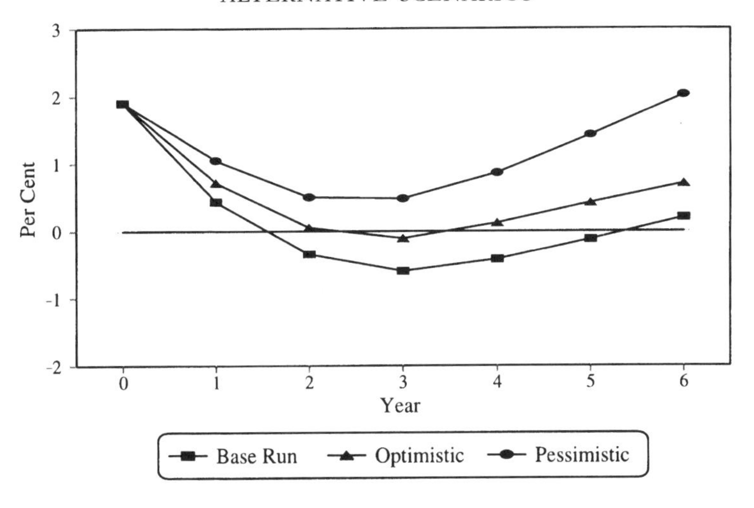

Figure 7.6 External resource balance (per cent of GDP)

both the base run and the optimistic scenario, but in the pessimistic scenario this share is only 22.6 per cent. In the pessimistic projection, more constrained capital inflows and the assumed poorer export performance put a limit on available external finance. This causes the real exchange rate to depreciate, although the less satisfactory growth performance also corresponds with a relative drop in imports.

The overall implication for the resource balance is that South Africa, as shown in Figure 7.6, will import less than is exported for the whole of the time horizon studied in the pessimistic scenario, and the resource balance is actually improving from the second year onwards. As regards the optimistic scenario, the resource balance remains positive except in the third year, but the surplus is much smaller than in the pessimistic scenario in response to the greater import demand and more favourable financing conditions.

Consequently, while the trade surplus in foreign currency terms disappears quickly in the base run, it takes somewhat longer in the optimistic scenario, and in the pessimistic scenario the balance decreases to a positive 4.4 billion rand in the second year from a base year level of 8.3 billion before improving even further. However, the relatively more positive resource balance in the pessimistic scenario is actually a condition imposed by the inability to borrow in international capital markets, rather than being a desired state of affairs. Thus, there is in the pessimistic scenario a considerable real resource outflow from South Africa amounting to between 0.5 per cent and 2.0 per cent of GDP per year. In contrast, the outflow quickly disappears in the base run, and in the last year of the optimistic scenario the outflow is limited to less than 0.7 per cent of GDP after a real resource inflow of 0.1 per cent of GDP in the middle of the period. In the circumstances facing South Africa there is a considerable need to ensure the availability of adequate real resources, so the very high positive trade balance in foreign currency terms could in the pessimistic scenario ignite inherent social difficulties and conflict. Hence, the trade and resource balance indicators must be interpreted with great care.

Turning to prices and the exchange rate, it may be recalled from Chapter 6 that the real exchange rate was assumed to remain constant, and that the annual inflation rate was at 6 per cent throughout in the construction of the base run. Thus, after the transition from the base year to the first year, where inflation drops to its new level, annual nominal devaluations of 2.9 per cent are required for the rest of the period as shown in Figure 7.7. In relation to the optimistic scenario, annual inflation was, as pointed out above, limited even further to 3 per cent. This implies initially a minor appreciation of the real rate of exchange as compared to the base run, which is mainly caused by the additional foreign currency inflows due to increased exports. Yet the real rate subsequently depreciates slowly to a level just above the base run level in the last year of the optimistic projection. As shown in Figure 7.7, this development in the real rate requires a transition from the base year to a situation where the nominal exchange rate remains almost constant throughout. This is consistent with the fact that domestic inflation is similar to world price inflation.

As regards the pessimistic scenario, it is assumed that the new government will have to finance a growing deficit through domestic credit as the only available source of finance. If the government, in addition, maintains the extension of nominal credit to the private sector as shown in Table 7.1, the implication is that annual inflation will gradually increase to 14.7 per cent. With the assumed rates of inflation in domestic and world prices, the pessimistic scenario requires annual nominal devaluations, which gradually grow to 12.7 per cent, so the real exchange rate depreciates by approximately 12 per cent over the projection period. Due to the terms of trade deterioration achieved by decreasing the export prices, it

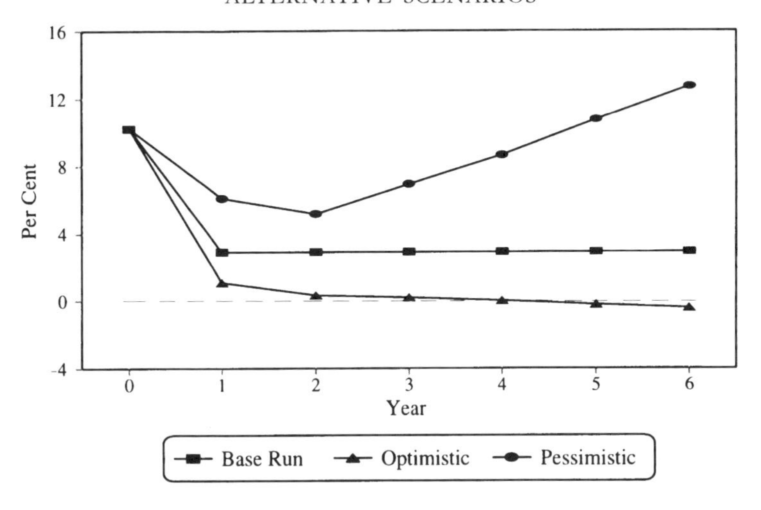

Figure 7.7 The exchange rate (annual changes in per cent)

becomes necessary to distinguish between the real rate of exchange for exports and imports, calculated as the nominal exchange rate divided by the domestic price level and multiplied by the export and import price level, respectively. On this basis it can be noted that while the real exchange rate for exports gradually depreciates to a level which differs by 6.5 per cent from the base year rate, the real rate of exchange for imports depreciates by a total of 12.1 per cent.

Developments in the resource balance were reviewed above, and it was noted that the trade balance in foreign currency terms is generally positive in the optimistic and pessimistic scenarios. However, due to interest payments, net factor payments and other transfers, the small deficit on the current account in the base year grows in all of the three scenarios as shown in Figure 7.8.

The easy access to foreign borrowing in the base run is reflected in current account deficits, which reach a level of 4.4 per cent of GDP in the last year, while the optimistic and pessimistic levels are projected to end up at around 3.3 per cent and 2.6 per cent of GDP, respectively. The underlying story is that government is able to bring down the current account deficit in the optimistic scenario without impairing growth and real resource inflows. In the pessimistic scenario, the deficit also appears under control, but in reality private foreign borrowing has become severely constrained. Similarly, in line with the total foreign borrowing projected, foreign

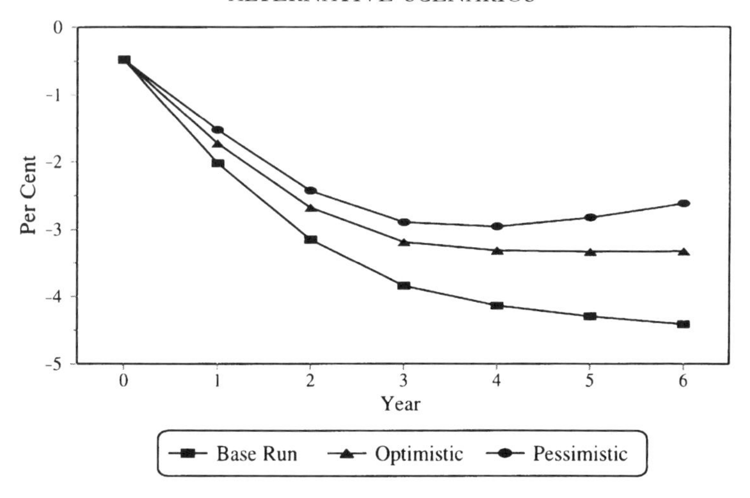

Figure 7.8 Current account (per cent of GDP)

interest payments will increase from 1.5 per cent of GDP in the base year to 3.7 per cent in the final year of the base run, whereas the corresponding shares in the optimistic and pessimistic scenarios are 3.2 per cent and 3.5 per cent, respectively.

As far as the government accounts are concerned, government domestic interest payments fall from 4.9 per cent to 4.0 per cent of GDP in the base run. They drop even further to only 3.0 per cent in the optimistic scenario, but increase to 6.7 per cent in the pessimistic scenario. Thus, taking account of foreign interest payments as well, total government interest payments as a share of GDP increase from 5.8 per cent of GDP in the base year to 5.9 per cent in the base run in the last year as shown in Figure 7.9. In the optimistic scenario total interest payments fall to only 4.5 per cent of GDP, whereas they increase in the pessimistic scenario to 9 per cent of GDP. This clearly reflects that while the government avoids the dangers of entering a debt trap in the base run and the optimistic scenario, this is certainly not the case in the pessimistic projection.

In line with the above observations, the government deficit falls from 5.3 per cent to 4.3 per cent of GDP in the base run, and in the optimistic scenario it is feasible to bring down the deficit even further to 2.5 per cent of GDP in the last year, as shown in Figure 7.10, without impairing growth. In contrast, the government deficit as a share of GDP increases to almost 8 per cent in the

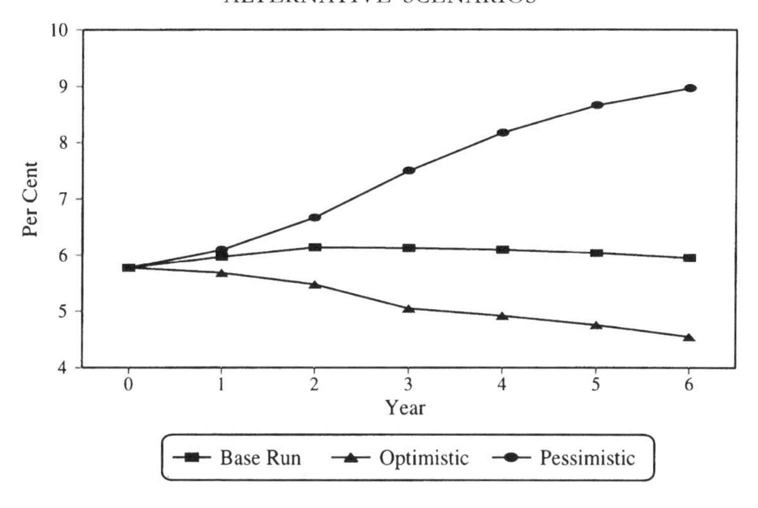

Figure 7.9 Total government interest payments (per cent of GDP)

pessimistic scenario, highlighting the very different characteristics of the three scenarios presented. Similarly, while the annual growth in the budget deficit stays at more than 15 per cent in the pessimistic scenario towards the end of the time horizon, it drops consistently in the optimistic scenario from the middle of the period, and in the base run the growth in the budget deficit is clearly under control, as discussed in Chapter 6.

In accordance with the above developments, the government does not rely on domestic credit in the base run and the optimistic scenario, as shown in Figure 7.11. The amount of real credit to the government in the latter scenario ends up at less than 15 billion rand, equivalent to around 2 per cent of GDP as compared to the base year level of 3.6 per cent. Yet in the pessimistic projection government will find itself forced to absorb a greater share of total domestic credit. Other sources cannot be tapped. Hence, government credit will grow in real terms to around 60 billion rand, or 12.2 per cent of GDP.

Moreover, as demonstrated in Figure 7.12, credit to the private sector is squeezed in the pessimistic scenario. This is not the case in the other two scenarios. In fact, taking account of inflation, real credit to the private sector falls in the pessimistic scenario to only 36.6 per cent of GDP, or 178.9 billion rand in real terms, as compared to 49.4 per cent, or 214.6 billion rand, in the base

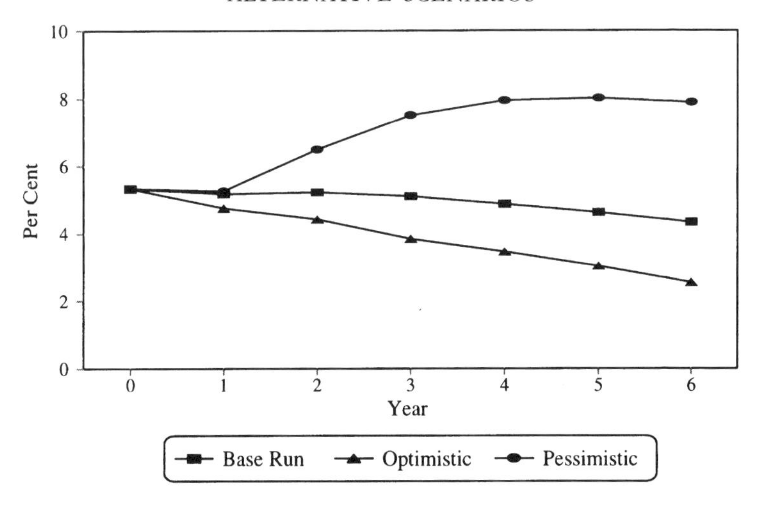

Figure 7.10 Government budget deficit (per cent of GDP)

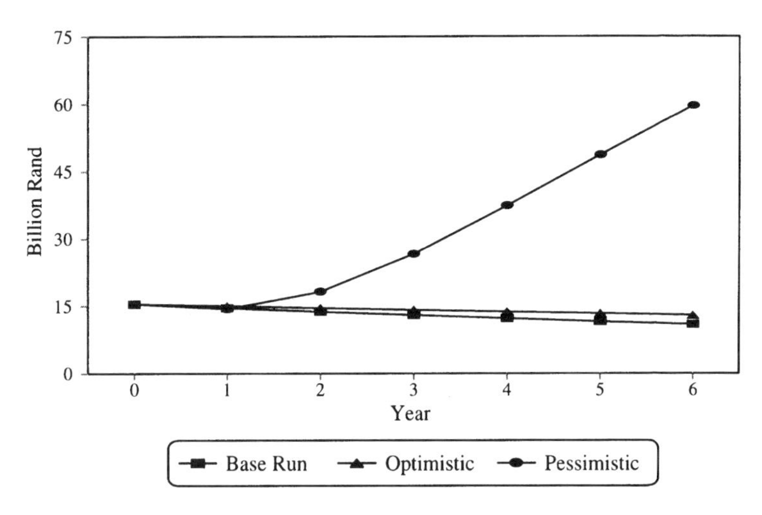

Figure 7.11 Government credit (constant 1994 prices)

year. In the base run and the optimistic scenario, real private credit increases to respectively 255.9 and 297.3 billion rand, corresponding to 47.9 per cent and 51.1 per cent of GDP. Thus, while credit extended to the private sector drops slightly in the base run as a

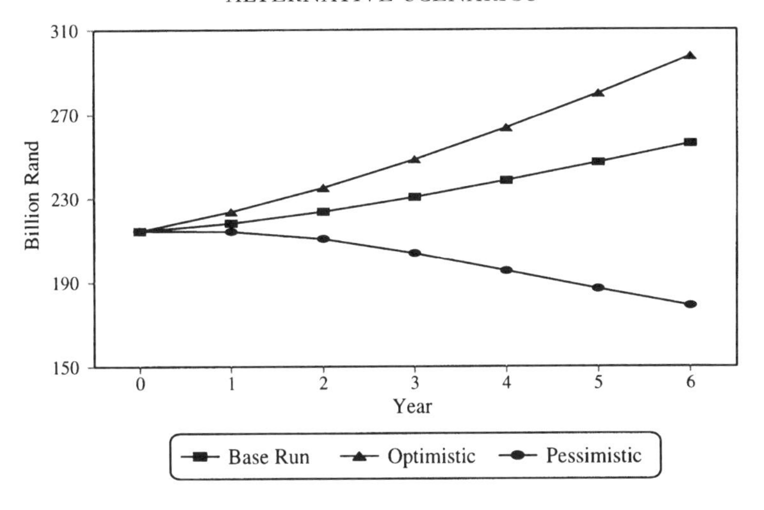

Figure 7.12 Private sector credit (constant 1994 prices)

share of GDP, despite the real increase in the amount of credit extended, the optimistic scenario makes it possible to let private credit grow as a share of GDP.

Domestic debt finance involving the issuance of government debt decreases as a share of GDP in all three scenarios from the level of 4.1 per cent in the base year. The underlying reason in the optimistic scenario is that government does not need to rely as much on this financing source, so this source can fall to 1.5 per cent in the last year. The drop to 2.2 per cent in the pessimistic scenario reflects, on the other hand, an assumed inability to raise more funds through this mechanism without having to raise interest rates considerably. Finally, while increased foreign borrowing is relied on to the extent feasible in the pessimistic scenario, government has the option of keeping this financing at a relatively low level in the optimistic scenario.

With the assumed decrease of the velocity of money circulation, the growth in nominal GDP translates in the optimistic scenario into a nominal money supply amounting to almost 415 billion rand in the final year of the projection. This is to be compared to a nominal money supply of 244.2 billion in the base year. Accordingly, as a share of GDP the money supply increases in the optimistic scenario from 56.2 per cent in the base year to 59.7 per cent in the final year, whereas it remains stable in both the base

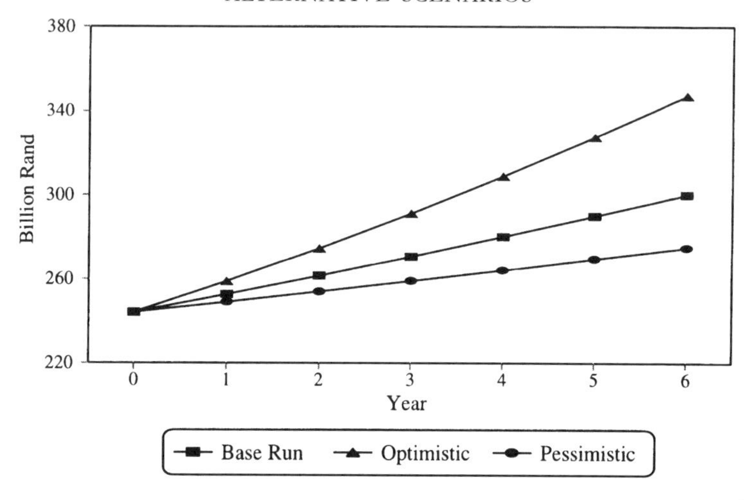

Figure 7.13 Money supply (constant 1994 prices)

run and the pessimistic scenario. The real increase in the money supply implied in the optimistic scenario is equal to 42.2 per cent over the six-year period in comparison with 22.9 per cent for the base run as illustrated in Figure 7.13.

In the pessimistic scenario, the nominal money supply expands to 485.3 billion rand in the last year of the projection. This reflects an increase of almost 98.7 per cent. However, as a share of GDP, the money supply remains constant since the velocity of money circulation is kept unchanged, and the real increase in the money supply in the pessimistic scenario amounts to only 12.5 per cent due to inflation. This increase amounts to only around half the increase in the base run and between one-third and one-quarter the increase in the optimistic scenario.

Finally, in relation to the composition of the money supply, it can be observed that the share of international reserves grows from 3.2 per cent to around 6.3 per cent in both the base run and the optimistic scenario, whereas the share in the final year of the pessimistic scenario is 7.5 per cent. Thus, domestic credit expands slightly more in relative terms in the last scenario as compared to the first two.

Together with the developments in the issuance of government domestic stock and net foreign borrowing by the government, total government debt as a share of GDP increases from 50.0 per cent

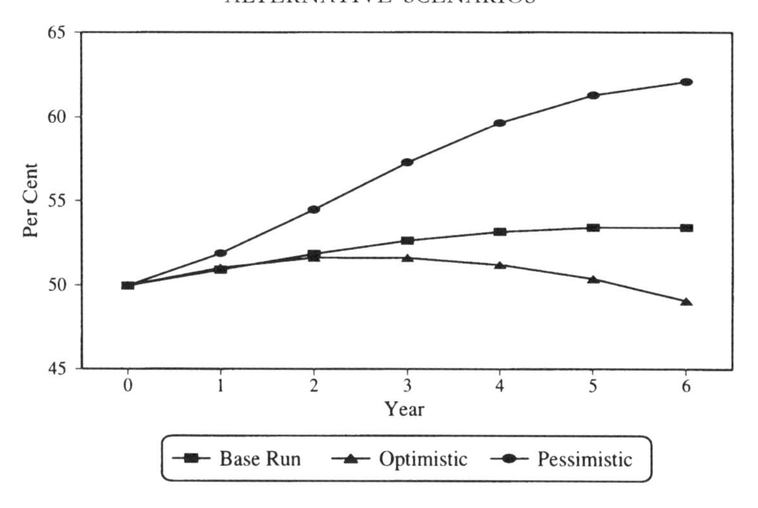

Figure 7.14 Total government debt (per cent of GDP)

in the base year to 53.4 per cent in the final year of the base run as shown in Figure 7.14. The corresponding debt/GDP ratios in the final year of the optimistic and pessimistic scenarios are 49.1 per cent and 62.1 per cent, respectively. Moreover, the composition of the debt among the three available sources of finance (i.e. domestic credit as well as government domestic foreign debt) is markedly different in the three scenarios. This reflects, *inter alia*, that the government is able to diminish its reliance on domestic financing in the optimistic scenario due to a favourable inflow of foreign capital. On the other hand, the pessimistic scenario presumes that government will find itself forced to absorb a greater share of total domestic credit. The reliance on domestic stock issues is constrained as is the access to foreign sources of finance.

SUMMING-UP

The implications of the alternative scenarios for the medium-term future in South Africa are, in sum, markedly different both from each other and from the macroeconomic conditions inherent in the moderately optimistic base run. The optimistic scenario involves a higher growth path in combination with more exports and an increased inflow of foreign capital resources. This inflow, together with more domestic savings, makes it possible to expand investment as required in support of growth and development. This can, moreover, be done without compressing government and private consumption, which expand in per capita terms, partly due to the fact that installed capacity is used more efficiently. In addition, such increases in consumption will in no way impair domestic macro balances, including the budget position of the government and the rate of inflation. On the contrary, inflation can drop to a level which is indeed very low by historic standards. The good news also includes the fact that credit extended to the private sector grows even further in real terms than in the base run. Hence, no crowding-out takes place, and both the government and the private sector can play an active role in the reconstruction of the country. The need for pursuing a well designed set of sectoral and microeconomic policies to maximize employment generation and income redistribution would be much easier in such a favourable macroeconomic context.

The pessimistic scenario, on the other hand, illustrates that if internal conflicts and management problems get out of hand and economic growth falters, badly needed economic restructuring and social reconciliation may become infeasible. This would, no doubt, limit domestic savings as well as capital inflows and could intensify capital flight, impairing import capacity. This, in turn, would depress investments, domestic output and exports even further. The government would be hard pressed to try to counteract such a trend, but its budget could easily reach a clearly unsustainable level. Moreover, while total foreign debt might be increasing less than in the base run due to foreign borrowing constraints, the government would soon find itself in a complex debt trap in which debt service assumes significant importance due to the increase in the domestic interest rates. Even stricter fiscal and monetary restraint may therefore become necessary, and this could lead to a critical worsening of the perspectives for socio-economic development. Moreover, government reliance on domestic credit will in the above process become hard to avoid, and without growth, inflation bounces upwards, squeezing real private credit even further, and impairing the contribution this sector can potentially make to growth and development.

8

CONCLUSION

This study took as its point of departure that aggregate models and quantified macroeconomic projections are indispensable tools in helping governments concerned with economic management and development planning. Moreover, when use is made of foreign finance in support of economic restructuring, recipient third world governments will have to relate to influential international financing institutions, including in particular the IMF and the World Bank. The two Bretton Woods organizations use a variety of analytical tools in their country economic work. Yet relatively little has been published on the Financial Programming (FP) and Revised Minimum Standard Modelling (RMSM) frameworks. This is so even though they have over the years been the two most common macroeconomic modelling frameworks used by IMF and World Bank staff in producing macro projections. This is unfortunate. The influence of the IMF and the World Bank over domestic policy making has increased considerably in developing countries. At the same time, it would appear that the relationship between the Bretton Woods institutions and the African countries, in particular, has not been an entirely happy one during the 1980s and early 1990s. There are many reasons for this (Tarp, 1993a), but the lack of transparency and capacity to elaborate independent macroeconomic projections has no doubt played a critical role in this process. Putting the FP and RMSM analytical models squarely into the public domain in a practical and easily replicable manner as done in this book is therefore an attempt to help students of development and practitioners involved in country economic analyses to come to grips with the fundamental perceptions of macroeconomic causality that are often implicit in the economic policy advice given by the IMF and the World Bank, and at the same time to assist in fostering a better balanced and more insightful policy dialogue in future.

Hence, this study has developed and fully documented how the FP and RMSM frameworks can be used in a rigorous manner in a concrete country context (i.e. South Africa). This was done by taking the reader carefully through all the methodological and practical steps necessary to produce a set of internally consistent projections. Relevant country background was provided in Chapter 2 from which it is clear that the debate on future economic policy and development strategy in South Africa has so far proven both controversial and complex as is the case elsewhere in the third world. Nevertheless, it is by now widely accepted that the priority issues to be addressed by the new government revolve around the possibilities for making the two objectives of growth and redistribution compatible. Stagnation set in at the beginning of the 1970s, and the South African economy has been on the decline for more than a decade. In addition, deep-seated structural weaknesses have developed alongside social imbalances. Inward-looking industrialization, based on the export of gold, and coupled with the exploitation of cheap black labour, was at the core of the economic plan of the apartheid regime. It was, moreover, the intention that South Africa should become a political and economic power house in a constellation of states in Southern Africa. Strategic rather than economic considerations were, therefore, allowed to play a major role in decision making. In addition, inefficiencies, generated by unviable project selection and a host of arbitrary apartheid laws and price controls, together with the extreme degree of conglomerate concentration, hindered an appropriate allocation of economic resources. Instead of concentrating on the development of its own economy, the apartheid regime initiated a destructive and extremely costly engagement in the region. Hence, the development challenges faced by South Africa are enormous. They can, however, be articulated using insights from standard economic theory and practice, and the basic policy frameworks identified in Chapter 2 are not different in any fundamental way from those used to inform the policy debate in other country contexts.

Having established, in Chapter 3, the necessary accounting framework and base year data set, the methodological step of this volume was to operationalise the FP and RMSM projection frameworks in Chapter 4. This was done in the computer programming language called GAMS, using common notation to facilitate comparisons. To be able to produce compatible and consistent medium-term projections on the basis of the two models, some modifications were introduced as compared to the very few standard presentations available in the literature. A few additional changes were necessary due to the specific South African context. However, the overall properties of the models were kept intact, and all the necessary detail is available in Appendix A.

What transpired from the analysis in Chapter 4 is that the FP and RMSM frameworks are very different in terms of content as well as focus. Yet what the two models have in common is that they are quite simple theoretical constructs. Simplicity implies that critical economic assumptions have been made in formulating the models, and due account must, at all times, be taken of these underlying presumptions in applied policy work if serious misjudgements are to be avoided.

In the short-term FP framework there are only two behavioural relationships which explain money and import demand, respectively, in addition to a number of equilibrium conditions relating to the money market and the balance of payments. The implication is an assumption that a single competitive, flex-price market for traded and non-traded goods exists. Hence, constraints and inflexibilities, often present in developing countries, are ignored. Moreover, there is no link between real (full employment) GDP and monetary variables, despite the often observed negative supply-side effects of a credit squeeze. In sum, important institutional and structural context is left to be specified by the analyst entirely outside the framework of the model. The policy advice, involving manipulations of domestic credit and the exchange rate, which can be derived from the FP framework, can as a consequence easily be both mistargeted and harmful unless great care is exercised.

The RMSM model is a medium- to long-term fix-price model in the two-gap tradition. Hence, in contrast to the monetary focus of the FP model, the real sector of the economy is at the core of the RMSM. Consequently, it represents another theoretical extreme in the sense that changes in demand have no price effects affecting economic behaviour. The RMSM is therefore a planning tool, which can yield estimates of the levels of investment, imports and external borrowing needed to reach a targeted rate of real output growth. Yet issues related to the degree of utilization of installed capacity are – as was the case in the FP framework – ignored. Similarly, distributional questions are not addressed within the narrow confines of the models *per se*. Thus, the RMSM is not an economic policy model which the policy analyst can use to demonstrate how policies should be changed to reach a desired growth path. To arrive at policy prescriptions, it is necessary to move outside the narrow confines of the model.

It follows from the above that the FP and RMSM frameworks can, justifiably, be criticized for being theoretically too simple. As such they should not be used in a mechanistic manner for detailed policy analysis at country level to trace the effects of marginal changes in exogenous variables and parameters on the endogenous variables. This point also emerged as a major conclusion from the policy experiments in Chapter 5. Yet the two models are certainly consistent and contain the central monetary and material national accounting identities, which any macroeconomic projection model must include. As such they can be used in a non-mechanistic and meaningful manner to produce illustrative medium-term scenarios, relying on additional qualitative and quantitative judgement from outside the models. This is so in particular when all variables are in fact treated as endogenous in scenario building, as has been done in this volume. Moreover, a good grasp of consistency is a minimum requirement in macroeconomic analysis (Easterly, 1989). Simplicity is also a strength in the sense that the two models require relatively few data and are easy to use, while complex models are of little relevance if the needed data are not available or are unreliable. Thus it was demonstrated in Chapter 3 how a complete data set for the base year of the two modelling frameworks can be compiled from official South African statistics. At the same time, a standard national accounting framework was outlined, and it was shown how it could be used to ensure the required consistency among the data originating from different sources. For this reason it is hoped that Chapter 3 could facilitate future updating of the analysis presented in this volume.

Any model of how an economy actually works is based on a set of underlying assumptions regarding the mechanisms, which together with a particular set of parameters and exogenous variables determine the economic outcome within the chosen time horizon. Thus, to more fully understand these mechanisms and assess the importance of the different variables it is useful to implement model experiments. This can be done, first, by changing parameters and exogenous variables one by one and noting the impact on the value of the endogenous variables as compared to what happens in the base run. In this context, the results from different models can also be compared with each other. Second, such individual experiments can be carried out under different closure rules, i.e. different sets of assumptions as to which variables take the necessary adjustments in the course of the experiment. Such model experiments were implemented in Chapter 5, and it was, by way of introduction, noted that standard practice in applications of the FP model is to assume an endogenous exchange rate and exogenous capital flows, reflecting the perception of the exchange rate as a policy instrument. The RMSM, on the other hand, is normally specified with the opposite closure, i.e. with an exogenous exchange rate and endogenous external borrowing by the government.

It can, on the basis of Chapter 5, be concluded that the choice of closure mechanism has significant influence on the properties of the two models. Moreover, while the closure rule in some experiments had the same qualitative impact on selected endogenous variables in the two models, there are also examples where the opposite is true. The FP and RMSM models do, as shown in Chapter 5, quite often lead to the same qualitative results as far as the endogenous variables are concerned, provided the closure rule is the same. Yet they also, at times, produce different economic outcomes following the same change in a parameter or exogenous variable. This is critical, since it can lead to contradictory policy advice.

Thus, different results can be obtained about the same reality, depending on the model in question and on how it is specified. This underlines the importance of making explicit one's assumptions about how the economy works, so they can be verified. The overall conclusion, emerging from Chapter 5, is therefore that great caution must be exercised in clarifying the empirical conditions relevant to the particular case in question, before models such as the FP framework and the RMSM are used to inform the macroeconomic policy debate. However, this is, as already noted above, mainly in relation to the analysis of marginal policy experiments. Thus, only limited specific policy advice can be drawn up on the analytic basis provided by the models in focus here. This is highlighted by the fact that the FP and RMSM models have nothing to say about the different distributional and employment consequences which may result from different growth paths, and which are of great importance in most third world countries.

Nevertheless, the FP and RMSM models described in Chapter 4 can be used sensibly in scenario building. They were therefore relied on together with the data set from Chapter 3 to generate the moderately optimistic base run in Chapter 6. It can in this regard be reiterated, first, that the base run was constructed through a consistent use of separate projections generated by the two underlying models. This is seldom – if ever – done in practice and serves to illustrate how a more complete picture can be obtained if the two approaches are merged. Second, the main conclusion of Chapter 6 is that the government of South Africa is not left without room for manoeuvre despite the critical problems listed in Chapter 2. The economy is potentially very rich, with a considerable human and physical infrastructure as well as a significant natural resource base, although gold might be a wasting asset. Moreover, installed capacity is probably not fully utilized, and South Africa's international debt is limited.

More specifically, the medium-term base scenario illustrates that government consumption can be expanded from 21.0 per cent to 21.8 per cent of GDP under moderately optimistic assumptions about the future. This corresponds to an increase in real terms of almost 25 billion rand over the six-year period. In addition, the public investment programme in the last year is about 20 per cent higher than in the base year. Thus, there is space for additional investments totalling 6 billion rand in real terms over the six-year forecasting period as compared to the level of the base year. Moreover, some of the increase in government consumption can be directed to investment if this proves possible and desirable. Finally, private investment in constant prices in the base run is expected to increase from an annual 68.7 billion rand in the base year to more than 104.8 billion at the end of the six-year forecast horizon.

These are important conclusions, which are in contrast with the present government strategy where exclusive emphasis is put on financing RDP initiatives through budget reallocations within the context of the Budget Reprioritization Programme (BRP). The BRP approach is bound, however, to result in more limited amounts of financing as the room for manoeuvre within the existing budget frame is limited by commitments already made. Yet it is underlined that little was said in definitive terms in Chapter 6 on the complex choices which the new South African government will have to make in striking a balance between existing competing – or maybe better, complementary – development strategies. Institutions such as the IMF and the World Bank argue for a development strategy based on export led growth (IMF, 1992; Fallon and Pereira de Silva, 1994). There are, however, other analysts, who focus their attention more on developing domestic markets and institutions (Padayachee, 1990; Zarenda, 1992; MERG, 1993). Nevertheless, it did transpire clearly from Chapter 6, that there is room under moderately optimistic conditions for an active developmental state to start addressing the needs of poor South African people directly without disturbing macroeconomic balances or crowding-out private sector activity.

In Chapter 7, a more optimistic as well as a more pessimistic scenario were established. The optimistic scenario involves a higher growth path made possible by increased exports in combination with more savings and investment. In addition to the higher level of government investment, private investment increases to a level which in the final year is more than 26 per cent higher than in the base run, and it is possible to expand both government and private consumption. This expansion does not impair domestic macro balances, including the budget position of the government and the rate of annual inflation, which can actually be brought down from 6 per cent to only 3 per cent.

The pessimistic scenario, on the other hand, illustrates that if access to foreign borrowing becomes more stringent and real resource inflows and growth falter, not even considerable moderation will be sufficient to maintain domestic macro balances. On the contrary, the government budget can easily reach an unsustainable level of almost 8 per cent of GDP, and government becomes more dependent on domestic credit. Without growth, inflation bounces upwards, and this will squeeze real private credit, so both government and private investment fall as compared to the base run. Even stricter fiscal and monetary restraint may quickly become necessary, and this could lead to a further critical worsening of the state of the economy.

The alternative scenarios in Chapter 7 were developed in the same manner as the base scenario contained in Chapter 6. Thus, the respective optimistic and pessimistic FP and RMSM projections are consistent with each other. This methodological approach made it possible to identify general reasons or circumstances which are behind the markedly different economic outcomes in terms of growth, inflation, the balance of payments and government finances, delineated in the two scenarios. However, the alternative scenarios put forward in Chapter 7 are, together with the base run in Chapter 6, merely three out of the numerous projections, which could be made on the basis of the analytical frameworks presented in Chapter 4. It is, in fact, highly unlikely that actual developments in South Africa will in the coming years precisely reproduce one of these selected combinations of macroeconomic variables and parameters. Thus, the exact quantification of the parameters and the exogenous and endogenous variables undertaken in previous chapters should not be interpreted too literally in a real life context. Hence, nothing can be taken for granted. South Africa will have to be on the look out to avoid dangers such as those inherent in the pessimistic scenario, while searching at the same time for a way to the base run, or even better, the optimistic scenario.

In this process, domestic and international players in the policy dialogue are well advised that similarly sized macroeconomic indicators may conceal very different underlying social and economic realities, as is evident when comparing the three scenarios put forward in Chapters 6 and 7. This should not be taken as an argument to avoid quantification. On the contrary, qualitative statements have problems of their own, and it is believed that the three scenarios presented capture the essential macroeconomic differences between the many possible directions which the South African economy may take. Actually, the scenarios identified are likely to cover a very substantial part of the range of probable economic medium-term outcomes in South Africa, in particular as each of them can be seen as a representative of a much larger sub-set of specific development paths. This together with the documentation provided in Appendices A–D, should facilitate not only further experimentation and updating, but also make it possible to interpret in a more coherent manner the overall macroeconomic framework within which the future development of South Africa will take place.

In this regard, it is by way of conclusion reiterated that macroeconomic stability and economic growth will be critical preconditions for development to succeed in South Africa as has been the case elsewhere. This is why these topics have been in focus in this study, which has in addition demonstrated how the FP and RMSM macro models can be applied in a relevant way. Nevertheless, issues such as employment, urban–rural divisions and income distribution as well as many non-economic factors are just as crucial measures of the development process and for the well-being of the population. To cover these issues in the analysis, applied macro models of the FP and RMSM kind are not appropriate tools. Instead, other analytical frameworks are required. It has been beyond the scope of the present study to cover these alternative modelling strategies, but their existence as well as the limitations of the FP and RMSM frameworks should be fully appreciated in any follow-up work based on the guidelines set out in this book.

APPENDIX A
Modelling frameworks in GAMS

A.1 INTRODUCTION

Both the Financial Programming (FP) framework and the Revised Minimum Standard Model (RMSM), which were described in Chapter 4, were programmed and solved using the software GAMS (Brooke *et al.*, 1988). This appendix contains the GAMS programs used to generate the base run and the scenarios, analysed in Chapters 6 and 7, respectively. The programs for each model consist of three files, all of which are reproduced below, and the same structure is used in the FP and RMSM frameworks. There are one main program and two table programs. The table programs are included by a GAMS command in the main program and generate a range of tables for, respectively, the base run and the scenarios. The actual files are available on disks, which can be obtained from the authors.

Whereas all programs are fairly straightforward given some knowledge of GAMS programming, a few comments are required as far as data inputs are concerned. Data are entered in step VII in the main programs of both models, beginning with the base year data described in Chapter 3. Thus in step VII.A, the necessary 1993 values of lagged variables are defined, while step VII.B takes care of the 1994 values of all variables. The only notable feature in these steps is that some variable values are calculated from other data (e.g. interest rates). This method ensures that the right-hand sides of all model equations are exactly equal to the left-hand side value in the base year. Therefore, the two models reproduce precisely all base year data. In stage VII.C, initial values are specified for all endogenous variables in the forecast horizon. The next data input in both models, VII.D, is values of all exogenous variables during the forecast horizon. An important element of the step is a table called *iniexo*, containing the values of most exogenous variables. They were either calculated outside the modelling frameworks from the specified assumption or obtained from the solution of the other model in order to ensure that the two models produce a consistent base run and scenarios.

Consistency implies here that variables appearing in both models have identical values. This was achieved by applying an iterative procedure involving both frameworks. First, assumptions were made concerning the exogenous variables that enter the FP framework, and their level values were calculated outside the program. Since most assumptions underlying the base run as well as the scenarios, cf. Chapters 6 and 7, have the form of a growth rate or a percentage of GDP, these calculations were straightforward. In the second step of the procedure, the FP framework was solved for its endogenous variables. Two types of assumptions were then imposed on the RMSM: (1) the values of variables, which are exogenous in both models, were entered in RMSM's *iniexo* table, and (2) the endogenous variables of the FP framework, which are exogenous in the RMSM, were taken from the solution of the FP framework and entered *iniexo* as well. To give an example, the exchange rate is endogenous in the FP framework, and its values were imported to RMSM, where the variable is exogenous. In the final step, the RMSM was solved and the results checked. Since the early attempts at constructing the base run as well as the scenarios did not give reasonable results for all variables, the procedure was repeated several times with modified assumptions until satisfactory outcomes were obtained. However, since only a limited number of decimals is used in the different data input tables, there are some minor deviations in variable values when the two models are solved. The last part of the data entry section of the frameworks concerns parameter values. They were either entered directly in tables or calibrated from base year data.

Finally, in order to obtain consistency between the two modelling frameworks in the scenarios, tables corresponding to *iniexo* appear in the programs. They are named *opprn* in the optimistic and *peppr* in the pessimistic scenario. Besides values of exogenous variables, these tables also include the values of parameters, which were changed when the two scenarios were generated.

A.2 FINANCIAL PROGRAMMING FRAMEWORK

Main program (FPSCEN.GMS)

```
$offsymlist offsymxref
*
* FP – Financial Programming Framework


*
* I Sets
*

SETS        tl           Long time horizon        /1993*2000/
            t(tl)        Model time horizon       /1994*2000/
            tf(tl)       Forecast time horizon    /1995*2000/;


*
* II Parameters
*

PARAMETERS  m0(tl)       Constant in import function
            m1(tl)       GDP elasticity of import
            m2(tl)       Real exchange rate elasticity of import
            theta        Weight in price index
            v(tl)        Money velocity;


*
* III Variables
*

VARIABLES   BRG(tl)      Government borrowing requirement
            CG(tl)       Government consumption
            CURBAL(tl)   Current account surplus
            DC(tl)       Total domestic credit
            DCG(tl)      Government domestic credit
            DCP(tl)      Private domestic credit
            E(tl)        Nominal exchange rate
            GDP(tl)      Real GDP
            GDPN(tl)     Nominal GDP
            GT(tl)       Other government expenditures
            INDG(tl)     Government interest payments on domestic debt
            INFG(tl)     Government interest payments on foreign debt
            INFP(tl)     Private interest payments on foreign debt
            IRD(tl)      Domestic interest rate
            IRF(tl)      Foreign interest rate
            IVG(tl)      Government investment
            M(tl)        Import
            MD(tl)       Money demand
            MPI(tl)      Import price index
            MS(tl)       Money supply
            NETFSY(tl)   Net factor services from abroad
            NDDG(tl)     Government net domestic debt
            NFDG(tl)     Government net foreign debt
            NFDP(tl)     Private net foreign debt
            NFP(tl)      Net other factor services
            NTRG(tl)     Net transfers to government from abroad
            NTRP(tl)     Net transfers to private sector from abroad
```

```
            OBJ          Objective
            P(tl)        General price level
            PD(tl)       Domestic price level
            R(tl)        Foreign exchange reserves
            RESBAL(tl)   Resource balance
            TG(tl)       Government revenue
            X(tl)        Export
            XPI(tl)      Export price index;

POSITIVE VARIABLES CG, E, GDP, GDPN, GT, M, MD, MPI, MS, NDDG, P, PD, TG, X,
XPI;
```

*

* *IV Equations*

*

```
EQUATIONS   EQ01(t)      General price index
            EQ02(t)      Nominal GDP
            EQ03(t)      Money demand
            EQ04(tl)     Money supply
            EQ05(t)      Total domestic credit
            EQ06(t)      Money market equilibrium condition
            EQ07(tl)     Government interest payments on foreign debt
            EQ08(tl)     Government interest payments on domestic debt
            EQ09(t)      Government borrowing requirement
            EQ10(tl)     Government finance constraint
            EQ11(t)      Import function
            EQ12(t)      Resource balance
            EQ13(tl)     Private interest payments on foreign debt
            EQ14(t)      Net factor services
            EQ15(t)      Current account
            EQ16(tl)     Balance of payments
            EQ99         Objective function;
```

*

* *V Model equations*

*

* A Prices and monetary sector

*

```
EQ01(t) . .
  P(t) =e= (1 - theta)*PD(t) + theta*E(t)*MPI(t);

EQ02(t) . .
  GDPN(t) =e= P(t)*GDP(t);

EQ03(t) . .
  MD(t) =e= (1/v(t))*GDPN(t);

EQ04(tl-1) . .
  MS(tl) - MS(tl-1) =e= E(tl)*(R(tl) - R(tl-1)) + (DC(tl) - DC(tl-1)) +
                        (E(tl) - E(tl-1))*R(tl-1);

EQ05(t) . .
  DC(t) =e= DCG(t) + DCP(t);

EQ06(t) . .
  MS(t) =e= MD(t);
```

```
*
* B Government accounts
*

EQ07(tl-1) . .
  INFG(tl) =e= IRF(tl)*NFDG(tl-1);

EQ08(tl-1) . .
  INDG(tl) =e= IRD(tl)*NDDG(tl-1);

EQ09(t) . .
  BRG(t) =e= P(t)*(CG(t) + IVG(t)) + GT(t) + INDG(t) + E(t)*INFG(t) -
             TG(t) - E(t)*NTRG(t);

EQ10(tl-1) . .
  BRG(tl) =e= (DCG(tl) - DCG(tl-1)) + (NDDG(tl) - NDDG(tl-1)) +
              E(tl)*(NFDG(tl) - NFDG(tl-1));


*
* C Balance of payments
*

EQ11(t) . .
  log(M(t)) =e= m0(t) + m1(t)*log(GDP(t)) + m2(t)*log((E(t)*MPI(t)/PD(t)));

EQ12(t) . .
  RESBAL(t) =e= X(t)*XPI(t) - M(t)*MPI(t);

EQ13(tl-1) . .
  INFP(tl) =e= IRF(tl)*NFDP(tl-1);

EQ14(t) . .
  NETFSY(t) =e= NFP(t) - INFG(t) - INFP(t);

EQ15(t) . .
  CURBAL(t) =e= RESBAL(t) + NETFSY(t) + NTRG(t) + NTRP(t);

EQ16(tl-1) . .
  R(tl) - R(tl-1) =e= CURBAL(tl) + (NFDG(tl) - NFDG(tl-1)) +
                      (NFDP(tl) - NFDP(tl-1));


*
* D Objective
*

EQ99 . .
  OBJ =e= sum(t, GDP(t));


*
* VI Model definitions
*

MODEL FP Financial Programming Model / all/;


*
* II Data
*
* A 1993 values of lagged variables
*

DC.fx("1993")              =     201.015;
```

```
DCG.fx("1993")          =   14.955;
DCP.fx("1993")          =  186.060;
E.fx("1993")            =    0.9072;
MD.fx("1993")           =  210.9778704;
MS.fx("1993")           =  210.9778704;
NDDG.fx("1993")         =  151.379;
NFDG.fx("1993")         =   27.510;
NFDP.fx("1993")         =   17.286;
R.fx("1993")            =   10.982;


*
* B 1994 values of all variables
*

BRG.fx("1994")          =   23.144;
CG.fx("1994")           =   91.349;
CURBAL.fx("1994")       =   -2.089;
DC.fx("1994")           =  230.047;
DCG.fx("1994")          =   15.487;
DCP.fx("1994")          =  214.560;
E.fx("1994")            =    1.000;
GDP.fx("1994")          =  434.246;
GDPN.fx("1994")         =  434.246;
GT.fx("1994")           =   15.421;
INDG.fx("1994")         =   21.193023172;
INFG.fx("1994")         =    3.887976828;
INFP.fx("1994")         =    2.443023172;
IRD.fx("1994")          = INDG.l("1994")/NDDG.l("1993");
IRF.fx("1994")          = INFG.l("1994")/NFDG.l("1993");
IVG.fx("1994")          =    9.620;
M.fx("1994")            =   94.415;
MD.fx("1994")           =  244.150;
MPI.fx("1994")          =    1.000;
MS.fx("1994")           =  244.150;
NETFSY.fx("1994")       =  -10.561;
NDDG.fx("1994")         =  169.190;
NFDG.fx("1994")         =   32.311;
NFDP.fx("1994")         =   17.695;
NFP.fx("1994")          =   -4.230;
NTRG.fx("1994")         =     .272;
NTRP.fx("1994")         =    -.067;
P.fx("1994")            =    1.000;
PD.fx("1994")           =    1.000;
R.fx("1994")            =   14.103;
RESBAL.fx("1994")       =    8.267;
TG.fx("1994")           =  118.055;
X.fx("1994")            =  102.682;
XPI.fx("1994")          =    1.000;


*
* C Initial values and bounds of endogenous variables in
* forecast horizon
*

BRG.l(tf)               = BRG.l("1994");
CG.l(tf)                = CG.l("1994");
CURBAL.l(tf)            = CURBAL.l("1994");
DC.l(tf)                = DC.l("1994");
```

```
DCG.l(tf)          =  DCG.l("1994");
E.l(tf)            =  E.l("1994");
E.lo(tf)           =  0.75;
GDPN.l(tf)         =  GDPN.l("1994");
INDG.l(tf)         =  INDG.l("1994");
INFG.l(tf)         =  INFG.l("1994");
INFP.l(tf)         =  INFP.l("1994");
M.l(tf)            =  M.l("1994");
MD.l(tf)           =  MD.l("1994");
MS.l(tf)           =  MS.l("1994");
NETFSY.l(tf)       =  NETFSY.l("1994");
PD.l(tf)           =  PD.l("1994");
PD.lo(tf)          =  0.75;
RESBAL.l(tf)       =  RESBAL.l("1994");
```

*
* D Values of exogenous variables in forecast horizon
* (calculated from assumptions outside model)
*

table iniexo(*,tf) Values of exogenous variables in forecast horizon

	1995	1996	1997	1998	1999	2000
DCP	231.462	251.420	274.637	301.014	330.436	362.968
GDP	449.445	465.175	481.456	498.307	515.748	533.799
GT	16.918	18.561	20.363	22.341	24.510	26.890
IRD	0.1404	0.1404	0.1354	0.1304	0.1254	0.1204
IRF	0.1413	0.1413	0.1413	0.1413	0.1413	0.1413
IVG	9.812	10.058	10.359	10.722	11.097	11.486
MPI	1.0300	1.0609	1.0927	1.1255	1.1593	1.1941
NDDG	186.611	203.319	219.841	236.545	254.568	273.880
NFDG	39.349	49.350	61.028	73.471	85.499	96.882
NFDP	26.224	36.904	49.597	63.904	80.895	100.948
NFP	−4.509	−4.807	−5.125	−5.463	−5.824	−6.209
NTRG	0.290	0.309	0.329	0.351	0.374	0.399
NTRP	−0.071	−0.075	−0.080	−0.086	−0.092	−0.098
P	1.0600	1.1236	1.1910	1.2625	1.3382	1.4185
R	20.317	25.455	29.612	33.168	36.493	39.793
TG	129.584	143.212	158.838	177.407	198.084	219.589
X	105.762	109.993	114.943	120.690	127.328	134.382
XPI	1.0300	1.0609	1.0927	1.1255	1.1593	1.1941

```
DCP.fx(tf)         =  iniexo("DCP",tf);
GDP.fx(tf)         =  iniexo("GDP",tf);
GT.fx(tf)          =  iniexo("GT",tf);
IRD.fx(tf)         =  iniexo("IRD",tf);
IRF.fx(tf)         =  iniexo("IRF",tf);
IVG.fx(tf)         =  iniexo("IVG",tf);
MPI.fx(tf)         =  iniexo("MPI",tf);
NDDG.fx(tf)        =  iniexo("NDDG",tf);
NFDG.fx(tf)        =  iniexo("NFDG",tf);
NFDP.fx(tf)        =  iniexo("NFDP",tf);
NFP.fx(tf)         =  iniexo("NFP",tf);
NTRG.fx(tf)        =  iniexo("NTRG",tf);
NTRP.fx(tf)        =  iniexo("NTRP",tf);
P.fx(tf)           =  iniexo("P",tf);
R.fx(tf)           =  iniexo("R",tf);
TG.fx(tf)          =  iniexo("TG",tf);
```

```
X.fx(tf)                    =  iniexo("X",tf);
XPI.fx(tf)                  =  iniexo("XPI",tf);
```

*
* E Parameter values and calibration
*

```
table inipar(*,*)  Parameter values in forecast horizon

             1995      1996      1997      1998      1999      2000

M0         -2.687    -2.656    -2.643    -2.643    -2.643    -2.6434

* Import function parameters (Source for elasticities: Kahn et al., 1992)

m1(t)       =  1.20;
m2(t)       = -0.73;
m0("1994") = log(M.l("1994")) - m1("1994")*log(GDP.l("1994"));
m0(tf)      = inipar("M0",tf);

* Weight in price index

theta       = 0.2;

* Money velocity v(t) calibrated to fit base year data

v(t)        = GDPN.l("1994")/MD.l("1994");
```

*
* *VIII Solve base run*
*

```
OPTION SOLPRINT=off,LIMROW=0,LIMCOL=0;

SOLVE FP MAXIMIZING OBJ USING NLP;
```

*
* *IX Report definitions*
*

```
SETS  r1  Government budget    /G-REV,G-ROW,G-CON,G-INV,G-TRA,G-IND,
                                 G-INF,G-TOT/
      r2  Government finance   /F-DCR,F-BON,F-FCR,F-TOT/
      r3  Balance of payments  /B-EXP,B-IMP,B-INT,B-TRA,B-FAC,B-CUA,
                                 B-GBO,B-PBO,B-RES/
      r4  Money supply         /M-MOS,M-RES,M-CRE,M-GCR,M-PCR/
      r5  Other assets         /O-GCR,O-GBO,O-FBG,O-GOD,O-FBP/
      r6  Prices               /P-GEN,P-DOM,P-IMP,P-EXP,P-EXR,P-RER/
      r7  Other variables      /V-IRD,V-IRF,V-NFDG,V-NFDP,V-R,V-GDPN/
      r8  Material balance     /Z-GDP,Z-CG,Z-IVG,Z-EXP,Z-IMP/;

PARAMETERS  govbud0(r1,tl)  Government budget - base run values
            govbud1(r1,tl)  Government budget - billion rand
            govbud2(r1,tl)  Government budget - per cent of GDP
            govbud3(r1,tl)  Government budget - growth rates
            govbud4(r1,tl)  Government budget - deviation from base run
            govfin0(r2,tl)  Government deficit finance - base run values
            govfin1(r2,tl)  Government deficit finance - billion rand
            govfin2(r2,tl)  Government deficit finance - per cent of GDP
```

```
              govfin3(r2,tl)    Government deficit finance – growth rates
              govfin4(r2,tl)    Government deficit finance – deviation base run
              baofpa0(r3,tl)    Balance of payments – base run values
              baofpa1(r3,tl)    Balance of payments – billion rand
              baofpa2(r3,tl)    Balance of payments – per cent of GDP
              baofpa3(r3,tl)    Balance of payments – growth rates
              baofpa4(r3,tl)    Balance of payments – deviation from base run
              baofus0(r3,tl)    Balance of payments – base run values
              baofus1(r3,tl)    Balance of payments – billion foreign currency
              baofus2(r3,tl)    Balance of payments – per cent of GDP
              baofus3(r3,tl)    Balance of payments – growth rates
              baofus4(r3,tl)    Balance of payments – deviation from base run
              monsup0(r4,tl)    Money supply – base run values
              monsup1(r4,tl)    Money supply – billion rand
              monsup2(r4,tl)    Money supply – per cent of GDP
              monsup3(r4,tl)    Money supply – growth rates
              monsup4(r4,tl)    Money supply – deviation from base run
              othass0(r5,tl)    Other asset stocks – base run values
              othass1(r5,tl)    Other asset stocks – billion rand
              othass2(r5,tl)    Other asset stocks – per cent of GDP
              othass3(r5,tl)    Other asset stocks – growth rates
              othass4(r5,tl)    Other asset stocks – deviation from base run
              pritab0(r6,tl)    Prices – base run values
              pritab1(r6,tl)    Prices – 1994=1
              pritab3(r6,tl)    Prices – growth rates
              pritab4(r6,tl)    Prices – deviation from base run
              othvar0(r7,tl)    Other variables – base run values
              othvar1(r7,tl)    Other variables
              othvar3(r7,tl)    Other variables – growth rates
              othvar4(r7,tl)    Other variables – deviation from base run
              matvar0(r8,tl)    Material balance var. – base run values
              matvar1(r8,tl)    Material balance var. – constant 1994 rand
              matvar2(r8,tl)    Material balance var. – per cent of GDP
              matvar3(r8,tl)    Material balance var. – growth rates
              matvar4(r8,tl)    Material balance var. – deviation from base run
              parame1(*,tl)     Parameter values;

$include fpscent1.gms
```

* *X Scenarios*

```
*
```

* 0 Parameters defining growth rates in base run

```
*

parameters    gdpgr(t)    GDP growth
              expgr(t)    Export growth
              ivggr(t)    Government investment growth;

gdpgr(t)$(ORD(t) GT 1)    =    GDP.l(t)/GDP.l(t−1) − 1;
expgr(t)$(ORD(t) GT 1)    =    X.l(t)/X.l(t−1) − 1;
ivggr(t)$(ORD(t) GT 1)    =    IVG.l(t)/IVG.l(t−1) −1;


*
```

* A The 'optimistic' scenario

```
*

*  1. GDP growth rates increased
*  2. Export growth rates increased
*  3. Government investment growth increased
```

```
*  4. Inflation rate reduced
*  5. Nominal government revenue reduced
*  6. Nominal other government expenditures reduced
*  7. Domestic interest rate reduced
*  8. Government external debt reduced
*  9. Money velocity reduced
* 10. Private credit reduced nominally
* 11. Government domestic debt reduced nominally
* 12. Foreign reserves increased

loop(t$(ORD(t) GT 1), GDP.fx(t)  =  (1 + gdpgr(t) + 0.015)*GDP.l(t-1););
loop(t$(ORD(t) GT 1), X.fx(t)    =  (1 + expgr(t) + 0.020)*X.l(t-1););
loop(t$(ORD(t) GT 1), IVG.fx(t)  =  (1 + ivggr(t) + 0.015)*IVG.l(t-1););

P.fx(tf)            =  1.03**ORD(tf);
TG.fx(tf)           =  TG.l(tf)*0.980**ORD(tf);
GT.fx(tf)           =  GT.l(tf)*0.985**ORD(tf);

IRD.fx(tf)          =  iniexo("IRD",tf) - 0.03;
IRD.fx("1995")      =  iniexo("IRD","1995") - 0.01;
IRD.fx("1996")      =  iniexo("IRD","1996") - 0.02;
NFDG.fx(tf)         =  NFDG.l(tf)*0.97**ORD(tf);
v(tf)               =  v(tf)/(1.01**ORD(tf));


table opprn(*,tf)  Selected exogenous variables

           1995      1996      1997      1998      1999      2000

DCP     230.512   249.440   271.483   296.498   324.343   355.048
NDDG    185.608   199.688   211.431   222.543   233.557   243.860
R        20.466    26.009    30.725    35.008    39.271    43.732;


DCP.fx(tf)          =  opprn("DCP",tf);
NDDG.fx(tf)         =  opprn("NDDG",tf);
R.fx(tf)            =  opprn("R",tf);

SOLVE FP MAXIMIZING OBJ USING NLP;

$include fpscent2.gms


*
* Base run values are reestablished
*

DCP.fx(tf)          =  iniexo("DCP",tf);
GDP.fx(tf)          =  iniexo("GDP",tf);
GT.fx(tf)           =  iniexo("GT",tf);
IRD.fx(tf)          =  iniexo("IRD",tf);
IVG.fx(tf)          =  iniexo("IVG",tf);
NDDG.fx(tf)         =  iniexo("NDDG",tf);
NFDG.fx(tf)         =  iniexo("NFDG",tf);
P.fx(tf)            =  iniexo("P",tf);
R.fx(tf)            =  iniexo("R",tf);
TG.fx(tf)           =  iniexo("TG",tf);
X.fx(tf)            =  iniexo("X",tf);
v(tf)               =  v("1994");
```

```
*
* B The 'pessimistic' scenario
*

*
*  0. Price level made endogenous. Instead exogenous gov. consumption
*  1. GDP growth rates reduced
*  2. Export growth rates reduced
*  3. Government investment growth reduced
*  4. Private foreign debt reduced
*  5. Growth in export price index reduced
*  6. Government consumption reduced
*  7. Private credit reduced
*  8. Nominal other government expenditures increased
*  9. Domestic interest rate increased
* 10. Nominal government revenue increased

P.lo(tf)                      =   0.5;
P.up(tf)                      =  +INF;

loop(t$(ORD(t) GT 1), GDP.fx(t)  =  (1 + gdpgr(t) - 0.015)*GDP.l(t-1););
loop(t$(ORD(t) GT 1), X.fx(t)    =  (1 + expgr(t) - 0.010)*X.l(t-1););
loop(t$(ORD(t) GT 1), IVG.fx(t)  =  (1 + ivggr(t) - 0.015)*IVG.l(t-1););

NFDP.fx(tf)                   =  NFDP.l(tf)*(0.90**ORD(tf));
XPI.fx(tf)                    =  XPI.l(tf)*0.99**ORD(tf);
CG.fx(tf)                     =  peprn("CG",tf);
DCP.fx(tf)                    =  peprn("DCP",tf);

table peprn(*,tf)  Selected exogenous variables

            1995      1996      1997      1998      1999      2000

CG        93.430    98.604   102.201   104.727   106.422   107.128
DCP      227.148   238.872   251.359   266.913   287.609   315.706
GT        16.673    18.185    20.184    22.798    26.205    30.651
IRD        .1404     .1497     .1686     .1878     .2073     .2272
TG       129.584   141.580   157.976   180.639   210.130   246.967;

GT.fx(tf)                     =  peprn("GT",tf);
IRD.fx(tf)                    =  peprn("IRD",tf);
TG.fx(tf)                     =  peprn("TG",tf);

SOLVE FP MAXIMIZING OBJ USING NLP;

$include fpscent2.gms
```

Program generating base run tables (FPSCENT1.GMS)

```
* This file calculates reporting values for the base run
* and save base run values in parameters "0"
*

govbud0("G-REV",t)            =  TG.l(t);
govbud0("G-ROW",t)            =  E.l(t)*NTRG.l(t);
govbud0("G-CON",t)            =  -P.l(t)*CG.l(t);
govbud0("G-INV",t)            =  -P.l(t)*IVG.l(t);
govbud0("G-TRA",t)            =  -GT.l(t);
govbud0("G-IND",t)            =  -INDG.l(t);
```

```
govbud0("G-INF",t)           =  -E.l(t)*INFG.l(t);
govbud0("G-TOT",t)           =  -BRG.l(t);

govbud1(r1,t)                =  govbud0(r1,t);
govbud2(r1,t)                =  100*govbud1(r1,t)/GDPN.l(t);
govbud3(r1,t)$(ord(t) GT 1)  =  (govbud1(r1,t)/govbud1(r1,t-1) - 1)*100;

govfin0("F-DCR",tl)$(ord(tl) GT 1)  =  DCG.l(tl) - DCG.l(tl-1);
govfin0("F-BON",tl)$(ord(tl) GT 1)  =  NDDG.l(tl) - NDDG.l(tl-1);
govfin0("F-FCR",tl)$(ord(tl) GT 1)  =  E.l(tl)*(NFDG.l(tl) - NFDG.l(tl-1));
govfin0("F-TOT",t)                  =  BRG.l(t);

govfin1(r2,t)                =  govfin0(r2,t);
govfin2(r2,t)                =  100*govfin1(r2,t)/GDPN.l(t);
govfin3(r2,t)$(ord(t) GT 1)  =  (govfin1(r2,t)/govfin1(r2,t-1) - 1)*100;

baofpa0("B-EXP",t)                  =  E.l(t)*XPI.l(t)*X.l(t);
baofpa0("B-IMP",t)                  =  -E.l(t)*MPI.l(t)*M.l(t);
baofpa0("B-INT",t)                  =  -E.l(t)*(INFG.l(t) + INFP.l(t));
baofpa0("B-TRA",t)                  =  E.l(t)*(NTRG.l(t) + NTRP.l(t));
baofpa0("B-FAC",t)                  =  E.l(t)*NFP.l(t);
baofpa0("B-CUA",t)                  =  E.l(t)*CURBAL.l(t);
baofpa0("B-GBO",tl)$(ord(tl) GT 1)  =  -E.l(tl)*(NFDG.l(tl) - NFDG.l(tl-1));
baofpa0("B-PBO",tl)$(ord(tl) GT 1)  =  -E.l(tl)*(NFDP.l(tl) - NFDP.l(tl-1));
baofpa0("B-RES",tl)$(ord(tl) GT 1)  =  E.l(tl)*(R.l(tl) - R.l(tl-1));

baofpa1(r3,t)                =  baofpa0(r3,t);
baofpa2(r3,t)                =  100*baofpa1(r3,t)/GDPN.l(t);
baofpa3(r3,t)$(ord(t) GT 1)  =  ((baofpa1(r3,t)/baofpa1(r3,t-1)-1)*100)$
                                baofpa1(r3,t-1);

baofus0("B-EXP",t)                  =  XPI.l(t)*X.l(t);
baofus0("B-IMP",t)                  =  -MPI.l(t)*M.l(t);
baofus0("B-INT",t)                  =  -(INFG.l(t) + INFP.l(t));
baofus0("B-TRA",t)                  =  NTRG.l(t) + NTRP.l(t);
baofus0("B-FAC",t)                  =  NFP.l(t);
baofus0("B-CUA",t)                  =  CURBAL.l(t);
baofus0("B-GBO",tl)$(ord(tl) GT 1)  =  -(NFDG.l(tl) - NFDG.l(tl-1));
baofus0("B-PBO",tl)$(ord(tl) GT 1)  =  -(NFDP.l(tl) - NFDP.l(tl-1));
baofus0("B-RES",tl)$(ord(tl) GT 1)  =  R.l(tl) - R.l(tl-1);

baofus1(r3,t)                =  baofus0(r3,t);
baofus2(r3,t)                =  100*E.l(t)*baofus1(r3,t)/GDPN.l(t);
baofus3(r3,t)$(ord(t) GT 1)  =  ((baofus1(r3,t)/baofus1(r3,t-1) - 1)*100)$
                                baofus1(r3,t-1);

monsup0("M-MOS",t)  =  MS.l(t);
monsup0("M-RES",t)  =  E.l(t)*R.l(t);
monsup0("M-CRE",t)  =  DC.l(t);
monsup0("M-GCR",t)  =  DCG.l(t);
monsup0("M-PCR",t)  =  DCP.l(t);

monsup1(r4,t)                =  monsup0(r4,t);
monsup2(r4,t)                =  100*monsup1(r4,t)/GDPN.l(t);
monsup3(r4,t)$(ord(t) GT 1)  =  100*(monsup1(r4,t)/monsup1(r4,t-1) - 1);

othass0("O-GCR",t)  =  DCG.l(t);
othass0("O-GBO",t)  =  NDDG.l(t);
othass0("O-FBG",t)  =  E.l(t)*NFDG.l(t);
othass0("O-GOD",t)  =  DCG.l(t) + NDDG.l(t) + E.l(t)*NFDG.l(t);
othass0("O-FBP",t)  =  E.l(t)*NFDP.l(t);
```

```
othass1(r5,t)                   =  othass0(r5,t);
othass2(r5,t)                   =  100*othass1(r5,t)/GDPN.l(t);
othass3(r5,t)$(ord(t) GT 1)     =  100*(othass1(r5,t)/othass1(r5,t-1) - 1);

pritab0("P-GEN",t)       =  P.l(t);
pritab0("P-DOM",t)       =  PD.l(t);
pritab0("P-IMP",t)       =  MPI.l(t);
pritab0("P-EXP",t)       =  XPI.l(t);
pritab0("P-EXR",t)       =  E.l(t);
pritab0("P-RER",t)       =  E.l(t)*MPI.l(t)/PD.l(t);

pritab1(r6,t)                   =  pritab0(r6,t);
pritab3(r6,t)$(ord(t) GT 1)     =  100*(pritab1(r6,t)/pritab1(r6,t-1) - 1);

othvar0("V-IRD",t)       =  100*IRD.l(t);
othvar0("V-IRF",t)       =  100*IRF.l(t);
othvar0("V-NFDG",t)      =  NFDG.l(t);
othvar0("V-NFDP",t)      =  NFDP.l(t);
othvar0("V-R",t)         =  R.l(t);
othvar0("V-GDPN",t)      =  GDPN.l(t);

othvar1(r7,t)                   =  othvar0(r7,t);
othvar3(r7,t)$(ord(t) GT 1)     =  (100*(othvar1(r7,t)/othvar1(r7,t-1) - 1))$
                                   othvar1(r7,t-1);

matvar0("Z-GDP",t)       =  GDP.l(t);
matvar0("Z-CG",t)        =  CG.l(t);
matvar0("Z-IVG",t)       =  IVG.l(t);
matvar0("Z-EXP",t)       =  X.l(t);
matvar0("Z-IMP",t)       =  M.l(t);

matvar1(r8,t)                   =  matvar0(r8,t);
matvar2(r8,t)                   =  100*matvar1(r8,t)/GDP.l(t);
matvar3(r8,t)$(ord(t) GT 1)     =  100*(matvar1(r8,t)/matvar1(r8,t-1) - 1);

parame1("Q-M0",t)        =  m0(t);
parame1("Q-M1",t)        =  m1(t);
parame1("Q-M2",t)        =  m2(t);
parame1("Q-THETA",t)     =  theta;
parame1("Q-V",t)         =  v(t);

*
* In order to get some nice data in our tables, most table values are
* rounded to 1 decimal.
*

govbud1(r1,t)   =  round(govbud1(r1,t), 1);
govbud2(r1,t)   =  round(govbud2(r1,t), 1);
govbud3(r1,t)   =  round(govbud3(r1,t), 1);
govfin1(r2,t)   =  round(govfin1(r2,t), 1);
govfin2(r2,t)   =  round(govfin2(r2,t), 1);
govfin3(r2,t)   =  round(govfin3(r2,t), 1);
baofpa1(r3,t)   =  round(baofpa1(r3,t), 1);
baofpa2(r3,t)   =  round(baofpa2(r3,t), 1);
baofpa3(r3,t)   =  round(baofpa3(r3,t), 1);
baofus1(r3,t)   =  round(baofus1(r3,t), 1);
baofus2(r3,t)   =  round(baofus2(r3,t), 1);
baofus3(r3,t)   =  round(baofus3(r3,t), 1);
monsup1(r4,t)   =  round(monsup1(r4,t), 1);
monsup2(r4,t)   =  round(monsup2(r4,t), 1);
monsup3(r4,t)   =  round(monsup3(r4,t), 1);
```

```
othass1(r5,t)    =  round(othass1(r5,t), 1);
othass2(r5,t)    =  round(othass2(r5,t), 1);
othass3(r5,t)    =  round(othass3(r5,t), 1);
pritab1(r6,t)    =  round(pritab1(r6,t), 3);
pritab3(r6,t)    =  round(pritab3(r6,t), 1);
othvar1(r7,t)    =  round(othvar1(r7,t), 1);
othvar3(r7,t)    =  round(othvar3(r7,t), 1);
matvar1(r8,t)    =  round(matvar1(r8,t), 1);
matvar2(r8,t)    =  round(matvar2(r8,t), 1);
matvar3(r8,t)    =  round(matvar3(r8,t), 1);

option   govbud1:1:1:1,govbud2:1:1:1,govbud3:1:1:1,
         govfin1:1:1:1,govfin2:1:1:1,govfin3:1:1:1,
         baofpa1:1:1:1,baofpa2:1:1:1,baofpa3:1:1:1,
         baofus1:1:1:1,baofus2:1:1:1,baofus3:1:1:1,
         monsup1:1:1:1,monsup2:1:1:1,monsup3:1:1:1,
         othass1:1:1:1,othass2:1:1:1,othass3:1:1:1,
         pritab1:3:1:1,pritab3:1:1:1,
         othvar1:1:1:1,othvar3:1:1:1,
         matvar1:1:1:1,matvar2:1:1:1,matvar3:1:1:1,
         parame1:4:1:1;

display  govbud1,govbud2,govbud3,govfin1,govfin2,govfin3,
         baofpa1,baofpa2,baofpa3,baofus1,baofus2,baofus3,
         monsup1,monsup2,monsup3,othass1,othass2,othass3,
         pritab1,pritab3,othvar1,othvar3,
         matvar1,matvar2,matvar3,parame1;
```

Program generating scenario tables (FPSCENT2.GMS)

```
* This file is used to generate report tables for scenarios
* Note: It is necessary to run "FPSCENT1.GMS" before this file to
* calculate deviations from base run
*

govbud1("G-REV",t)    =  TG.l(t);
govbud1("G-ROW",t)    =  E.l(t)*NTRG.l(t);
govbud1("G-CON",t)    =  -P.l(t)*CG.l(t);
govbud1("G-INV",t)    =  -P.l(t)*IVG.l(t);
govbud1("G-TRA",t)    =  -GT.l(t);
govbud1("G-IND",t)    =  -INDG.l(t);
govbud1("G-INF",t)    =  -E.l(t)*INFG.l(t);
govbud1("G-TOT",t)    =  -BRG.l(t);

govbud2(r1,t)                  =  100*govbud1(r1,t)/GDPN.l(t);
govbud3(r1,t)$(ord(t) GT 1)    =  (govbud1(r1,t)/govbud1(r1,t-1) - 1)*100;
govbud4(r1,t)                  =  (govbud1(r1,t)/govbud0(r1,t) - 1)*100;

govfin1("F-DCR",tl)$(ord(tl) GT 1)   =  DCG.l(tl) - DCG.l(tl-1);
govfin1("F-BON",tl)$(ord(tl) GT 1)   =  NDDG.l(tl) - NDDG.l(tl-1);
govfin1("F-FCR",tl)$(ord(tl) GT 1)   =  E.l(tl)*(NFDG.l(tl) - NFDG.l(tl-1));
govfin1("F-TOT",t)                   =  BRG.l(t);

govfin2(r2,t)                  =  100*govfin1(r2,t)/GDPN.l(t);
govfin3(r2,t)$(ord(t) GT 1)    =  (govfin1(r2,t)/govfin1(r2,t-1) - 1)*100;
govfin4(r2,t)                  =  (govfin1(r2,t)/govfin0(r2,t) - 1)*100;

baofpa1("B-EXP",t)                   =  E.l(t)*XPI.l(t)*X.l(t);
baofpa1("B-IMP",t)                   =  -E.l(t)*MPI.l(t)*M.l(t);
```

```
baofpa1("B-INT",t)                     =  -E.l(t)*(INFG.l(t) + INFP.l(t));
baofpa1("B-TRA",t)                     =  E.l(t)*(NTRG.l(t) + NTRP.l(t));
baofpa1("B-FAC",t)                     =  E.l(t)*NFP.l(t);
baofpa1("B-CUA",t)                     =  E.l(t)*CURBAL.l(t);
baofpa1("B-GBO",tl)$(ord(tl) GT 1)  =  -E.l(tl)*(NFDG.l(tl) - NFDG.l(tl-1));
baofpa1("B-PBO",tl)$(ord(tl) GT 1)  =  -E.l(tl)*(NFDP.l(tl) - NFDP.l(tl-1));
baofpa1("B-RES",tl)$(ord(tl) GT 1)  =  E.l(tl)*(R.l(tl) - R.l(tl-1));

baofpa2(r3,t)                  =  100*baofpa1(r3,t)/GDPN.l(t);
baofpa3(r3,t)$(ord(t) GT 1)    =  ((baofpa1(r3,t)/baofpa1(r3,t-1) - 1)*100)$
                                  baofpa1(r3,t-1);
baofpa4(r3,t)                  =  ((baofpa1(r3,t)/baofpa0(r3,t) - 1)*100)$baofpa0(r3,t);

baofus1("B-EXP",t)                     =  XPI.l(t)*X.l(t);
baofus1("B-IMP",t)                     =  -MPI.l(t)*M.l(t);
baofus1("B-INT",t)                     =  -(INFG.l(t) + INFP.l(t));
baofus1("B-TRA",t)                     =  NTRG.l(t) + NTRP.l(t);
baofus1("B-FAC",t)                     =  NFP.l(t);
baofus1("B-CUA",t)                     =  CURBAL.l(t);
baofus1("B-GBO",tl)$(ord(tl) GT 1)  =  -(NFDG.l(tl) - NFDG.l(tl-1));
baofus1("B-PBO",tl)$(ord(tl) GT 1)  =  -(NFDP.l(tl) - NFDP.l(tl-1));
baofus1("B-RES",tl)$(ord(tl) GT 1)  =  R.l(tl) - R.l(tl-1);

baofus2(r3,t)                  =  100*E.l(t)*baofus1(r3,t)/GDPN.l(t);
baofus3(r3,t)$(ord(t) GT 1)    =  ((baofus1(r3,t)/baofus1(r3,t-1) - 1)*100)$
                                  baofus1(r3,t-1);
baofus4(r3,t)                  =  ((baofus1(r3,t)/baofus0(r3,t) - 1)*100)$baofus0(r3,t);

monsup1("M-MOS",t)  =  MS.l(t);
monsup1("M-RES",t)  =  E.l(t)*R.l(t);
monsup1("M-CRE",t)  =  DC.l(t);
monsup1("M-GCR",t)  =  DCG.l(t);
monsup1("M-PCR",t)  =  DCP.l(t);

monsup2(r4,t)                  =  100*monsup1(r4,t)/GDPN.l(t);
monsup3(r4,t)$(ord(t) GT 1)    =  100*(monsup1(r4,t)/monsup1(r4,t-1) - 1);
monsup4(r4,t)                  =  (monsup1(r4,t)/monsup0(r4,t) - 1)*100;

othass1("O-GCR",t)  =  DCG.l(t);
othass1("O-GBO",t)  =  NDDG.l(t);
othass1("O-FBG",t)  =  E.l(t)*NFDG.l(t);
othass1("O-GOD",t)  =  DCG.l(t) + NDDG.l(t) + E.l(t)*NFDG.l(t);
othass1("O-FBP",t)  =  E.l(t)*NFDP.l(t);

othass2(r5,t)                  =  100*othass1(r5,t)/GDPN.l(t);
othass3(r5,t)$(ord(t) GT 1)    =  100*(othass1(r5,t)/othass1(r5,t-1) - 1);
othass4(r5,t)                  =  (othass1(r5,t)/othass0(r5,t) - 1)*100;

pritab1("P-GEN",t)  =  P.l(t);
pritab1("P-DOM",t)  =  PD.l(t);
pritab1("P-IMP",t)  =  MPI.l(t);
pritab1("P-EXP",t)  =  XPI.l(t);
pritab1("P-EXR",t)  =  E.l(t);
pritab1("P-RER",t)  =  E.l(t)*MPI.l(t)/PD.l(t);

pritab3(r6,t)$(ord(t) GT 1)    =  100*(pritab1(r6,t)/pritab1(r6,t-1) - 1);
pritab4(r6,t)                  =  (pritab1(r6,t)/pritab0(r6,t) - 1)*100;

othvar1("V-IRD",t)    =  100*IRD.l(t);
othvar1("V-IRF",t)    =  100*IRF.l(t);
othvar1("V-NFDG",t)   =  NFDG.l(t);
```

```
othvar1("V-NFDP",t)     =  NFDP.l(t);
othvar1("V-R",t)        =  R.l(t);
othvar1("V-GDPN",t)     =  GDPN.l(t);

othvar3(r7,t)$(ord(t) GT 1)   =  100*(othvar1(r7,t)/othvar1(r7,t-1) - 1);
othvar4(r7,t)                 =  (othvar1(r7,t)/othvar0(r7,t) - 1)*100;

matvar1("Z-GDP",t)      =  GDP.l(t);
matvar1("Z-CG",t)       =  CG.l(t);
matvar1("Z-IVG",t)      =  IVG.l(t);
matvar1("Z-EXP",t)      =  X.l(t);
matvar1("Z-IMP",t)      =  M.l(t);

matvar2(r8,t)                 =  100*matvar1(r8,t)/GDP.l(t);
matvar3(r8,t)$(ord(t) GT 1)   =  100*(matvar1(r8,t)/matvar1(r8,t-1) - 1);
matvar4(r8,t)                 =  (matvar1(r8,t)/matvar0(r8,t) - 1)*100;

parame1("Q-M0",t)       =  m0(t);
parame1("Q-M1",t)       =  m1(t);
parame1("Q-M2",t)       =  m2(t);
parame1("Q-THETA",t)    =  theta;
parame1("Q-V",t)        =  v(t);

* In order to get some nice data in our tables, most table values are
* rounded to 1 decimal.

govbud1(r1,t)   =  round(govbud1(r1,t), 1);
govbud2(r1,t)   =  round(govbud2(r1,t), 1);
govbud3(r1,t)   =  round(govbud3(r1,t), 1);
govbud4(r1,t)   =  round(govbud4(r1,t), 1);
govfin1(r2,t)   =  round(govfin1(r2,t), 1);
govfin2(r2,t)   =  round(govfin2(r2,t), 1);
govfin3(r2,t)   =  round(govfin3(r2,t), 1);
govfin4(r2,t)   =  round(govfin4(r2,t), 1);
baofpa1(r3,t)   =  round(baofpa1(r3,t), 1);
baofpa2(r3,t)   =  round(baofpa2(r3,t), 1);
baofpa3(r3,t)   =  round(baofpa3(r3,t), 1);
baofpa4(r3,t)   =  round(baofpa4(r3,t), 1);
baofus1(r3,t)   =  round(baofus1(r3,t), 1);
baofus2(r3,t)   =  round(baofus2(r3,t), 1);
baofus3(r3,t)   =  round(baofus3(r3,t), 1);
baofus4(r3,t)   =  round(baofus4(r3,t), 1);
monsup1(r4,t)   =  round(monsup1(r4,t), 1);
monsup2(r4,t)   =  round(monsup2(r4,t), 1);
monsup3(r4,t)   =  round(monsup3(r4,t), 1);
monsup4(r4,t)   =  round(monsup4(r4,t), 1);
othass1(r5,t)   =  round(othass1(r5,t), 1);
othass2(r5,t)   =  round(othass2(r5,t), 1);
othass3(r5,t)   =  round(othass3(r5,t), 1);
othass4(r5,t)   =  round(othass4(r5,t), 1);
pritab1(r6,t)   =  round(pritab1(r6,t), 3);
pritab3(r6,t)   =  round(pritab3(r6,t), 1);
pritab4(r6,t)   =  round(pritab4(r6,t), 1);
othvar1(r7,t)   =  round(othvar1(r7,t), 1);
othvar3(r7,t)   =  round(othvar3(r7,t), 1);
othvar4(r7,t)   =  round(othvar4(r7,t), 1);
matvar1(r8,t)   =  round(matvar1(r8,t), 1);
matvar2(r8,t)   =  round(matvar2(r8,t), 1);
matvar3(r8,t)   =  round(matvar3(r8,t), 1);
matvar4(r8,t)   =  round(matvar4(r8,t), 1);
```

```
option  govbud1:1:1:1,govbud2:1:1:1,govbud3:1:1:1,govbud4:1:1:1,
        govfin1:1:1:1,govfin2:1:1:1,govfin3:1:1:1,govfin4:1:1:1,
        baofpa1:1:1:1,baofpa2:1:1:1,baofpa3:1:1:1,baofpa4:1:1:1,
        baofus1:1:1:1,baofus2:1:1:1,baofus3:1:1:1,baofus4:1:1:1,
        monsup1:1:1:1,monsup2:1:1:1,monsup3:1:1:1,monsup4:1:1:1,
        othass1:1:1:1,othass2:1:1:1,othass3:1:1:1,othass4:1:1:1,
        pritab1:3:1:1,pritab3:1:1:1,pritab4:1:1:1,
        othvar1:1:1:1,othvar3:1:1:1,othvar4:1:1:1,
        matvar1:1:1:1,matvar2:1:1:1,matvar3:1:1:1,matvar4:1:1:1,
        parame1:4:1:1;

display govbud1,govbud2,govbud3,govbud4,govfin1,govfin2,govfin3,govfin4,
        baofpa1,baofpa2,baofpa3,baofpa4,baofus1,baofus2,baofus3,baofus4,
        monsup1,monsup2,monsup3,monsup4,othass1,othass2,othass3,othass4,
        pritab1,pritab3,pritab4,othvar1,othvar3,othvar4,
        matvar1,matvar2,matvar3,matvar4,parame1;
```

A.3 REVISED MINIMUM STANDARD MODEL

Main program (RMSMSCEN.GMS)

```
$offsymlist offsymxref
*
* RMSM - Revised Minimum Standard Model
*


*
* I Sets
*

SETS        i           GDP disaggregation
                        /AGR    Agriculture
                         MIN    Mining
                         MAN    Manufacturing
                         OTH    Other sectors/

            ie          Export categories
                        /AGR    Agriculture
                         GOL    Gold
                         MET    Basic metals and minerals
                         OTH    Other/

            tl          Long time horizon       /1993*2000/
            t(tl)       Model time horizon      /1994*2000/
            tf(tl)      Forecast horizon        /1995*2000/;


*
* II Parameters
*

PARAMETERS  b(tl)           Private saving propensity
            d(tl)           Ratio of reserve changes to import changes
            expgr(ie,tl)    Export growth rates
            gdpgr(i,tl)     Sectoral GDP growth rates
            k0(tl)          Constant in investment function
            k1(tl)          Capital-output ratio
```

```
            m0(tl)       Constant in import function
            m1(tl)       GDP elasticity of import
            m2(tl)       Real exchange rate elasticity of import
            theta        Weight in price index;


*
* III Variables
*

VARIABLES   C(tl)        Total consumption
            CG(tl)       Government consumption
            CP(tl)       Private consumption
            CURBAL(tl)   Current account surplus
            E(tl)        Nominal exchange rate
            GDP(tl)      Real GDP
            GDPS(i,tl)   Sectoral real GDP
            GDS(tl)      Gross domestic saving
            GDY(tl)      Gross domestic income
            GT(tl)       Other government expenditures
            INFG(tl)     Government interest payments on foreign debt
            INFP(tl)     Private interest payments on foreign debt
            IRF(tl)      Foreign interest rate
            IV(tl)       Total investment
            IVG(tl)      Government investment
            IVP(tl)      Private investment
            M(tl)        Import
            MPI(tl)      Import price index
            NETFSY(tl)   Net factor services from abroad
            NFDG(tl)     Government net foreign debt
            NFDP(tl)     Private net foreign debt
            NFP(tl)      Net other factor payments from abroad
            NTRG(tl)     Net transfers to government from abroad
            NTRP(tl)     Net transfers to private sector from abroad
            OBJ          Objective
            P(tl)        General price level
            PD(tl)       Domestic price level
            R(tl)        Foreign exchange reserve
            RESBAL(tl)   Resource balance
            RG(tl)       Resource gap
            TG(tl)       Government revenue
            TTADJ(tl)    Terms-of-trade adjustment
            X(tl)        Total export
            XPI(tl)      Export price index
            XS(ie,tl)    Export by category
            XTTADJ(tl)   Terms-of-trade adjusted export;

POSITIVE VARIABLES C, E, GDP, GDPS, IV, M, P, PD, X, XS;


*
* IV Equations
*
EQUATIONS   EQ01(tl)     Total real GDP
            EQ02(i,tl)   Sectoral GDP
            EQ03(tl)     Total export
            EQ04(ie,tl)  Export by category
            EQ05(tl)     Investment function
            EQ06(tl)     Import function
            EQ07(t)      Total consumption
            EQ08(t)      Total investment
```

```
EQ09(t)      Private consumption
EQ10(t)      Material balance
EQ11(t)      Terms-of-trade adjusted export
EQ12(t)      Terms-of-trade adjustment
EQ13(t)      Gross domestic income
EQ14(t)      Gross domestic saving
EQ15(t)      Resource gap
EQ16(t)      Resource balance
EQ17(tl)     Government interest payments on foreign debt
EQ18(tl)     Private interest payments on foreign debt
EQ19(t)      Net factor services
EQ20(t)      Current account
EQ21(tl)     Balance of payments
EQ22(tl)     Foreign reserves
EQ23(tl)     General price index
EQ99         Objective function;
```

```
*
* V Model equations
*
*
* A Real sector
*

EQ01(t) . .
  GDP(t) =e= sum(i, GDPS(i,t));

EQ02(i,tl-1) . .
  GDPS(i,tl) =e= (1 + gdpgr(i,tl))*GDPS(i,tl-1);

EQ03(t) . .
  X(t) =e= sum(ie, XS(ie,t));

EQ04(ie,tl-1) . .
  XS(ie,tl) =e= (1 + expgr(ie,tl))*XS(ie,tl-1);

EQ05(tl-1) . .
  IV(tl)/GDP(tl) =e= k0(tl) + k1(tl)*((GDP(tl) - GDP(tl-1))/GDP(tl));

EQ06(t) . .
  log(M(t)) =e= m0(t) + m1(t)*log(GDP(t)) + m2(t)*log(E(t)*MPI(t)/PD(t));

EQ07(t) . .
  C(t) =e= CP(t) + CG(t);

EQ08(t) . .
  IV(t) =e= IVP(t) + IVG(t);

EQ09(t) . .
  P(t)*CP(t) =e= (1 - b(t))*(P(t)*GDY(t)  TG(t) + GT(t));

EQ10(t) . .
  C(t) =e= GDP(t) - IV(t) - X(t) + M(t);


*
* B Income effects from terms-of-trade
*

EQ11(t) . .
  XTTADJ(t) =e= X(t)*XPI(t)/MPI(t);

EQ12(t) . .
  TTADJ(t) =e= XTTADJ(t) - X(t);
```

```
EQ13(t) . .
  GDY(t) =e= GDP(t) + TTADJ(t);

EQ14(t) . .
  GDS(t) =e= GDY(t) - C(t);

EQ15(t) . .
  RG(t) =e= M(t) - XTTADJ(t);


*
* C Balance of payments
*

EQ16(t) . .
  RESBAL(t) =e= X(t)*XPI(t) - M(t)*MPI(t);

EQ17(tl-1) . .
  INFG(tl) =e= IRF(tl)*NFDG(tl-1);

EQ18(tl-1) . .
  INFP(tl) =e= IRF(tl)*NFDP(tl-1);

EQ19(t) . .
  NETFSY(t) =e= NFP(t) - INFG(t) - INFP(t);

EQ20(t) . .
  CURBAL(t) =e= RESBAL(t) + NETFSY(t) + NTRG(t) + NTRP(t);

EQ21(tl-1) . .
  R(tl) - R(tl-1) =e= CURBAL(tl) + (NFDG(tl) - NFDG(tl-1)) + (NFDP(tl) - NFDP(tl-1));

EQ22(tl-1) . .
  R(tl) - R(tl-1) =e= (M(tl)*MPI(tl) - M(tl-1)*MPI(tl-1))/d(tl);

EQ23(t) . .
  P(t) =e= (1 - theta)*PD(t) + theta*E(t)*MPI(t);


*
* D Objective function
*

EQ99 . .
  OBJ =e= sum(t, C(t));


*
* VI Model definitions
*

MODEL RMSM Revised Minimum Standard Model / all/;


*
* VII Data
*
*
* A 1993 values of lagged variables
*

GDP.fx("1993")                =    426.813;
GDPS.fx("AGR","1993")         =     17.405;
GDPS.fx("MIN","1993")         =     35.943;
GDPS.fx("MAN","1993")         =     92.368;
```

```
GDPS.fx("OTH","1993")     =    281.097;
M.fx("1993")              =     81.968;
MPI.fx("1993")            =      1.024;
NFDG.fx("1993")           =     27.510;
NFDP.fx("1993")           =     17.286;
R.fx("1993")              =     10.982;
XS.fx("AGR","1993")       =      3.366;
XS.fx("GOL","1993")       =     25.462;
XS.fx("MET","1993")       =     36.064;
XS.fx("OTH","1993")       =     37.208;


*
* B 1994 values of all variables
*

C.fx("1994")              =    347.669;
CG.fx("1994")             =     91.349;
CP.fx("1994")             =    256.320;
CURBAL.fx("1994")         =     -2.089;
E.fx("1994")              =      1.000;
GDP.fx("1994")            =    434.246;
GDPS.fx("AGR","1994")     =     18.865;
GDPS.fx("MIN","1994")     =     34.908;
GDPS.fx("MAN","1994")     =     94.282;
GDPS.fx("OTH","1994")     =    286.191;
GDS.fx("1994")            =     86.577;
GDY.fx("1994")            =    434.246;
GT.fx("1994")             =     15.421;
INFG.fx("1994")           =      3.887976828;
INFP.fx("1994")           =      2.443023172;
IRF.fx("1994")            =   INFG.l("1994")/NFDG.l("1993");
IV.fx("1994")             =     78.310;
IVG.fx("1994")            =      9.620;
IVP.fx("1994")            =     68.690;
M.fx("1994")              =     94.415;
MPI.fx("1994")            =      1.000;
NETFSY.fx("1994")         =    -10.561;
NFDG.fx("1994")           =     32.311;
NFDP.fx("1994")           =     17.695;
NFP.fx("1994")            =     -4.230;
NTRG.fx("1994")           =      0.272;
NTRP.fx("1994")           =     -0.067;
P.fx("1994")              =      1.000;
PD.fx("1994")             =      1.000;
R.fx("1994")              =     14.103;
RESBAL.fx("1994")         =      8.267;
RG.fx("1994")             =     -8.267;
TG.fx("1994")             =    118.055;
TTADJ.fx("1994")          =      0.000;
X.fx("1994")              =    102.682;
XPI.fx("1994")            =      1.000;
XS.fx("AGR","1994")       =      6.292;
XS.fx("GOL","1994")       =     22.661;
XS.fx("MET","1994")       =     33.110;
XS.fx("OTH","1994")       =     40.619;
XTTADJ.fx("1994")         =    102.682;
```

```
*
* C Initial values of endogenous variables in forecast horizon
*

C.l(tf)              = C.l("1994");
CG.l(tf)             = CG.l("1994");
CP.l(tf)             = CP.l("1994");
CURBAL.l(tf)         = CURBAL.l("1994");
GDP.l(tf)            = GDP.l("1994");
GDPS.l(i,tf)         = GDPS.l(i,"1994");
GDS.l(tf)            = GDS.l("1994");
GDY.l(tf)            = GDY.l("1994");
INFG.l(tf)           = INFG.l("1994");
INFP.l(tf)           = INFP.l("1994");
IV.l(tf)             = IV.l("1994");
IVP.l(tf)            = IVP.l("1994");
M.l(tf)              = M.l("1994");
NETFSY.l(tf)         = NETFSY.l("1994");
NFDG.l(tf)           = NFDG.l("1994");
PD.l(tf)             = PD.l("1994");
RESBAL.l(tf)         = RESBAL.l("1994");
R.l(tf)              = R.l("1994");
RG.l(tf)             = RG.l("1994");
TTADJ.l(tf)          = TTADJ.l("1994");
X.l(tf)              = X.l("1994");
XS.l(ie,tf)          = XS.l(ie,"1994");
XTTADJ.l(tf)         = XTTADJ.l("1994");


*
* D Values of exogenous variables in forecast horizon
* (calculated from assumptions outside model)
*

table iniexo(*,tf)  Values of exogenous variables in forecast horizon
            1995      1996      1997      1998      1999      2000

E         1.0291    1.0591    1.0899    1.1217    1.1544    1.1880
GT        16.918    18.561    20.363    22.341    24.510    26.890
IRF       0.1413    0.1413    0.1413    0.1413    0.1413    0.1413
IVG        9.812    10.058    10.359    10.722    11.097    11.486
MPI       1.0300    1.0609    1.0927    1.1255    1.1593    1.1941
NFDP      26.224    36.904    49.597    63.904    80.895   100.948
NFP       -4.509    -4.807    -5.125    -5.463    -5.824    -6.209
NTRG       0.290     0.309     0.329     0.351     0.374     0.399
NTRP      -0.071    -0.075    -0.080    -0.086    -0.092    -0.098
P         1.0600    1.1236    1.1910    1.2625    1.3382    1.4185
TG       129.584   143.212   158.838   177.407   198.084   219.589
XPI       1.0300    1.0609    1.0927    1.1255    1.1593    1.1941;

E.fx(tf)             = iniexo("E",tf);
GT.fx(tf)            = iniexo("GT",tf);
IRF.fx(tf)           = IRF.l("1994");
IVG.fx(tf)           = iniexo("IVG",tf);
MPI.fx(tf)           = iniexo("MPI",tf);
NFDP.fx(tf)          = iniexo("NFDP",tf);
NFP.fx(tf)           = iniexo("NFP",tf);
NTRG.fx(tf)          = iniexo("NTRG",tf);
```

```
NTRP.fx(tf)            = iniexo("NTRP",tf);
P.fx(tf)               = iniexo("P",tf);
TG.fx(tf)              = iniexo("TG",tf);
XPI.fx(tf)             = iniexo("XPI",tf);
```

*
* E Export and GDP growth rates in forecast horizon
*

table gdpgro(i,tf) Sectoral GDP growth rates in forecast horizon

	1995	1996	1997	1998	1999	2000
AGR	.0250	.0250	.0250	.0250	.0250	.0250
MIN	.0000	.0000	.0000	.0000	.0000	.0000
MAN	.0500	.0500	.0500	.0500	.0500	.0500
OTH	.0350	.0348	.0345	.0343	.0341	.0339;

table expgro(ie,tf) Export growth rates in forecast horizon

	1995	1996	1997	1998	1999	2000
AGR	.0200	.0200	.0200	.0200	.0200	.0200
GOL	.0000	.0000	.0000	.0000	.0000	.0000
MET	.0300	.0350	.0400	.0450	.0450	.0450
OTH	.0483	.0683	.0749	.0810	.0903	.0887;

```
gdpgr(i,"1994")        = GDPS.l(i,"1994")/GDPS.l(i,"1993") - 1;
gdpgr(i,tf)            = gdpgro(i,tf);
expgr(ie,"1994")       = XS.l(ie,"1994")/XS.l(ie,"1993") - 1;
expgr(ie,tf)           = expgro(ie,tf);
```

*
* F Parameter values and calibration
*

table inipar(*,*) Values of selected parameters in forecast horizon

	1995	1996	1997	1998	1999	2000
B	0.2299	0.2328	0.2363	0.2397	0.2427	0.2454
D	2.0141	2.2312	2.4906	2.6580	3.0513	3.2807
K0	0.1243	0.1348	0.1403	0.1418	0.1418	0.1418
M0	−2.6870	−2.6560	−2.6430	−2.6430	−2.6430	−2.6434;

```
* Private saving propensity

b("1994")   = 1 - P.l("1994")*CP.l("1994")/
              (P.l("1994")*GDP.l("1994") - (TG.l("1994") - GT.l("1994")));
b(tf)       = inipar("B",tf);

* Ratio of foreign reserve to import changes

d("1994")   = (M.l("1994")*MPI.l("1994") - M.l("1993")*MPI.l("1993"))/
              (R.l("1994") - R.l("1993"));
d(tf)       = inipar("D",tf);
```

```
* Investment function parameters (Sources: Kahn et al., 1992,
* and Fallon et al., 1993)

k1(t)       =  2.25;
k0("1994")  =  IV.l("1994")/GDP.l("1994") - k1("1994")*((GDP.l("1994") -
               GDP.l("1993"))/GDP.l("1994"));
k0(tf)      =  inipar("K0",tf);

* Import function parameters (Source for elasticities: Kahn et al., 1992)

m1(t)       =   1.20;
m2(t)       =  -0.73;
m0("1994")  =   log(M.l("1994")) - m1("1994")*log(GDP.l("1994"));
m0(tf)      =   inipar("M0",tf);

* Weight in price index

theta       =  0.2;


*
* VIII Solve
*

OPTION SOLPRINT=off,LIMROW=0,LIMCOL=0;

SOLVE RMSM MAXIMIZING OBJ USING NLP;


*
* IX Report definitions
*

SETS  r1  Material balance      /M-CPR,M-CGO,M-IPR,M-IGO,M-EXP,M-IMP,
                                 M-GDP/
      r2  Sectoral GDP          /G-AGR,G-MIN,G-MAN,G-OTH,G-TOT/
      r3  Sectoral export       /E-AGR,E-GOL,E-MET,E-OTH,E-TOT/
      r4  Balance of payments   /B-EXP,B-IMP,B-INT,B-TRA,B-FAC,B-CUA, B-GBO,
                                 B-PBO,B-RES/
      r5  Foreign assets        /O-FBG,O-FBP,O-RES/
      r6  Prices                /P-GEN,P-DOM,P-IMP,P-EXP,P-EXR,P-RER/
      r7  Other variables       /T-TG,T-GT,T-NFDG,T-NFDP,T-R,T-TTA,T-GDY/;

PARAMETERS  matbal0(r1,tl)   Material balance - base run values
            matbal1(r1,tl)   Material balance - constant 1994 rand
            matbal2(r1,tl)   Material balance - per cent of GDP
            matbal3(r1,tl)   Material balance - real growth rates
            matbal4(r1,tl)   Material balance - deviation from base run
            secgdp0(r2,tl)   Sectoral GDP - base run values
            secgdp1(r2,tl)   Sectoral GDP - constant 1994 rand
            secgdp2(r2,tl)   Sectoral GDP - per cent of total
            secgdp3(r2,tl)   Sectoral GDP - real growth rates
            secgdp4(r2,tl)   Sectoral GDP - deviation from base run
            secexp0(r3,tl)   Sectoral export - base run values
            secexp1(r3,tl)   Sectoral export - constant 1994 rand
            secexp2(r3,tl)   Sectoral export - per cent of total
            secexp3(r3,tl)   Sectoral export - real growth rates
            secexp4(r3,tl)   Sectoral export - deviation from base run
            baofpa0(r4,tl)   Balance of payments - base run values
            baofpa1(r4,tl)   Balance of payments - billion rand
            baofpa2(r4,tl)   Balance of payments - per cent of GDP
            baofpa3(r4,t)    Balance of payments - growth rates
            baofpa4(r4,t)    Balance of payments - deviation from base run
```

```
          baofus0(r4,tl)    Balance of payments – base run values
          baofus1(r4,tl)    Balance of payments – billion foreign currency
          baofus2(r4,tl)    Balance of payments – per cent of GDP
          baofus3(r4,t)     Balance of payments – growth rates
          baofus4(r4,t)     Balance of payments – deviation from base run
          othass0(r5,t)     Foreign asset stocks – base run values
          othass1(r5,t)     Foreign asset stocks – billion rand
          othass2(r5,t)     Foreign asset stocks – per cent of GDP
          othass3(r5,t)     Foreign asset stocks – growth rates
          othass4(r5,t)     Foreign asset stocks – deviation from base run
          pritab0(r6,t)     Prices – base run values
          pritab1(r6,t)     Prices – 1994 = 1
          pritab3(r6,t)     Prices – growth rates
          pritab4(r6,t)     Prices – deviation from base run
          othvar0(r7,t)     Other variables – base run values
          othvar1(r7,t)     Other variables
          othvar3(r7,t)     Other variables – growth rates
          othvar4(r7,t)     Other variables – deviation from base run
          parame1(*,tl)     Parameter values;

$include rmsmsct1.gms


*
* X Scenarios
*
*
* 0 Parameter defining government investment growth in base run
*

parameter ivggr(tl) Government investment growth in base run;

ivggr(t)$(ORD(t) GT 1) = IVG.l(t)/IVG.l(t-1) - 1;


*
* A The 'optimistic' scenario
*

*  1. GDP growth rates increased
*  2. Export growth rates increased
*  3. Private savings propensity increased
*  4. Constant in investment decreased
*  5. Government investment growth increased
*  6. Inflation rate reduced
*  7. Nominal government revenue reduced
*  8. Nominal government expenditures reduced
*  9. Nominal exchange rate reduced
* 10. Foreign reserves increased

gdpgr(i,tf)      =  gdpgr(i,tf) + 0.015;
expgr(ie,tf)     =  expgr(ie,tf) + 0.020;

b("1995")        =  b("1995") + 0.0099;
b("1996")        =  b("1996") + 0.0195;
b("1997")        =  b("1997") + 0.0290;
b("1998")        =  b("1998") + 0.0363;
b("1999")        =  b("1999") + 0.0414;
b("2000")        =  b("2000") + 0.0391;

k0("1995")       =  k0("1995") - 0.0246;
```

```
k0("1996")     = k0("1996") - 0.0180;
k0("1997")     = k0("1997") - 0.0110;
k0("1998")     = k0("1998") - 0.0050;

loop(t$(ORD(t) GT 1), IVG.fx(t) = (1 + ivggr(t) + 0.015)*IVG.l(t-1););

P.fx(tf)       = 1.03**ORD(tf);
TG.fx(tf)      = TG.l(tf)*0.980**ORD(tf);
GT.fx(tf)      = GT.l(tf)*0.985**ORD(tf);

table opprn(*,tf)  Values of exchange rate and foreign reserve parameter

            1995      1996      1997      1998      1999      2000

E         1.0109    1.0143    1.0164    1.0166    1.0143    1.0101
D         2.0903    2.3916    2.6749    2.8672    3.2304    3.4274;

E.fx(tf)       = opprn("E",tf);
d(tf)          = opprn("D",tf);

SOLVE RMSM MAXIMIZING OBJ USING NLP;

$include rmsmsct2.gms


*
* Base run values are reestablished
*

E.fx(tf)       = iniexo("E",tf);
GT.fx(tf)      = iniexo("GT",tf);
IVG.fx(tf)     = iniexo("IVG",tf);
P.fx(tf)       = iniexo("P",tf);
TG.fx(tf)      = iniexo("TG",tf);
gdpgr(i,tf)    = gdpgro(i,tf);
expgr(ie,tf)   = expgro(ie,tf);
b(tf)          = inipar("B",tf);
d(tf)          = inipar("D",tf);
k0(tf)         = inipar("K0",tf);


* B The 'pessimistic' scenario
*

*  1. GDP growth rates decreased
*  2. Export growth rates decreased
*  3. Private savings propensity reduced
*  4. Constant in investment function increased
*  5. Government investment reduced
*  6. Private foreign debt reduced
*  7. Growth in export price index reduced
*  8. Nominal exchange rate increased
*  9. Inflation rate increased
* 10. Nominal government revenue increased
* 11. Nominal government expenditures increased
* 12. Foreign reserves maintained by higher values of "d"

gdpgr(i,tf)    = gdpgr(i,tf) - 0.015;
expgr(ie,tf)   = expgr(ie,tf) - 0.010;
b(tf)          = b(tf) - 0.010;
```

```
k0(tf)          = k0("1994");

loop(t$(ORD(t) GT 1), IVG.fx(t) = (1 + ivggr(t) - 0.015)*IVG.l(t-1););

NFDP.fx(tf)     = NFDP.l(tf)*0.90**ORD(tf);
XPI.fx(tf)      = XPI.l(tf)*0.99**ORD(tf);

table peprn(*,tf)  Selected exogenous variables and parameters
```

	1995	1996	1997	1998	1999	2000
D	1.2482	1.4952	1.5005	1.4561	1.5640	1.6237
E	1.0611	1.1158	1.1930	1.2961	1.4354	1.6178
GT	16.673	18.185	20.184	22.798	26.205	30.651
P	1.0600	1.1335	1.2334	1.3658	1.5391	1.7650
TG	129.584	141.580	157.976	180.639	210.130	246.967;

```
E.fx(tf)        = peprn("E",tf);
P.fx(tf)        = peprn("P",tf);
GT.fx(tf)       = peprn("GT",tf);
TG.fx(tf)       = peprn("TG",tf);
d(tf)           = peprn("D",tf);

SOLVE RMSM MAXIMIZING OBJ USING NLP;

$include rmsmsct2.gms
```

Program generating base run tables (RMSMSCT1.GMS)

```
* This file calculates reporting values for the base run
* and save base run values in parameters "0".
*

matbal0("M-CPR",t)   =  CP.l(t);
matbal0("M-CGO",t)   =  CG.l(t);
matbal0("M-IPR",t)   =  IVP.l(t);
matbal0("M-IGO",t)   =  IVG.l(t);
matbal0("M-EXP",t)   =  X.l(t);
matbal0("M-IMP",t)   =  -M.l(t);
matbal0("M-GDP",t)   =  GDP.l(t);

matbal1(r1,t)                 =  matbal0(r1,t);
matbal2(r1,t)                 =  (matbal1(r1,t)/GDP.l(t))*100;
matbal3(r1,t)$(ord(t) gt 1)   =  (matbal1(r1,t)/matbal1(r1,t-1) - 1)*100;

secgdp0("G-AGR",t)   =  GDPS.l("AGR",t);
secgdp0("G-MIN",t)   =  GDPS.l("MIN",t);
secgdp0("G-MAN",t)   =  GDPS.l("MAN",t);
secgdp0("G-OTH",t)   =  GDPS.l("OTH",t);
secgdp0("G-TOT",t)   =  GDP.l(t);

secgdp1(r2,t)                 =  secgdp0(r2,t);
secgdp2(r2,t)                 =  (secgdp1(r2,t)/GDP.l(t))*100;
secgdp3(r2,t)$(ord(t) gt 1)   =  (secgdp1(r2,t)/secgdp1(r2,t-1) - 1)*100;

secexp0("E-AGR",t)   =  XS.l("AGR",t);
secexp0("E-GOL",t)   =  XS.l("GOL",t);
secexp0("E-MET",t)   =  XS.l("MET",t);
```

```
secexp0("E-OTH",t)      =  XS.l("OTH",t);
secexp0("E-TOT",t)      =  X.l(t);

secexp1(r3,t)               =  secexp0(r3,t);
secexp2(r3,t)               =  (secexp1(r3,t)/X.l(t))*100;
secexp3(r3,t)$(ord(t) gt 1) =  (secexp1(r3,t)/secexp1(r3,t-1) - 1)*100;

baofpa0("B-EXP",t)                      =  E.l(t)*XPI.l(t)*X.l(t);
baofpa0("B-IMP",t)                      =  -E.l(t)*MPI.l(t)*M.l(t);
baofpa0("B-INT",t)                      =  -E.l(t)*(INFG.l(t) + INFP.l(t));
baofpa0("B-TRA",t)                      =  E.l(t)*(NTRG.l(t) + NTRP.l(t));
baofpa0("B-FAC",t)                      =  E.l(t)*NFP.l(t);
baofpa0("B-CUA",t) = E.l(t)*CURBAL.l(t);
baofpa0("B-GBO",tl)$(ord(tl) GT 1) =  -E.l(tl)*(NFDG.l(tl) - NFDG.l(tl-1));
baofpa0("B-PBO",tl)$(ord(tl) GT 1) =  -E.l(tl)*(NFDP.l(tl) - NFDP.l(tl-1));
baofpa0("B-RES",tl)$(ord(tl) GT 1) =  E.l(tl)*(R.l(tl) - R.l(tl-1));

baofpa1(r4,t)               =  baofpa0(r4,t);
baofpa2(r4,t)               =  (baofpa1(r4,t)/(P.l(t)*GDP.l(t)))*100;
baofpa3(r4,t)$(ord(t) GT 1) =  ((baofpa1(r4,t)/baofpa1(r4,t-1) - 1)*100)$
                               baofpa1(r4,t-1);

baofus0("B-EXP",t)                      =  XPI.l(t)*X.l(t);
baofus0("B-IMP",t)                      =  -MPI.l(t)*M.l(t);
baofus0("B-INT",t)                      =  -(INFG.l(t) + INFP.l(t));
baofus0("B-TRA",t)                      =  NTRG.l(t) + NTRP.l(t);
baofus0("B-FAC",t)                      =  NFP.l(t);
baofus0("B-CUA",t)                      =  CURBAL.l(t);
baofus0("B-GBO",tl)$(ord(tl) GT 1) =  -(NFDG.l(tl) - NFDG.l(tl-1));
baofus0("B-PBO",tl)$(ord(tl) GT 1) =  -(NFDP.l(tl) - NFDP.l(tl-1));
baofus0("B-RES",tl)$(ord(tl) GT 1) =  R.l(tl) - R.l(tl-1);

baofus1(r4,t)               =  baofus0(r4,t);
baofus2(r4,t)               =  (E.l(t)*baofus1(r4,t)/(P.l(t)*GDP.l(t)))*100;
baofus3(r4,t)$(ord(t) GT 1) =  ((baofus1(r4,t)/baofus1(r4,t-1) - 1)*100)$
                               baofus1(r4,t-1);

othass0("O-FBG",t)      =  E.l(t)*NFDG.l(t);
othass0("O-FBP",t)      =  E.l(t)*NFDP.l(t);
othass0("O-RES",t)      =  E.l(t)*R.l(t);

othass1(r5,t)               =  othass0(r5,t);
othass2(r5,t)               =  100*othass1(r5,t)/(P.l(t)*GDP.l(t));
othass3(r5,t)$(ord(t) GT 1) =  (100*(othass1(r5,t)/othass1(r5,t-1) - 1))$
                               othass1(r5,t-1);

pritab0("P-GEN",t)      =  P.l(t);
pritab0("P-DOM",t)      =  PD.l(t);
pritab0("P-IMP",t)      =  MPI.l(t);
pritab0("P-EXP",t)      =  XPI.l(t);
pritab0("P-EXR",t)      =  E.l(t);
pritab0("P-RER",t)      =  E.l(t)*MPI.l(t)/PD.l(t);

pritab1(r6,t)               =  pritab0(r6,t);
pritab3(r6,t)$(ord(t) GT 1) =  (100*(pritab1(r6,t)/pritab1(r6,t-1) - 1))$
                               pritab1(r6,t-1);

othvar0("T-TG",t)       =  TG.l(t);
othvar0("T-GT",t)       =  GT.l(t);
othvar0("T-NFDG",t)     =  NFDG.l(t);
othvar0("T-NFDP",t)     =  NFDP.l(t);
```

```
othvar0("T-R",t)          =  R.l(t);
othvar0("T-TTA",t)        =  TTADJ.l(t);
othvar0("T-GDY",t)        =  GDY.l(t);

othvar1(r7,t)                   =  othvar0(r7,t);
othvar3(r7,t)$(ord(t) GT 1)     =  (100*(othvar1(r7,t)/othvar1(r7,t-1) - 1))$
                                   othvar1(r7,t-1);

parame1("P-B",t)          =  b(t);
parame1("P-D",t)          =  d(t);
parame1("P-K0",t)         =  k0(t);
parame1("P-K1",t)         =  k1(t);
parame1("P-M0",t)         =  m0(t);
parame1("P-M1",t)         =  m1(t);
parame1("P-M2",t)         =  m2(t);
parame1("P-THETA",t)      =  theta;

*
* In order to get some nice data in our tables, most table values are
* rounded to 1 decimal.
*

matbal1(r1,t)    =  round(matbal1(r1,t), 1);
matbal2(r1,t)    =  round(matbal2(r1,t), 1);
matbal3(r1,t)    =  round(matbal3(r1,t), 1);
secgdp1(r2,t)    =  round(secgdp1(r2,t), 1);
secgdp2(r2,t)    =  round(secgdp2(r2,t), 1);
secgdp3(r2,t)    =  round(secgdp3(r2,t), 1);
secexp1(r3,t)    =  round(secexp1(r3,t), 1);
secexp2(r3,t)    =  round(secexp2(r3,t), 1);
secexp3(r3,t)    =  round(secexp3(r3,t), 1);
baofpa1(r4,t)    =  round(baofpa1(r4,t), 1);
baofpa2(r4,t)    =  round(baofpa2(r4,t), 1);
baofpa3(r4,t)    =  round(baofpa3(r4,t), 1);
baofus1(r4,t)    =  round(baofus1(r4,t), 1);
baofus2(r4,t)    =  round(baofus2(r4,t), 1);
baofus3(r4,t)    =  round(baofus3(r4,t), 1);
othass1(r5,t)    =  round(othass1(r5,t), 1);
othass2(r5,t)    =  round(othass2(r5,t), 1);
othass3(r5,t)    =  round(othass3(r5,t), 1);
pritab1(r6,t)    =  round(pritab1(r6,t), 3);
pritab3(r6,t)    =  round(pritab3(r6,t), 1);
othvar1(r7,t)    =  round(othvar1(r7,t), 1);
othvar3(r7,t)    =  round(othvar3(r7,t), 1);

option   matbal1:1:1:1,matbal2:1:1:1,matbal3:1:1:1,
         secgdp1:1:1:1,secgdp2:1:1:1,secgdp3:1:1:1,
         secexp1:1:1:1,secexp2:1:1:1,secexp3:1:1:1,
         baofpa1:1:1:1,baofpa2:1:1:1,baofpa3:1:1:1,
         baofus1:1:1:1,baofus2:1:1:1,baofus3:1:1:1,
         othass1:1:1:1,othass2:1:1:1,othass3:1:1:1,
         pritab1:3:1:1,pritab3:1:1:1,
         othvar1:1:1:1,othvar3:1:1:1,
         parame1:4:1:1,gdpgr:4:1:1,expgr:4:1:1;

display  matbal1,matbal2,matbal3,secgdp1,secgdp2,secgdp3,
         secexp1,secexp2,secexp3,baofpa1,baofpa2,baofpa3,
         baofus1,baofus2,baofus3,othass1,othass2,othass3,
         pritab1,pritab3,othvar1,othvar3,parame1,gdpgr,expgr;
```

APPENDIX A

Program generating scenario tables (RMSMSCT2.GMS)

```
* This file is used to generate report tables for scenarios
* Note: It is necessary to run "RMSMSCT1.GMS" before this file
* to calculate deviations from base run
*

matbal1("M-CPR",t)    =  CP.l(t);
matbal1("M-CGO",t)    =  CG.l(t);
matbal1("M-IPR",t)    =  IVP.l(t);
matbal1("M-IGO",t)    =  IVG.l(t);
matbal1("M-EXP",t)    =  X.l(t);
matbal1("M-IMP",t)    =  -M.l(t);
matbal1("M-GDP",t)    =  GDP.l(t);

matbal2(r1,t)                    =  (matbal1(r1,t)/GDP.l(t))*100;
matbal3(r1,t)$(ord(t) gt 1)      =  (matbal1(r1,t)/matbal1(r1,t-1) - 1)*100;
matbal4(r1,t)                    =  ((matbal1(r1,t)/matbal0(r1,t) - 1)*100)$matbal0(r1,t);

secgdp1("G-AGR",t)    =  GDPS.l("AGR",t);
secgdp1("G-MIN",t)    =  GDPS.l("MIN",t);
secgdp1("G-MAN",t)    =  GDPS.l("MAN",t);
secgdp1("G-OTH",t)    =  GDPS.l("OTH",t);
secgdp1("G-TOT",t)    =  GDP.l(t);

secgdp2(r2,t)                    =  (secgdp1(r2,t)/GDP.l(t))*100;
secgdp3(r2,t)$(ord(t) gt 1)      =  (secgdp1(r2,t)/secgdp1(r2,t-1) - 1)*100;
secgdp4(r2,t)                    =  ((secgdp1(r2,t)/secgdp0(r2,t) - 1)*100)$secgdp0(r2,t);

secexp1("E-AGR",t)    =  XS.l("AGR",t);
secexp1("E-GOL",t)    =  XS.l("GOL",t);
secexp1("E-MET",t)    =  XS.l("MET",t);
secexp1("E-OTH",t)    =  XS.l("OTH",t);
secexp1("E-TOT",t)    =  X.l(t);

secexp2(r3,t)                    =  (secexp1(r3,t)/X.l(t))*100;
secexp3(r3,t)$(ord(t) gt 1)      =  (secexp1(r3,t)/secexp1(r3,t-1) - 1)*100;
secexp4(r3,t)                    =  ((secexp1(r3,t)/secexp0(r3,t) - 1)*100)$
                                    secexp0(r3,t);

baofpa1("B-EXP",t)    =  E.l(t)*XPI.l(t)*X.l(t);
baofpa1("B-IMP",t)    =  -E.l(t)*MPI.l(t)*M.l(t);
baofpa1("B-INT",t)    =  -E.l(t)*(INFG.l(t) + INFP.l(t));
baofpa1("B-TRA",t)    =  E.l(t)*(NTRG.l(t) + NTRP.l(t));
baofpa1("B-FAC",t)    =  E.l(t)*NFP.l(t);
baofpa1("B-CUA",t)    =  E.l(t)*CURBAL.l(t);
baofpa1("B-GBO",tl)   =  (-E.l(tl)*(NFDG.l(tl)-NFDG.l(tl-1)))$(ord(tl) GT 1);
baofpa1("B-PBO",tl)   =  (-E.l(tl)*(NFDP.l(tl)-NFDP.l(tl-1)))$(ord(tl) GT 1);
baofpa1("B-RES",tl)   =  (E.l(tl)*(R.l(tl) - R.l(tl-1)))$(ord(tl) GT 1);

baofpa2(r4,t)                    =  (baofpa1(r4,t)/(P.l(t)*GDP.l(t)))*100;
baofpa3(r4,t)$(ord(t) GT 1)      =  ((baofpa1(r4,t)/baofpa1(r4,t-1) - 1)*100)$
                                    baofpa1(r4,t-1);
baofpa4(r4,t)                    =  ((baofpa1(r4,t)/baofpa0(r4,t) - 1)*100)$
                                    baofpa0(r4,t);

baofus1("B-EXP",t)    =  XPI.l(t)*X.l(t);
baofus1("B-IMP",t)    =  -MPI.l(t)*M.l(t);
baofus1("B-INT",t)    =  -(INFG.l(t) + INFP.l(t));
baofus1("B-TRA",t)    =  NTRG.l(t) + NTRP.l(t);
baofus1("B-FAC",t)    =  NFP.l(t);
```

```
baofus1("B-CUA",t)     =  CURBAL.l(t);
baofus1("B-GBO",tl)    =  -(NFDG.l(tl) - NFDG.l(tl-1))$(ord(tl) GT 1);
baofus1("B-PBO",tl)    =  -(NFDP.l(tl) - NFDP.l(tl-1))$(ord(tl) GT 1);
baofus1("B-RES",tl)    =  (R.l(tl) - R.l(tl-1))$(ord(tl) GT 1);

baofus2(r4,t)                  =  (E.l(t)*baofus1(r4,t)/(P.l(t)*GDP.l(t)))*100;
baofus3(r4,t)$(ord(t) GT 1)    =  ((baofus1(r4,t)/baofus1(r4,t-1) - 1)*100)$
                                  baofus1(r4,t-1);
baofus4(r4,t)                  =  ((baofus1(r4,t)/baofus0(r4,t) - 1)*100)$
                                  baofus0(r4,t);

othass1("O-FBG",t)     =  E.l(t)*NFDG.l(t);
othass1("O-FBP",t)     =  E.l(t)*NFDP.l(t);
othass1("O-RES",t)     =  E.l(t)*R.l(t);

othass2(r5,t)                  =  100*othass1(r5,t)/(P.l(t)*GDP.l(t));
othass3(r5,t)$(ord(t) GT 1)    =  (100*(othass1(r5,t)/othass1(r5,t-1) - 1))$
                                  othass1(r5,t-1);
othass4(r5,t)                  =  ((othass1(r5,t)/othass0(r5,t) - 1)*100)$
                                  othass0(r5,t);

pritab1("P-GEN",t)     =  P.l(t);
pritab1("P-DOM",t)     =  PD.l(t);
pritab1("P-IMP",t)     =  MPI.l(t);
pritab1("P-EXP",t)     =  XPI.l(t);
pritab1("P-EXR",t)     =  E.l(t);
pritab1("P-RER",t)     =  E.l(t)*MPI.l(t)/PD.l(t);

pritab3(r6,t)$(ord(t) GT 1)    =  (100*(pritab1(r6,t)/pritab1(r6,t-1) - 1))$
                                  pritab1(r6,t-1);
pritab4(r6,t)                  =  ((pritab1(r6,t)/pritab0(r6,t) - 1)*100)$
                                  pritab0(r6,t);

othvar1("T-TG",t)      =  TG.l(t);
othvar1("T-GT",t)      =  GT.l(t);
othvar1("T-NFDG",t)    =  NFDG.l(t);
othvar1("T-NFDP",t)    =  NFDP.l(t);
othvar1("T-R",t)       =  R.l(t);
othvar1("T-TTA",t)     =  TTADJ.l(t);
othvar1("T-GDY",t)     =  GDY.l(t);

othvar3(r7,t)$(ord(t) GT 1)    =  (100*(othvar1(r7,t)/othvar1(r7,t-1) - 1))$
                                  othvar1(r7,t-1);
othvar4(r7,t)                  =  ((othvar1(r7,t)/othvar0(r7,t) - 1)*100)$
                                  othvar0(r7,t);

parame1("P-B",t)       =  b(t);
parame1("P-D",t)       =  d(t);
parame1("P-K0",t)      =  k0(t);
parame1("P-K1",t)      =  k1(t);
parame1("P-M0",t)      =  m0(t);
parame1("P-M1",t)      =  m1(t);
parame1("P-M2",t)      =  m2(t);
parame1("P-THETA",t)   =  theta;

* In order to get some nice data in our tables, most table values are
* rounded to 1 decimal.

matbal1(r1,t)   =  round(matbal1(r1,t), 1);
matbal2(r1,t)   =  round(matbal2(r1,t), 1);
matbal3(r1,t)   =  round(matbal3(r1,t), 1);
```

```
matbal4(r1,t)   =  round(matbal4(r1,t), 1);
secgdp1(r2,t)   =  round(secgdp1(r2,t), 1);
secgdp2(r2,t)   =  round(secgdp2(r2,t), 1);
secgdp3(r2,t)   =  round(secgdp3(r2,t), 1);
secgdp4(r2,t)   =  round(secgdp4(r2,t), 1);
secexp1(r3,t)   =  round(secexp1(r3,t), 1);
secexp2(r3,t)   =  round(secexp2(r3,t), 1);
secexp3(r3,t)   =  round(secexp3(r3,t), 1);
secexp4(r3,t)   =  round(secexp4(r3,t), 1);
baofpa1(r4,t)   =  round(baofpa1(r4,t), 1);
baofpa2(r4,t)   =  round(baofpa2(r4,t), 1);
baofpa3(r4,t)   =  round(baofpa3(r4,t), 1);
baofpa4(r4,t)   =  round(baofpa4(r4,t), 1);
baofus1(r4,t)   =  round(baofus1(r4,t), 1);
baofus2(r4,t)   =  round(baofus2(r4,t), 1);
baofus3(r4,t)   =  round(baofus3(r4,t), 1);
baofus4(r4,t)   =  round(baofus4(r4,t), 1);
othass1(r5,t)   =  round(othass1(r5,t), 1);
othass2(r5,t)   =  round(othass2(r5,t), 1);
othass3(r5,t)   =  round(othass3(r5,t), 1);
othass4(r5,t)   =  round(othass4(r5,t), 1);
pritab1(r6,t)   =  round(pritab1(r6,t), 3);
pritab3(r6,t)   =  round(pritab3(r6,t), 1);
pritab4(r6,t)   =  round(pritab4(r6,t), 1);
othvar1(r7,t)   =  round(othvar1(r7,t), 1);
othvar3(r7,t)   =  round(othvar3(r7,t), 1);
othvar4(r7,t)   =  round(othvar4(r7,t), 1);

option   matbal1:1:1:1,matbal2:1:1:1,matbal3:1:1:1,matbal4:1:1:1,
         secgdp1:1:1:1,secgdp2:1:1:1,secgdp3:1:1:1,secgdp4:1:1:1,
         secexp1:1:1:1,secexp2:1:1:1,secexp3:1:1:1,secexp4:1:1:1,
         baofpa1:1:1:1,baofpa2:1:1:1,baofpa3:1:1:1,baofpa4:1:1:1,
         baofus1:1:1:1,baofus2:1:1:1,baofus3:1:1:1,baofus4:1:1:1,
         othass1:1:1:1,othass2:1:1:1,othass3:1:1:1,othass4:1:1:1,
         pritab1:3:1:1,pritab3:1:1:1,pritab4:1:1:1,
         othvar1:1:1:1,othvar3:1:1:1,othvar4:1:1:1,
         parame1:4:1:1,gdpgr:4:1:1,expgr:4:1:1;

display  matbal1,matbal2,matbal3,matbal4,secgdp1,secgdp2,secgdp3,secgdp4,
         secexp1,secexp2,secexp3,secexp4,baofpa1,baofpa2,baofpa3,baofpa4,
         baofus1,baofus2,baofus3,baofus4,othass1,othass2,othass3,othass4,
         pritab1,pritab3,pritab4,othvar1,othvar3,othvar4,
         parame1,gdpgr,expgr;
```

APPENDIX B
Base Run

Table B.1 Material balance

	Year 0	*Year 1*	*Year 2*	*Year 3*	*Year 4*	*Year 5*	*Year 6*
				Constant 1994 billion rand			
Private consumption	256.3	264.3	271.8	278.9	285.5	292.3	300.3
Public consumption	91.3	93.2	96.9	101.3	106.4	111.7	116.1
Private investment	68.7	80.3	88.1	93.8	97.8	101.3	104.8
Public investment	9.6	9.8	10.1	10.4	10.7	11.1	11.5
Export	102.7	105.8	110.0	114.9	120.7	127.3	134.4
Import	−94.4	−103.8	−111.6	−117.8	−122.8	−128.0	−133.3
GDP	434.2	449.4	465.2	481.5	498.3	515.7	533.8
				Per cent of GDP			
Private consumption	59.0	58.8	58.4	57.9	57.3	56.7	56.3
Public consumption	21.0	20.7	20.8	21.0	21.3	21.7	21.8
Private investment	15.8	17.9	18.9	19.5	19.6	19.6	19.6
Public investment	2.2	2.2	2.2	2.2	2.2	2.2	2.2
Export	23.6	23.5	23.6	23.9	24.2	24.7	25.2
Import	−21.7	−23.1	−24.0	−24.5	−24.6	−24.8	−25.0
GDP	100.0	100.0	100.0	100.0	100.0	100.0	100.0
				Real growth rates in per cent			
Private consumption		3.1	2.8	2.6	2.4	2.4	2.7
Public consumption		2.0	4.0	4.5	5.0	5.0	4.0
Private investment		16.8	9.7	6.5	4.3	3.5	3.5
Public investment		2.0	2.5	3.0	3.5	3.5	3.5
Export		3.0	4.0	4.5	5.0	5.5	5.5
Import		10.0	7.5	5.6	4.2	4.2	4.2
GDP		3.5	3.5	3.5	3.5	3.5	3.5

Table B.2. Sectoral GDP

	Year 0	*Year 1*	*Year 2*	*Year 3*	*Year 4*	*Year 5*	*Year 6*
				Constant 1994 billion rand			
Agriculture	18.9	19.3	19.8	20.3	20.8	21.3	21.9
Mining	34.9	34.9	34.9	34.9	34.9	34.9	34.9
Manufacturing	94.3	99.0	103.9	109.1	114.6	120.3	126.3
Other	286.2	296.2	306.5	317.1	328.0	339.2	350.6
Total	434.2	449.4	465.2	481.5	498.3	515.7	533.8
				Per cent of GDP			
Agriculture	4.3	4.3	4.3	4.2	4.2	4.1	4.1
Mining	8.0	7.8	7.5	7.3	7.0	6.8	6.5
Manufacturing	21.7	22.0	22.3	22.7	23.0	23.3	23.7
Other	65.9	65.9	65.9	65.9	65.8	65.8	65.7
Total	100.0	100.0	100.0	100.0	100.0	100.0	100.0
				Real growth rates in per cent			
Agriculture		2.5	2.5	2.5	2.5	2.5	2.5
Mining		0.0	0.0	0.0	0.0	0.0	0.0
Manufacturing		5.0	5.0	5.0	5.0	5.0	5.0
Other		3.5	3.5	3.4	3.4	3.4	3.4
Total		3.5	3.5	3.5	3.5	3.5	3.5

Table B.3. Export Categories

	Year 0	*Year 1*	*Year 2*	*Year 3*	*Year 4*	*Year 5*	*Year 6*
				Constant 1994 billion rand			
Agriculture	6.3	6.4	6.5	6.7	6.8	6.9	7.1
Gold	22.7	22.7	22.7	22.7	22.7	22.7	22.7
Basic metals and minerals	33.1	34.1	35.3	36.7	38.4	40.1	41.9
Other exports	40.6	42.6	45.5	48.9	52.9	57.6	62.7
Total	102.7	105.8	110.0	114.9	120.7	127.3	134.4
				Per cent of export			
Agriculture	6.1	6.1	6.0	5.8	5.6	5.5	5.3
Gold	22.1	21.4	20.6	19.7	18.8	17.8	16.9
Basic metals and minerals	32.2	32.2	32.1	31.9	31.8	31.5	31.2
Other exports	39.6	40.3	41.4	42.5	43.8	45.3	46.7
Total	100.0	100.0	100.0	100.0	100.0	100.0	100.0
				Real growth rates			
Agriculture		2.0	2.0	2.0	2.0	2.0	2.0
Gold		0.0	0.0	0.0	0.0	0.0	0.0
Basic metals and minerals		3.0	3.5	4.0	4.5	4.5	4.5
Other exports		4.8	6.8	7.5	8.1	9.0	8.9
Total		3.0	4.0	4.5	5.0	5.5	5.5

Table B.4. Public sector budget

	Year 0	Year 1	Year 2	Year 3	Year 4	Year 5	Year 6
				Billion rand			
Domestic revenue	118.1	129.6	143.2	158.8	177.4	198.1	219.6
Transfers from ROW	0.3	0.3	0.3	0.4	0.4	0.4	0.5
Consumption	−91.3	−98.8	−108.9	−120.6	−134.3	−149.4	−164.7
Investment	−9.6	−10.4	−11.3	−12.3	−13.5	−14.9	−16.3
Transfers	−15.4	−16.9	−18.6	−20.4	−22.3	−24.5	−26.9
Domestic interest payments	−21.2	−23.8	−26.2	−27.5	−28.7	−29.7	−30.6
Foreign interest payments	−3.9	−4.7	−5.9	−7.6	−9.7	−12.0	−14.4
Budget surplus	−23.1	−24.7	−27.3	−29.2	−30.7	−31.9	−32.8
				Per cent of GDP			
Domestic revenue	27.2	27.2	27.4	27.7	28.2	28.7	29.0
Transfers from ROW	0.1	0.1	0.1	0.1	0.1	0.1	0.1
Consumption	−21.0	−20.7	−20.8	−21.0	−21.3	−21.6	−21.8
Investment	−2.2	−2.2	−2.2	−2.2	−2.2	−2.2	−2.2
Transfers	−3.6	−3.6	−3.6	−3.6	−3.6	−3.6	−3.6
Domestic interest payments	−4.9	−5.0	−5.0	−4.8	−4.6	−4.3	−4.0
Foreign interest payments	−0.9	−1.0	−1.1	−1.3	−1.5	−1.7	−1.9
Budget surplus	−5.3	−5.2	−5.2	−5.1	−4.9	−4.6	−4.3
				Growth rates in per cent			
Domestic revenue		9.8	10.5	10.9	11.7	11.7	10.9
Transfers from ROW		9.7	9.7	9.6	9.8	9.6	9.8
Consumption		8.1	10.2	10.8	11.3	11.3	10.2
Investment		8.1	8.7	9.2	9.7	9.7	9.7
Transfers		9.7	9.7	9.7	9.7	9.7	9.7
Domestic interest payments		12.1	10.3	5.1	4.1	3.5	3.3
Foreign interest payments		20.8	25.3	29.1	27.3	23.9	19.8
Budget surplus		6.6	10.7	7.1	4.9	4.0	2.9

Table B.5. Public sector deficit finance

	Year 0	*Year 1*	*Year 2*	*Year 3*	*Year 4*	*Year 5*	*Year 6*
				Billion rand			
Domestic credit	0.5	0.0	0.0	0.0	0.0	0.0	0.0
Domestic debt	17.8	17.4	16.7	16.5	16.7	18.0	19.3
Foreign credit	4.8	7.2	10.6	12.7	14.0	13.9	13.5
Total	23.1	24.7	27.3	29.2	30.7	31.9	32.8
				Per cent of GDP			
Domestic credit	0.1	0.0	0.0	0.0	0.0	0.0	0.0
Domestic debt	4.1	3.7	3.2	2.9	2.7	2.6	2.6
Foreign credit	1.1	1.5	2.0	2.2	2.2	2.0	1.8
Total	5.3	5.2	5.2	5.1	4.9	4.6	4.3
				Growth rates in per cent			
Domestic credit		−100.0	0.0	0.0	0.0	0.0	0.0
Domestic debt		−2.2	−4.1	−1.1	1.1	7.9	7.2
Foreign credit		50.9	46.2	20.2	9.7	−0.5	−2.6
Total		6.6	10.7	7.1	4.9	4.0	2.9

Table B.6. Balance of Payments

	Year 0	*Year 1*	*Year 2*	*Year 3*	*Year 4*	*Year 5*	*Year 6*
			Billion foreign currency units				
Export	102.7	108.9	116.7	125.6	135.8	147.6	160.5
Import	−94.4	−106.9	−118.4	−128.7	−138.2	−148.4	−159.2
Interest payments	−6.3	−7.1	−9.3	−12.2	−15.6	−19.4	−23.5
Net transfers	0.2	0.2	0.2	0.2	0.3	0.3	0.3
Other factor services	−4.2	−4.5	−4.8	−5.1	−5.5	−5.8	−6.2
Current account surplus	−2.1	−9.4	−15.5	−20.2	−23.2	−25.7	−28.1
Public sector borrowing	−4.8	−7.0	−10.0	−11.7	−12.4	−12.0	−11.4
Private sector borrowing	−0.4	−8.5	−10.7	−12.7	−14.3	−17.0	−20.1
Change in reserves	3.1	6.2	5.1	4.2	3.6	3.3	3.3
			Per cent of GDP				
Export	23.6	23.5	23.6	23.9	24.2	24.7	25.2
Import	−21.7	−23.1	−24.0	−24.5	−24.6	−24.8	−25.0
Interest payments	−1.5	−1.5	−1.9	−2.3	−2.8	−3.2	−3.7
Net transfers	0.0	0.0	0.0	0.0	0.0	0.0	0.0
Other factor services	−1.0	−1.0	−1.0	−1.0	−1.0	−1.0	−1.0
Current account surplus	−0.5	−2.0	−3.1	−3.8	−4.1	−4.3	−4.4
Public sector borrowing	−1.1	−1.5	−2.0	−2.2	−2.2	−2.0	−1.8
Private sector borrowing	−0.1	−1.8	−2.2	−2.4	−2.6	−2.8	−3.1
Change in reserves	0.7	1.3	1.0	0.8	0.6	0.6	0.5

	Growth rates in per cent					
Export	6.1	7.1	7.6	8.2	8.7	8.7
Import	13.3	10.7	8.7	7.3	7.3	7.3
Interest payments	11.6	31.1	31.5	28.3	24.2	21.1
Net transfers	6.8	6.8	6.4	6.4	6.4	6.7
Other factor services	6.6	6.6	6.6	6.6	6.6	6.6
Current account surplus	347.7	66.2	30.1	14.7	10.8	9.5
Public sector borrowing	46.6	42.1	16.8	6.6	−3.3	−5.4
Private sector borrowing	1985.3	25.2	18.8	12.7	18.8	18.0
Change in reserves	99.1	−17.3	−19.1	−14.5	−6.5	−0.8

Table B.7 Money supply

	Year 0	*Year 1*	*Year 2*	*Year 3*	*Year 4*	*Year 5*	*Year 6*
				Billion rand			
Money supply	244.2	267.9	293.9	322.4	353.7	388.0	425.7
Foreign reserves	14.1	20.9	27.0	32.3	37.2	42.1	47.3
Total domestic credit	230.0	246.9	266.9	290.1	316.5	345.9	378.5
Public sector credit	15.5	15.5	15.5	15.5	15.5	15.5	15.5
Private sector credit	214.6	231.5	251.4	274.6	301.0	330.4	363.0
				Per cent of GDP			
Money supply	56.2	56.2	56.2	56.2	56.2	56.2	56.2
Foreign reserves	3.2	4.4	5.2	5.6	5.9	6.1	6.2
Total domestic credit	53.0	51.8	51.1	50.6	50.3	50.1	50.0
Public sector credit	3.6	3.3	3.0	2.7	2.5	2.2	2.0
Private sector credit	49.4	48.6	48.1	47.9	47.8	47.9	47.9
				Growth rates in per cent			
Money supply		9.7	9.7	9.7	9.7	9.7	9.7
Foreign reserves		48.3	28.9	19.7	15.3	13.2	12.2
Total domestic credit		7.3	8.1	8.7	9.1	9.3	9.4
Public sector credit		0.0	0.0	0.0	0.0	0.0	0.0
Private sector credit		7.9	8.6	9.2	9.6	9.8	9.8

Table B.8 Other asset stocks

	Year 0	*Year 1*	*Year 2*	*Year 3*	*Year 4*	*Year 5*	*Year 6*
				Billion rand			
Public sector credit	15.5	15.5	15.5	15.5	15.5	15.5	15.5
Public sector domestic debt	169.2	186.6	203.3	219.8	236.5	254.6	273.9
Public sector foreign debt	32.3	40.5	52.3	66.5	82.4	98.7	115.1
Total public sector debt	217.0	242.6	271.1	301.8	334.5	368.7	404.5
Private sector foreign debt	17.7	27.0	39.1	54.1	71.7	93.4	119.9
				Per cent of GDP			
Public sector credit	3.6	3.3	3.0	2.7	2.5	2.2	2.0
Public sector domestic debt	39.0	39.2	38.9	38.3	37.6	36.9	36.2
Public sector foreign debt	7.4	8.5	10.0	11.6	13.1	14.3	15.2
Total public sector debt	50.0	50.9	51.9	52.6	53.2	53.4	53.4
Private sector foreign debt	4.1	5.7	7.5	9.4	11.4	13.5	15.8
				Growth rates in per cent			
Public sector credit		0.0	0.0	0.0	0.0	0.0	0.0
Public sector domestic debt		10.3	9.0	8.1	7.6	7.6	7.6
Public sector foreign debt		25.3	29.1	27.3	23.9	19.8	16.6
Total public sector debt		11.8	11.7	11.4	10.8	10.3	9.7
Private sector foreign debt		52.5	44.8	38.3	32.6	30.3	28.4

Table B.9 Prices and exchange rates

	Year 0	*Year 1*	*Year 2*	*Year 3*	*Year 4*	*Year 5*	*Year 6*
			Index 1994 = 1.000				
General price index	1.000	1.060	1.124	1.191	1.263	1.338	1.419
Domestic price level	1.000	1.060	1.124	1.191	1.263	1.338	1.419
Import price level	1.000	1.030	1.061	1.093	1.126	1.159	1.194
Export price level	1.000	1.030	1.061	1.093	1.126	1.159	1.194
Nominal exchange rate	1.000	1.029	1.059	1.090	1.122	1.154	1.188
Real exchange rate	1.000	1.000	1.000	1.000	1.000	1.000	1.000
			Growth rates in per cent				
General price index		6.0	6.0	6.0	6.0	6.0	6.0
Domestic price level		6.0	6.0	6.0	6.0	6.0	6.0
Import price level		3.0	3.0	3.0	3.0	3.0	3.0
Export price level		3.0	3.0	3.0	3.0	3.0	3.0
Nominal exchange rate		2.9	2.9	2.9	2.9	2.9	2.9
Real exchange rate		0.0	0.0	0.0	0.0	0.0	0.0

Table B.10 Other variables

	Year 0	*Year 1*	*Year 2*	*Year 3*	*Year 4*	*Year 5*	*Year 6*
				Per cent			
Domestic interest rate	14.0	14.0	14.0	13.5	13.0	12.5	12.0
Foreign interest rate	14.1	14.1	14.1	14.1	14.1	14.1	14.1
				Billion rand			
Nominal GDP	434.2	476.4	522.7	573.4	629.1	690.2	757.2
				Constant 1994 billion rand			
Public sector revenue	118.1	122.2	127.5	133.4	140.5	148.0	154.8
Other public sector expenditure	15.4	16.0	16.5	17.1	17.7	18.3	19.0
Terms of trade adjustment	0.0	0.0	0.0	0.0	0.0	0.0	0.0
Real GDY	434.2	449.4	465.2	481.5	498.3	515.7	533.8
				Billion foreign currency units			
Public sector foreign debt	32.3	39.3	49.4	61.0	73.5	85.5	96.9
Private sector foreign debt	17.7	26.2	36.9	49.6	63.9	80.9	100.9
International reserves	14.1	20.3	25.5	29.6	33.2	36.5	39.8
				Growth rates			
Nominal GDP		9.7	9.7	9.7	9.7	9.7	9.7
Public sector revenue		3.6	4.3	4.6	5.4	5.3	4.6
Other public sector expenditure		3.5	3.5	3.5	3.5	3.5	3.5
Terms of trade adjustment		0.0	0.0	0.0	0.0	0.0	0.0
Real GDY		3.5	3.5	3.5	3.5	3.5	3.5
Public sector foreign debt		21.8	25.4	23.7	20.4	16.4	13.3
Private sector foreign debt		48.2	40.7	34.4	28.8	26.6	24.8
International reserves		44.1	25.3	16.3	12.0	10.0	9.0

APPENDIX C
Optimistic Scenario

Table C.1 Material balance

	Year 0	*Year 1*	*Year 2*	*Year 3*	*Year 4*	*Year 5*	*Year 6*
			Constant 1994 billion rand				
Private consumption	256.3	265.2	273.7	281.9	290.4	300.2	314.5
Public consumption	91.3	93.2	97.5	102.5	108.1	113.8	118.5
Private investment	68.7	84.4	96.9	108.0	117.4	126.0	132.3
Public investment	9.6	10.0	10.4	10.8	11.4	11.9	12.5
Export	102.7	107.8	114.3	121.7	130.2	140.0	150.5
Import	−94.4	−104.6	−114.0	−122.3	−129.6	−137.7	−146.5
GDP	434.2	456.0	478.8	502.7	527.8	554.2	581.9
			Per cent of GDP				
Private consumption	59.0	58.2	57.2	56.1	55.0	54.2	54.0
Public consumption	21.0	20.4	20.4	20.4	20.5	20.5	20.4
Private investment	15.8	18.5	20.2	21.5	22.2	22.7	22.7
Public investment	2.2	2.2	2.2	2.2	2.2	2.2	2.2
Export	23.6	23.6	23.9	24.2	24.7	25.3	25.9
Import	−21.7	−22.9	−23.8	−24.3	−24.6	−24.8	−25.2
GDP	100.0	100.0	100.0	100.0	100.0	100.0	100.0
			Real growth rates in per cent				
Private consumption		3.5	3.2	3.0	3.0	3.4	4.8
Public consumption		2.0	4.6	5.1	5.4	5.3	4.2
Private investment		22.8	14.8	11.5	8.7	7.4	5.0
Public investment		3.5	4.0	4.5	5.0	5.0	5.0
Export		5.0	6.0	6.5	7.0	7.5	7.5
Import		10.8	9.0	7.2	6.0	6.2	6.4
GDP		5.0	5.0	5.0	5.0	5.0	5.0

Table C.1 continued

	Year 0	*Year 1*	*Year 2*	*Year 3*	*Year 4*	*Year 5*	*Year 6*
	Deviations from base run in per cent						
Private consumption		0.4	0.7	1.1	1.7	2.7	4.7
Public consumption		0.1	0.7	1.2	1.6	1.9	2.1
Private investment		5.1	10.0	15.2	20.0	24.4	26.2
Public investment		1.5	3.0	4.5	6.0	7.5	9.1
Export		1.9	3.9	5.9	7.9	9.9	12.0
Import		0.7	2.2	3.8	5.5	7.6	9.9
GDP		1.4	2.9	4.4	5.9	7.5	9.0

Table C.2 Sectoral GDP

	Year 0	*Year 1*	*Year 2*	*Year 3*	*Year 4*	*Year 5*	*Year 6*
				Constant 1994 billion rand			
Agriculture	18.9	19.6	20.4	21.2	22.1	23.0	23.9
Mining	34.9	35.4	36.0	36.5	37.1	37.6	38.2
Manufacturing	94.3	100.4	106.9	113.9	121.3	129.2	137.6
Other	286.2	300.5	315.5	331.1	347.4	364.5	382.3
Total	434.2	456.0	478.8	502.7	527.8	554.2	581.9
				Per cent of GDP			
Agriculture	4.3	4.3	4.3	4.2	4.2	4.1	4.1
Mining	8.0	7.8	7.5	7.3	7.0	6.8	6.6
Manufacturing	21.7	22.0	22.3	22.7	23.0	23.3	23.6
Other	65.9	65.9	65.9	65.9	65.8	65.8	65.7
Total	100.0	100.0	100.0	100.0	100.0	100.0	100.0
				Real growth rates in per cent			
Agriculture		4.0	4.0	4.0	4.0	4.0	4.0
Mining		1.5	1.5	1.5	1.5	1.5	1.5
Manufacturing		6.5	6.5	6.5	6.5	6.5	6.5
Other		5.0	5.0	5.0	4.9	4.9	4.9
Total		5.0	5.0	5.0	5.0	5.0	5.0
				Deviations from base run in per cent			
Agriculture		1.5	2.9	4.5	6.0	7.5	9.1
Mining		1.5	3.0	4.6	6.1	7.7	9.3
Manufacturing		1.4	2.9	4.3	5.8	7.3	8.9
Other		1.4	2.9	4.4	5.9	7.5	9.0
Total		1.4	2.9	4.4	5.9	7.5	9.0

Table C.3 Export categories

	Year 0	Year 1	Year 2	Year 3	Year 4	Year 5	Year 6
				Constant 1994 billion rand			
Agriculture	6.3	6.5	6.8	7.1	7.4	7.7	8.0
Gold	22.7	23.1	23.6	24.0	24.5	25.0	25.5
Basic metals and minerals	33.1	34.8	36.7	38.9	41.4	44.1	47.0
Other exports	40.6	43.4	47.2	51.7	56.9	63.2	70.1
Total	102.7	107.8	114.3	121.7	130.2	140.0	150.5
				Per cent of export			
Agriculture	6.1	6.1	6.0	5.8	5.7	5.5	5.3
Gold	22.1	21.4	20.6	19.8	18.8	17.9	17.0
Basic metals and minerals	32.2	32.2	32.1	31.9	31.8	31.5	31.2
Other exports	39.6	40.2	41.3	42.5	43.7	45.2	46.6
Total	100.0	100.0	100.0	100.0	100.0	100.0	100.0
				Real growth rates			
Agriculture		4.0	4.0	4.0	4.0	4.0	4.0
Gold		2.0	2.0	2.0	2.0	2.0	2.0
Basic metals and minerals		5.0	5.5	6.0	6.5	6.5	6.5
Other exports		6.8	8.8	9.5	10.1	11.0	10.9
Total		5.0	6.0	6.5	7.0	7.5	7.5
				Deviations from base run in per cent			
Agriculture		2.0	4.0	6.0	8.1	10.2	12.4
Gold		2.0	4.0	6.1	8.2	10.4	12.6
Basic metals and minerals		1.9	3.9	5.9	7.9	10.0	12.1
Other exports		1.9	3.8	5.7	7.7	9.7	11.7
Total		1.9	3.9	5.9	7.9	9.9	12.0

Table C.4 Public sector budget

	Year 0	*Year 1*	*Year 2*	*Year 3*	*Year 4*	*Year 5*	*Year 6*
Billion rand							
Domestic revenue	118.1	127.0	137.5	149.5	163.6	179.1	194.5
Transfers from ROW	0.3	0.3	0.3	0.3	0.4	0.4	0.4
Consumption	−91.3	−96.0	−103.5	−112.0	−121.6	−131.8	−141.5
Investment	−9.6	−10.3	−11.0	−11.8	−12.8	−13.8	−15.0
Transfers	−15.4	−16.7	−18.0	−19.5	−21.0	−22.7	−24.6
Domestic interest payments	−21.2	−22.1	−22.3	−21.0	−21.2	−21.2	−21.1
Foreign interest payments	−3.9	−4.6	−5.5	−6.7	−8.0	−9.3	−10.5
Budget surplus	−23.1	−22.3	−22.5	−21.2	−20.6	−19.5	−17.7
Per cent of GDP							
Domestic revenue	27.2	27.0	27.1	27.2	27.5	27.9	28.0
Transfers from ROW	0.1	0.1	0.1	0.1	0.1	0.1	0.1
Consumption	−21.0	−20.4	−20.4	−20.4	−20.5	−20.5	−20.4
Investment	−2.2	−2.2	−2.2	−2.2	−2.2	−2.2	−2.2
Transfers	−3.6	−3.5	−3.5	−3.5	−3.5	−3.5	−3.5
Domestic interest payments	−4.9	−4.7	−4.4	−3.8	−3.6	−3.3	−3.0
Foreign interest payments	−0.9	−1.0	−1.1	−1.2	−1.3	−1.5	−1.5
Budget surplus	−5.3	−4.8	−4.4	−3.9	−3.5	−3.0	−2.5

Table C.4 continued

	Year 0	Year 1	Year 2	Year 3	Year 4	Year 5	Year 6
				Growth rates in per cent			
Domestic revenue		7.6	8.3	8.7	9.5	9.4	8.6
Transfers from ROW		7.8	6.9	6.7	6.7	6.3	6.2
Consumption		5.1	7.8	8.2	8.5	8.5	7.3
Investment		6.6	7.1	7.6	8.2	8.1	8.2
Transfers		8.1	8.1	8.1	8.1	8.1	8.1
Domestic interest payments		4.1	1.3	−5.8	0.9	0.0	−0.6
Foreign interest payments		18.7	18.5	21.9	20.0	16.5	12.4
Budget surplus		−3.5	0.6	−5.8	−2.6	−5.3	−9.5
				Deviations from base run in per cent			
Domestic revenue		−2.0	−4.0	−5.9	−7.8	−9.6	−11.4
Transfers from ROW		−1.8	−4.2	−6.7	−9.4	−12.1	−15.0
Consumption		−2.8	−4.9	−7.1	−9.5	−11.8	−14.1
Investment		−1.4	−2.8	−4.2	−5.5	−6.9	−8.2
Transfers		−1.5	−3.0	−4.4	−5.9	−7.3	−8.7
Domestic interest payments		−7.1	−14.7	−23.5	−26.0	−28.4	−31.1
Foreign interest payments		−1.8	−7.1	−12.3	−17.3	−22.2	−27.0
Budget surplus		−9.4	−17.7	−27.7	−32.8	−38.8	−46.2

Table C.5 Public sector deficit finance

	Year 0	*Year 1*	*Year 2*	*Year 3*	*Year 4*	*Year 5*	*Year 6*
				Billion rand			
Domestic credit	0.5	0.0	0.0	0.0	0.0	0.0	0.0
Domestic debt	17.8	16.4	14.1	11.7	11.1	11.0	10.3
Foreign credit	4.8	5.9	8.4	9.4	9.5	8.5	7.4
Total	23.1	22.3	22.5	21.2	20.6	19.5	17.7
				Per cent of GDP			
Domestic credit	0.1	0.0	0.0	0.0	0.0	0.0	0.0
Domestic debt	4.1	3.5	2.8	2.1	1.9	1.7	1.5
Foreign credit	1.1	1.3	1.7	1.7	1.6	1.3	1.1
Total	5.3	4.8	4.4	3.9	3.5	3.0	2.5
				Growth rates in per cent			
Domestic credit		−100.0	0.0	0.0	0.0	0.0	0.0
Domestic debt		−7.8	−14.2	−16.6	−5.4	−0.9	−6.5
Foreign credit		23.3	41.6	12.3	0.9	−10.6	−13.5
Total		−3.5	0.6	−5.8	−2.6	−5.3	−9.5
				Deviations from base run in per cent			
Domestic credit		0.0	0.0	0.0	0.0	0.0	0.0
Domestic debt		−5.8	−15.7	−28.9	−33.5	−38.9	−46.6
Foreign credit		−18.2	−20.9	−26.0	−31.9	−38.8	−45.6
Total		−9.4	−17.7	−27.7	−32.8	−38.8	−46.2

Table C.6 Balance of payments

	Year 0	*Year 1*	*Year 2*	*Year 3*	*Year 4*	*Year 5*	*Year 6*
				Billion foreign currency units			
Export	102.7	111.1	121.2	133.0	146.6	162.3	179.8
Import	−94.4	−107.7	−121.0	−133.6	−145.9	−159.6	−174.9
Interest payments	−6.3	−7.1	−9.1	−11.8	−14.9	−18.2	−21.8
Net transfers	0.2	0.2	0.2	0.2	0.3	0.3	0.3
Other factor services	−4.2	−4.5	−4.8	−5.1	−5.5	−5.8	−6.2
Current account surplus	−2.1	−8.0	−13.4	−17.2	−19.4	−21.1	−22.9
Public sector borrowing	−4.8	−5.9	−8.3	−9.3	−9.3	−8.4	−7.3
Private sector borrowing	−0.4	−8.5	−10.7	−12.7	−14.3	−17.0	−20.1
Change in reserves	3.1	6.4	5.5	4.7	4.3	4.3	4.5
				Per cent of GDP			
Export	23.6	23.9	24.2	24.6	25.1	25.6	26.1
Import	−21.7	−23.2	−24.2	−24.7	−25.0	−25.2	−25.4
Interest payments	−1.5	−1.5	−1.8	−2.2	−2.5	−2.9	−3.2
Net transfers	0.0	0.0	0.0	0.0	0.0	0.0	0.0
Other factor services	−1.0	−1.0	−1.0	−0.9	−0.9	−0.9	−0.9
Current account surplus	−0.5	−1.7	−2.7	−3.2	−3.3	−3.3	−3.3
Public sector borrowing	−1.1	−1.3	−1.7	−1.7	−1.6	−1.3	−1.1
Private sector borrowing	−0.1	−1.8	−2.1	−2.3	−2.4	−2.7	−2.9
Change in reserves	0.7	1.4	1.1	0.9	0.7	0.7	0.6

	Growth rates in per cent					
Export	8.1	9.2	9.7	10.2	10.7	10.8
Import	14.1	12.3	10.4	9.2	9.4	9.6
Interest payments	11.6	28.8	29.4	26.3	22.5	19.7
Net transfers	6.8	6.8	6.4	6.4	6.4	6.7
Other factor services	6.6	6.6	6.6	6.6	6.6	6.6
Current account surplus	284.1	67.0	28.7	12.3	9.0	8.4
Public sector borrowing	22.0	41.1	12.1	0.9	−10.4	−13.1
Private sector borrowing	1985.3	25.2	18.8	12.7	18.8	18.0
Change in reserves	103.9	−12.9	−14.9	−9.2	−0.5	4.6
	Deviations from base run in per cent					
Export	1.9	3.9	5.9	7.9	10.0	12.0
Import	0.7	2.2	3.8	5.5	7.6	9.9
Interest payments	0.0	−1.8	−3.4	−4.8	−6.1	−7.3
Net transfers	0.0	0.0	0.0	0.0	0.0	0.0
Other factor services	0.0	0.0	0.0	0.0	0.0	0.0
Current account surplus	−14.2	−13.8	−14.7	−16.5	−17.9	−18.7
Public sector borrowing	−16.8	−17.4	−20.7	−24.9	−30.3	−36.1
Private sector borrowing	0.0	0.0	0.0	0.0	0.0	0.0
Change in reserves	2.4	7.9	13.4	20.4	28.2	35.5

Table C.7 Money supply

	Year 0	*Year 1*	*Year 2*	*Year 3*	*Year 4*	*Year 5*	*Year 6*
				Billion rand			
Money supply	244.2	266.7	291.3	318.2	347.6	379.7	414.7
Foreign reserves	14.1	20.7	26.4	31.2	35.6	39.8	44.2
Total domestic credit	230.0	246.0	264.9	287.0	312.0	339.8	370.5
Public sector credit	15.5	15.5	15.5	15.5	15.5	15.5	15.5
Private sector credit	214.6	230.5	249.4	271.5	296.5	324.3	355.0
				Per cent of GDP			
Money supply	56.2	56.8	57.4	57.9	58.5	59.1	59.7
Foreign reserves	3.2	4.4	5.2	5.7	6.0	6.2	6.4
Total domestic credit	53.0	52.4	52.2	52.2	52.5	52.9	53.3
Public sector credit	3.6	3.3	3.0	2.8	2.6	2.4	2.2
Private sector credit	49.4	49.1	49.1	49.4	49.9	50.5	51.1
				Growth rates in per cent			
Money supply		9.2	9.2	9.2	9.2	9.2	9.2
Foreign reserves		46.7	27.5	18.4	14.0	11.9	10.9
Total domestic credit		6.9	7.7	8.3	8.7	8.9	9.0
Public sector credit		0.0	0.0	0.0	0.0	0.0	0.0
Private sector credit		7.4	8.2	8.8	9.2	9.4	9.5
				Deviations from base run in per cent			
Money supply		−0.4	−0.9	−1.3	−1.7	−2.2	−2.6
Foreign reserves		−1.0	−2.1	−3.2	−4.3	−5.4	−6.6
Total domestic credit		−0.4	−0.7	−1.1	−1.4	−1.8	−2.1
Public sector credit		0.0	0.0	0.0	0.0	0.0	0.0
Private sector credit		−0.4	−0.8	−1.1	−1.5	−1.8	−2.2

Table C.8 Other asset stocks

	Year 0	*Year 1*	*Year 2*	*Year 3*	*Year 4*	*Year 5*	*Year 6*
				Billion rand			
Public sector credit	15.5	15.5	15.5	15.5	15.5	15.5	15.5
Public sector domestic debt	169.2	185.6	199.7	211.4	222.5	233.6	243.9
Public sector foreign debt	32.3	38.6	47.1	56.6	66.1	74.5	81.5
Total public sector debt	217.0	239.7	262.3	283.5	304.2	323.5	340.9
Private sector foreign debt	17.7	26.5	37.4	50.4	65.0	82.0	102.0
				Per cent of GDP			
Public sector credit	3.6	3.3	3.0	2.8	2.6	2.4	2.2
Public sector domestic debt	39.0	39.5	39.3	38.5	37.5	36.4	35.1
Public sector foreign debt	7.4	8.2	9.3	10.3	11.1	11.6	11.7
Total public sector debt	50.0	51.0	51.6	51.6	51.2	50.4	49.1
Private sector foreign debt	4.1	5.6	7.4	9.2	10.9	12.8	14.7
				Growth rates in per cent			
Public sector credit		0.0	0.0	0.0	0.0	0.0	0.0
Public sector domestic debt		9.7	7.6	5.9	5.3	4.9	4.4
Public sector foreign debt		19.4	22.1	20.2	16.8	12.6	9.5
Total public sector debt		10.5	9.4	8.1	7.3	6.4	5.4
Private sector foreign debt		49.8	41.2	34.7	28.9	26.3	24.3
				Deviations from base run in per cent			
Public sector credit		0.0	0.0	0.0	0.0	0.0	0.0
Public sector domestic debt		−0.5	−1.8	−3.8	−5.9	−8.3	−11.0
Public sector foreign debt		−4.7	−9.9	−14.9	−19.8	−24.5	−29.2
Total public sector debt		−1.2	−3.2	−6.1	−9.1	−12.3	−15.7
Private sector foreign debt		−1.8	−4.2	−6.7	−9.4	−12.1	−15.0

Table C.9 Prices and exchange rates

	Year 0	*Year 1*	*Year 2*	*Year 3*	*Year 4*	*Year 5*	*Year 6*
				Index 1994 = 1.000			
General price index	1.000	1.030	1.061	1.093	1.126	1.159	1.194
Domestic price level	1.000	1.027	1.057	1.088	1.121	1.155	1.191
Import price level	1.000	1.030	1.061	1.093	1.126	1.159	1.194
Export price level	1.000	1.030	1.061	1.093	1.126	1.159	1.194
Nominal exchange rate	1.000	1.011	1.014	1.016	1.017	1.014	1.010
Real exchange rate	1.000	1.014	1.018	1.021	1.021	1.018	1.013
				Growth rates in per cent			
General price index		3.0	3.0	3.0	3.0	3.0	3.0
Domestic price level		2.7	2.9	2.9	3.0	3.1	3.1
Import price level		3.0	3.0	3.0	3.0	3.0	3.0
Export price level		3.0	3.0	3.0	3.0	3.0	3.0
Nominal exchange rate		1.1	0.3	0.2	0.0	−0.2	−0.4
Real exchange rate		1.4	0.4	0.3	0.0	−0.3	−0.5
				Deviations from base run in per cent			
General price index		−2.8	−5.6	−8.3	−10.9	−13.4	−15.8
Domestic price level		−3.1	−5.9	−8.6	−11.2	−13.7	−16.0
Import price level		0.0	0.0	0.0	0.0	0.0	0.0
Export price level		0.0	0.0	0.0	0.0	0.0	0.0
Nominal exchange rate		−1.8	−4.2	−6.7	−9.4	−12.1	−15.0
Real exchange rate		1.4	1.8	2.1	2.1	1.8	1.3

Table C.10 Other variables

	Year 0	*Year 1*	*Year 2*	*Year 3*	*Year 4*	*Year 5*	*Year 6*
				Per cent			
Domestic interest rate	14.0	13.0	12.0	10.5	10.0	9.5	9.0
Foreign interest rate	14.1	14.1	14.1	14.1	14.1	14.1	14.1
				Billion rand			
Nominal GDP	434.2	469.6	507.9	549.3	594.1	642.5	694.9
				Constant 1994 billion rand			
Public sector revenue	118.1	123.3	129.6	136.8	145.4	154.5	162.9
Other public sector expenditure	15.4	16.2	17.0	17.8	18.7	19.6	20.6
Terms of trade adjustment	0.0	0.0	0.0	0.0	0.0	0.0	0.0
Real GDY	434.2	456.0	478.8	502.7	527.8	554.2	581.9
				Billion foreign currency units			
Public sector foreign debt	32.3	38.2	46.4	55.7	65.0	73.4	80.7
Private sector foreign debt	17.7	26.2	36.9	49.6	63.9	80.9	100.9
International reserves	14.1	20.5	26.0	30.7	35.0	39.3	43.7
				Growth rates			
Nominal GDP		8.2	8.1	8.1	8.2	8.2	8.1
Public sector revenue		4.4	5.2	5.5	6.3	6.2	5.5
Other public sector expenditure		4.9	4.9	4.9	4.9	4.9	4.9
Terms of trade adjustment		0.0	0.0	0.0	0.0	0.0	0.0
Real GDY		5.0	5.0	5.0	5.0	5.0	5.0
Public sector foreign debt		18.1	21.7	20.0	16.8	12.9	9.9
Private sector foreign debt		48.2	40.7	34.4	28.8	26.6	24.8
International reserves		45.1	27.1	18.1	13.9	12.2	11.4

Table C.10 Other variables continued

	Year 0	*Year 1*	*Year 2*	*Year 3*	*Year 4*	*Year 5*	*Year 6*
		Deviations from base run in per cent					
Nominal GDP		−1.4	−2.8	−4.2	−5.6	−6.9	−8.2
Public sector revenue		0.9	1.7	2.6	3.5	4.3	5.2
Other public sector expenditure		1.4	2.8	4.2	5.6	7.0	8.5
Terms of trade adjustment		0.0	0.0	0.0	0.0	0.0	0.0
Real GDY		1.4	2.9	4.4	5.9	7.5	9.0
Public sector foreign debt		−3.0	−5.9	−8.7	−11.5	−14.1	−16.7
Private sector foreign debt		0.0	0.0	0.0	0.0	0.0	0.0
International reserves		0.7	2.2	3.8	5.5	7.6	9.9

APPENDIX D
Pessimistic scenario

Table D.1 Material balance

	Year 0	*Year 1*	*Year 2*	*Year 3*	*Year 4*	*Year 5*	*Year 6*
				Constant 1994 billion rand			
Private consumption	256.3	261.6	264.9	267.5	269.5	271.6	274.5
Public consumption	91.3	93.4	98.6	102.2	104.8	106.4	107.1
Private investment	68.7	72.7	74.3	75.7	77.3	78.8	80.4
Public investment	9.6	9.7	9.8	9.9	10.1	10.3	10.5
Export	102.7	104.7	107.9	111.7	116.1	121.4	126.9
Import	−94.4	−99.2	−103.6	−106.2	−107.7	−109.1	−110.4
GDP	434.2	442.9	451.8	460.8	470.0	479.4	489.0
				Per cent of GDP			
Private consumption	59.0	59.1	58.6	58.1	57.3	56.7	56.1
Public consumption	21.0	21.1	21.8	22.2	22.3	22.2	21.9
Private investment	15.8	16.4	16.4	16.4	16.4	16.4	16.4
Public investment	2.2	2.2	2.2	2.2	2.2	2.2	2.2
Export	23.6	23.6	23.9	24.2	24.7	25.3	25.9
Import	−21.7	−22.4	−22.9	−23.1	−22.9	−22.8	−22.6
GDP	100.0	100.0	100.0	100.0	100.0	100.0	100.0

	Real growth rates in per cent					
Private consumption	2.1	1.2	1.0	0.7	0.8	1.1
Public consumption	2.3	5.5	3.7	2.5	1.6	0.6
Private investment	5.8	2.2	2.0	2.0	2.0	2.0
Public investment	0.5	1.0	1.5	2.0	2.0	2.0
Export	2.0	3.0	3.5	4.0	4.5	4.5
Import	5.1	4.4	2.6	1.4	1.2	1.2
GDP	2.0	2.0	2.0	2.0	2.0	2.0
	Deviations from base run in per cent					
Private consumption	−1.0	−2.5	−4.1	−5.6	−7.1	−8.6
Public consumption	0.3	1.7	0.9	−1.5	−4.7	−7.8
Private investment	−9.4	−15.7	−19.2	−21.0	−22.2	−23.3
Public investment	−1.5	−2.9	−4.3	−5.7	−7.1	−8.4
Export	−1.0	−1.9	−2.9	−3.8	−4.7	−5.6
Import	−4.5	−7.2	−9.8	−12.2	−14.7	−17.2
GDP	−1.4	−2.9	−4.3	−5.7	−7.0	−8.4

Table D.2 Sectoral GDP

	Year 0	*Year 1*	*Year 2*	*Year 3*	*Year 4*	*Year 5*	*Year 6*
				Constant 1994 billion rand			
Agriculture	18.9	19.1	19.2	19.4	19.6	19.8	20.0
Mining	34.9	34.4	33.9	33.4	32.9	32.4	31.9
Manufacturing	94.3	97.6	101.0	104.5	108.2	112.0	115.9
Other	286.2	291.9	297.7	303.5	309.4	315.3	321.2
Total	434.2	442.9	451.8	460.8	470.0	479.4	489.0
				Per cent of GDP			
Agriculture	4.3	4.3	4.3	4.2	4.2	4.1	4.1
Mining	8.0	7.8	7.5	7.2	7.0	6.8	6.5
Manufacturing	21.7	22.0	22.4	22.7	23.0	23.4	23.7
Other	65.9	65.9	65.9	65.9	65.8	65.8	65.7
Total	100.0	100.0	100.0	100.0	100.0	100.0	100.0
				Real growth rates in per cent			
Agriculture		1.0	1.0	1.0	1.0	1.0	1.0
Mining		−1.5	−1.5	−1.5	−1.5	−1.5	−1.5
Manufacturing		3.5	3.5	3.5	3.5	3.5	3.5
Other		2.0	2.0	2.0	1.9	1.9	1.9
Total		2.0	2.0	2.0	2.0	2.0	2.0
				Deviations from base run in per cent			
Agriculture		−1.5	−2.9	−4.3	−5.7	−7.1	−8.5
Mining		−1.5	−3.0	−4.4	−5.9	−7.3	−8.7
Manufacturing		−1.4	−2.8	−4.2	−5.6	−6.9	−8.3
Other		−1.4	−2.9	−4.3	−5.7	−7.0	−8.4
Total		−1.4	−2.9	−4.3	−5.7	−7.0	−8.4

Table D.3 Export categories

	Year 0	*Year 1*	*Year 2*	*Year 3*	*Year 4*	*Year 5*	*Year 6*
				Constant 1994 billion rand			
Agriculture	6.3	6.4	6.4	6.5	6.5	6.6	6.7
Gold	22.7	22.4	22.2	22.0	21.8	21.6	21.3
Basic metals and minerals	33.1	33.8	34.6	35.7	36.9	38.2	39.5
Other exports	40.6	42.2	44.6	47.5	50.9	55.0	59.3
Total	102.7	104.7	107.9	111.7	116.1	121.4	126.9
				Per cent of export			
Agriculture	6.1	6.1	5.9	5.8	5.6	5.4	5.3
Gold	22.1	21.4	20.6	19.7	18.7	17.8	16.8
Basic metals and minerals	32.2	32.2	32.1	31.9	31.8	31.5	31.2
Other exports	39.6	40.3	41.4	42.6	43.8	45.3	46.8
Total	100.0	100.0	100.0	100.0	100.0	100.0	100.0
				Real growth rates			
Agriculture		1.0	1.0	1.0	1.0	1.0	1.0
Gold		−1.0	−1.0	−1.0	−1.0	−1.0	−1.0
Basic metals and minerals		2.0	2.5	3.0	3.5	3.5	3.5
Other exports		3.8	5.8	6.5	7.1	8.0	7.9
Total		2.0	3.0	3.5	4.0	4.5	4.5
				Deviations from base run in per cent			
Agriculture		−1.0	−2.0	−2.9	−3.9	−4.8	−5.7
Gold		−1.0	−2.0	−3.0	−3.9	−4.9	−5.9
Basic metals and minerals		−1.0	−1.9	−2.9	−3.8	−4.7	−5.6
Other exports		−1.0	−1.9	−2.8	−3.7	−4.6	−5.5
Total		−1.0	−1.9	−2.9	−3.8	−4.7	−5.6

Table D.4 Public sector budget

	Year 0	*Year 1*	*Year 2*	*Year 3*	*Year 4*	*Year 5*	*Year 6*
				Billion rand			
Domestic revenue	118.1	129.6	141.6	158.0	180.6	210.1	247.0
Transfers from ROW	0.3	0.3	0.3	0.4	0.5	0.5	0.6
Consumption	−91.3	−99.0	−111.7	−126.0	−143.0	−163.7	−188.9
Investment	−9.6	−10.2	−11.1	−12.2	−13.8	−15.9	−18.5
Transfers	−15.4	−16.7	−18.2	−20.2	−22.8	−26.2	−30.7
Domestic interest payments	−21.2	−23.8	−27.9	−34.3	−41.3	−49.0	−57.8
Foreign interest payments	−3.9	−4.8	−6.2	−8.3	−11.2	−14.9	−19.5
Budget surplus	−23.1	−24.7	−33.2	−42.7	−51.0	−59.0	−67.9
				Per cent of GDP			
Domestic revenue	27.2	27.6	27.7	27.8	28.1	28.5	28.6
Transfers from ROW	0.1	0.1	0.1	0.1	0.1	0.1	0.1
Consumption	−21.0	−21.1	−21.8	−22.2	−22.3	−22.2	−21.9
Investment	−2.2	−2.2	−2.2	−2.2	−2.2	−2.2	−2.2
Transfers	−3.6	−3.6	−3.6	−3.6	−3.6	−3.6	−3.6
Domestic interest payments	−4.9	−5.1	−5.5	−6.0	−6.4	−6.6	−6.7
Foreign interest payments	−0.9	−1.0	−1.2	−1.5	−1.7	−2.0	−2.3
Budget surplus	−5.3	−5.3	−6.5	−7.5	−7.9	−8.0	−7.9

	Growth rates in per cent					
Domestic revenue	9.8	9.3	11.6	14.3	16.3	17.5
Transfers from ROW	13.1	12.0	13.8	15.9	18.0	20.2
Consumption	8.4	12.8	12.8	13.5	14.5	15.4
Investment	6.5	8.0	10.4	12.9	14.9	16.9
Transfers	8.1	9.1	11.0	13.0	14.9	17.0
Domestic interest payments	12.1	17.6	22.7	20.4	18.8	18.0
Foreign interest payments	24.6	28.1	34.1	34.3	33.3	31.1
Budget surplus	6.5	34.7	28.4	19.4	15.9	15.0
	Deviations from base run in per cent					
Domestic revenue	0.0	−1.1	−0.5	1.8	6.1	12.5
Transfers from ROW	3.1	5.3	9.4	15.5	24.3	36.1
Consumption	0.3	2.6	4.5	6.5	9.6	14.7
Investment	−1.5	−2.1	−0.9	2.0	6.8	13.8
Transfers	−1.4	−2.0	−0.9	2.0	6.9	14.0
Domestic interest payments	0.0	6.6	24.5	44.0	65.3	88.7
Foreign interest payments	3.1	5.3	9.4	15.5	24.3	36.1
Budget surplus	0.0	21.7	45.9	66.1	85.1	106.7

Table D.5 Public sector deficit finance

	Year 0	*Year 1*	*Year 2*	*Year 3*	*Year 4*	*Year 5*	*Year 6*
				Billion rand			
Domestic credit	0.5	−0.2	5.3	12.2	18.1	23.8	30.2
Domestic debt	17.8	17.4	16.7	16.5	16.7	18.0	19.3
Foreign credit	4.8	7.5	11.2	13.9	16.1	17.3	18.4
Total	23.1	24.7	33.2	42.7	51.0	59.0	67.9
				Per cent of GDP			
Domestic credit	0.1	0.0	1.0	2.1	2.8	3.2	3.5
Domestic debt	4.1	3.7	3.3	2.9	2.6	2.4	2.2
Foreign credit	1.1	1.6	2.2	2.5	2.5	2.3	2.1
Total	5.3	5.3	6.5	7.5	7.9	8.0	7.9
				Growth rates in per cent			
Domestic credit		nd	nd	128.2	48.5	31.0	27.0
Domestic debt		−2.2	−4.1	−1.1	1.1	7.9	7.2
Foreign credit		55.5	49.4	24.8	15.7	7.0	6.6
Total		6.5	34.7	28.4	19.4	15.9	15.0
				Deviations from base run in per cent			
Domestic credit		nd	nd	nd	nd	nd	nd
Domestic debt		0.0	0.0	0.0	0.0	0.0	0.0
Foreign credit		3.1	5.3	9.4	15.5	24.3	36.1
Total		0.0	21.7	45.9	66.1	85.1	106.7

Note: nd denotes values not defined

Table D.6 Balance of payments

	Year 0	*Year 1*	*Year 2*	*Year 3*	*Year 4*	*Year 5*	*Year 6*
				Billion foreign currency units			
Export	102.7	106.8	112.2	118.4	125.5	133.8	142.6
Import	−94.4	−102.2	−109.9	−116.1	−121.3	−126.5	−131.8
Interest payments	−6.3	−7.1	−8.9	−11.2	−13.7	−16.3	−18.8
Net transfers	0.2	0.2	0.2	0.2	0.2	0.3	0.3
Other factor services	−4.2	−4.5	−4.8	−5.1	−5.5	−5.8	−6.2
Current account surplus	−2.1	−6.7	−11.2	−13.8	−14.7	−14.5	−14.0
Public sector borrowing	−4.8	−7.0	−10.0	−11.7	−12.4	−12.0	−11.4
Private sector borrowing	−0.4	−5.9	−6.3	−6.3	−5.8	−5.8	−5.9
Change in reserves	3.1	6.2	5.1	4.2	3.6	3.3	3.3
				Per cent of GDP			
Export	23.6	24.1	24.4	24.8	25.3	26.0	26.7
Import	−21.7	−23.1	−23.9	−24.4	−24.5	−24.6	−24.7
Interest payments	−1.5	−1.6	−1.9	−2.4	−2.8	−3.2	−3.5
Net transfers	0.0	0.0	0.1	0.1	0.1	0.1	0.1
Other factor services	−1.0	−1.0	−1.0	−1.1	−1.1	−1.1	−1.2
Current account surplus	−0.5	−1.5	−2.4	−2.9	−3.0	−2.8	−2.6
Public sector borrowing	−1.1	−1.6	−2.2	−2.5	−2.5	−2.3	−2.1
Private sector borrowing	−0.1	−1.3	−1.4	−1.3	−1.2	−1.1	−1.1
Change in reserves	0.7	1.4	1.1	0.9	0.7	0.6	0.6

Table D.6 continued

	Year 0	Year 1	Year 2	Year 3	Year 4	Year 5	Year 6
				Growth rates in per cent			
Export		4.0	5.0	5.5	6.1	6.6	6.6
Import		8.2	7.5	5.7	4.5	4.3	4.2
Interest payments		11.6	25.9	25.9	22.6	18.7	15.5
Net transfers		6.8	6.8	6.4	6.4	6.4	6.7
Other factor services		6.6	6.6	6.6	6.6	6.6	6.6
Current account surplus		222.2	65.7	23.6	6.3	−0.8	−4.0
Public sector borrowing		46.6	42.1	16.8	6.6	−3.3	−5.4
Private sector borrowing		1344.2	6.5	−0.4	−7.9	1.2	0.7
Change in reserves		99.1	−17.3	−19.1	−14.5	−6.5	−0.8
				Deviations from base run in per cent			
Export		−2.0	−3.9	−5.7	−7.6	−9.4	−11.1
Import		−4.5	−7.2	−9.8	−12.3	−14.7	−17.2
Interest payments		0.0	−4.0	−8.1	−12.1	−16.0	−19.9
Net transfers		0.0	0.0	0.0	0.0	0.0	0.0
Other factor services		0.0	0.0	0.0	0.0	0.0	0.0
Current account surplus		−28.0	−28.2	−31.8	−36.8	−43.4	−50.4
Public sector borrowing		0.0	0.0	0.0	0.0	0.0	0.0
Private sector borrowing		−30.7	−41.1	−50.7	−59.7	−65.6	−70.7
Change in reserves		0.0	0.0	0.0	0.0	0.0	0.0

Table D.7 Money supply

	Year 0	Year 1	Year 2	Year 3	Year 4	Year 5	Year 6
				Billion rand			
Money supply	244.2	264.0	287.9	319.5	360.8	414.6	484.9
Foreign reserves	14.1	21.6	28.4	35.3	43.0	52.4	64.3
Total domestic credit	230.0	242.4	259.5	284.2	317.9	362.3	420.6
Public sector credit	15.5	15.3	20.6	32.8	50.9	74.7	104.9
Private sector credit	214.6	227.1	238.9	251.4	266.9	287.6	315.7
				Per cent of GDP			
Money supply	56.2	56.2	56.2	56.2	56.2	56.2	56.2
Foreign reserves	3.2	4.6	5.5	6.2	6.7	7.1	7.5
Total domestic credit	53.0	51.6	50.7	50.0	49.5	49.1	48.8
Public sector credit	3.6	3.2	4.0	5.8	7.9	10.1	12.2
Private sector credit	49.4	48.4	46.7	44.2	41.6	39.0	36.6
				Growth rates in per cent			
Money supply		8.1	9.1	11.0	12.9	14.9	16.9
Foreign reserves		52.8	31.7	24.4	21.7	21.8	22.9
Total domestic credit		5.4	7.0	9.5	11.9	14.0	16.1
Public sector credit		−1.5	35.1	59.2	55.2	46.6	40.4
Private sector credit		5.9	5.2	5.2	6.2	7.8	9.8
				Deviations from base run in per cent			
Money supply		−1.5	−2.0	−0.9	2.0	6.9	13.9
Foreign reserves		3.1	5.3	9.4	15.5	24.3	36.1
Total domestic credit		−1.8	−2.8	−2.1	0.4	4.7	11.1
Public sector credit		−1.5	33.0	111.9	228.8	382.4	577.1
Private sector credit		−1.9	−5.0	−8.5	−11.3	−13.0	−13.0

Table D.8 Other asset stocks

	Year 0	*Year 1*	*Year 2*	*Year 3*	*Year 4*	*Year 5*	*Year 6*
				Billion rand			
Public sector credit	15.5	15.3	20.6	32.8	50.9	74.7	104.9
Public sector domestic debt	169.2	186.6	203.3	219.8	236.5	254.6	273.9
Public sector foreign debt	32.3	41.7	55.1	72.8	95.2	122.7	156.6
Total public sector debt	217.0	243.6	279.0	325.4	382.7	451.9	535.3
Private sector foreign debt	17.7	25.0	33.3	43.1	54.3	68.5	86.7
				Per cent of GDP			
Public sector credit	3.6	3.2	4.0	5.8	7.9	10.1	12.2
Public sector domestic debt	39.0	39.7	39.7	38.7	36.9	34.5	31.8
Public sector foreign debt	7.4	8.9	10.8	12.8	14.8	16.6	18.2
Total public sector debt	50.0	51.9	54.5	57.3	59.6	61.3	62.1
Private sector foreign debt	4.1	5.3	6.5	7.6	8.5	9.3	10.1
				Growth rates in per cent			
Public sector credit		−1.5	35.1	59.2	55.2	46.6	40.4
Public sector domestic debt		10.3	9.0	8.1	7.6	7.6	7.6
Public sector foreign debt		29.2	31.9	32.2	30.8	28.8	27.7
Total public sector debt		12.3	14.5	16.7	17.6	18.1	18.5
Private sector foreign debt		41.5	33.2	29.3	26.0	26.1	26.5
				Deviations from base run in per cent			
Public sector credit		−1.5	33.0	111.9	228.8	382.4	577.1
Public sector domestic debt		0.0	0.0	0.0	0.0	0.0	0.0
Public sector foreign debt		3.1	5.3	9.4	15.5	24.3	36.1
Total public sector debt		0.4	2.9	7.8	14.4	22.6	32.4
Private sector foreign debt		−7.2	−14.7	−20.2	−24.2	−26.6	−27.7

Table D.9 Prices and exchange rates

	Year 0	*Year 1*	*Year 2*	*Year 3*	*Year 4*	*Year 5*	*Year 6*
				Index 1994 = 1.000			
General price index	1.000	1.060	1.133	1.233	1.365	1.538	1.763
Domestic price level	1.000	1.052	1.121	1.216	1.342	1.507	1.722
Import price level	1.000	1.030	1.061	1.093	1.126	1.159	1.194
Export price level	1.000	1.020	1.040	1.060	1.081	1.102	1.124
Nominal exchange rate	1.000	1.061	1.116	1.193	1.296	1.435	1.616
Real exchange rate	1.000	1.039	1.056	1.072	1.087	1.104	1.121
				Growth rates in per cent			
General price index		6.0	6.9	8.8	10.7	12.7	14.6
Domestic price level		5.2	6.6	8.5	10.4	12.3	14.3
Import price level		3.0	3.0	3.0	3.0	3.0	3.0
Export price level		2.0	2.0	2.0	2.0	2.0	2.0
Nominal exchange rate		6.1	5.1	6.9	8.6	10.7	12.7
Real exchange rate		3.9	1.6	1.5	1.3	1.6	1.6
				Deviations from base run in per cent			
General price index		0.0	0.9	3.5	8.1	14.9	24.3
Domestic price level		−0.8	−0.3	2.1	6.3	12.6	21.4
Import price level		0.0	0.0	0.0	0.0	0.0	0.0
Export price level		−1.0	−2.0	−3.0	−3.9	−4.9	−5.9
Nominal exchange rate		3.1	5.3	9.4	15.5	24.3	36.1
Real exchange rate		3.9	5.6	7.2	8.7	10.4	12.1

Table D.10 Other variables

	Year 0	*Year 1*	*Year 2*	*Year 3*	*Year 4*	*Year 5*	*Year 6*
				Per cent			
Domestic interest rate	14.0	14.0	15.0	16.9	18.8	20.7	22.7
Foreign interest rate	14.1	14.1	14.1	14.1	14.1	14.1	14.1
				Billion rand			
Nominal GDP	434.2	469.5	512.0	568.2	641.8	737.5	862.4
				Constant 1994 billion rand			
Public sector revenue	118.1	122.2	124.9	128.1	132.3	136.5	139.9
Other public sector expenditure	15.4	15.7	16.0	16.4	16.7	17.0	17.4
Terms of trade adjustment	0.0	−1.0	−2.1	−3.3	−4.6	−5.9	−7.4
Real GDY	434.2	441.9	449.7	457.5	465.5	473.5	481.6
				Billion foreign currency units			
Public sector foreign debt	32.3	39.3	49.4	61.0	73.5	85.5	96.9
Private sector foreign debt	17.7	23.6	29.9	36.2	41.9	47.8	53.6
International reserves	14.1	20.3	25.5	29.6	33.2	36.5	39.8

			Growth rates			
Nominal GDP	8.1	9.1	11.0	12.9	14.9	16.9
Public sector revenue	3.6	2.2	2.5	3.3	3.2	2.5
Other public sector expenditure	2.0	2.0	2.0	2.0	2.0	2.0
Terms of trade adjustment	nd	105.0	54.5	38.0	30.0	24.8
Real GDY	1.8	1.8	1.7	1.7	1.7	1.7
Public sector foreign debt	21.8	25.4	23.7	20.4	16.4	13.3
Private sector foreign debt	33.4	26.7	21.0	16.0	13.9	12.3
International reserves	44.1	25.3	16.3	12.0	10.0	9.0
			Deviations from base run in per cent			
Nominal GDP	−1.5	−2.0	−0.9	2.0	6.9	13.9
Public sector revenue	0.0	−2.0	−4.0	−5.9	−7.8	−9.6
Other public sector expenditure	−1.4	−2.9	−4.3	−5.7	−7.0	−8.4
Terms of trade adjustment	nd	nd	nd	nd	nd	nd
Real GDY	−1.7	−3.3	−5.0	−6.6	−8.2	−9.8
Public sector foreign debt	0.0	0.0	0.0	0.0	0.0	0.0
Private sector foreign debt	−10.0	−19.0	−27.1	−34.4	−41.0	−46.9
International reserves	0.0	0.0	0.0	0.0	0.0	0.0

Note: nd denotes values not defined

BIBLIOGRAPHY

Addison, D. (1989) 'The World Bank Revised Minimum Standard Model – Concepts and Issues', Policy, Planning and Research Paper WPS 231, Washington, DC: World Bank.

African National Congress (ANC) (1992) 'Ready to Govern: ANC Policy Guidelines for a Democratic South Africa', Adopted at the National Conference 28–31 May.

—— (1994) *The Reconstruction and Development Program*, Johannesburg.

Bacha, E. L. (1990) 'A Three-Gap Model of Foreign Transfers and the GDP Growth Rate in Developing Countries', *Journal of Development Economics,* vol. 32, pp. 279–96.

Brooke, D. A., Kendrick, D. and Meeraus, A. (1988) *GAMS – A User's Guide*, San Francisco: Scientific Press.

Central Economic Advisory Service (CEAS) (1993) 'The Restructuring of the South African Economy: A Normative Model Approach', Pretoria: Government Printers.

Chenery, H. B. and Strout, A. M. (1966) 'Foreign Assistance and Economic Development', *American Economic Review*, vol. 56, no. 4, pp. 679–733.

COSATU (1992) 'Our Political Economy: Understanding the Problems', Johannesburg: COSATU.

Department of Finance (1995) *Budget Review*, Cape Town: Republic of South Africa.

Dornbusch, R. and Edwards, S. (eds) (1991) *The Macroeconomics of Populism in Latin America*, Chicago: University of Chicago Press.

Easterly, W. (1989) 'A Consistency Framework for Macroeconomic Policy Analysis', Policy, Planning and Research Paper WPS 234, Washington, DC: World Bank.

Eckert, G. (1991) 'An Evolving Crisis: Income Inequalities in South Africa', mimeo, Johannesburg.

Edwards, S. (1989) 'The International Monetary Fund and the Developing Countries: A Critical Evaluation', Working Paper no. 2909, Cambridge, Mass.: National Bureau of Economic Research.

Everaert, L., Garcia-Pinto, F. and Ventura, J. (1990) 'A RMSM-X Model for Turkey', Policy, Research, and External Affairs Working Paper WPS 486, Washington, DC: World Bank.

Fallon, P. and Pereira de Silva, L. A. (1994) 'South Africa: Economic Performance and Policies', Informal Discussion Papers on Aspects of the Economy of South Africa, no. 7, Washington, DC: World Bank.

Financial Mail (1995) 'State of the RDP: Modesty is its Virtue', 7 April.

Frenkel, J. A. and Johnson, H. G. (eds) (1976) *The Monetary Approach to the Balance of Payments*, London: George Allen & Unwin.

Gelb, S. (ed.) (1991) *South Africa's Economic Crisis*, Cape Town: David Phillip.

Gibson, B. and van Seventer, D. E. (1995a) 'Towards a Growth Strategy for the South African Economy', mimeo, Halfway House: Development Bank of Southern Africa.

—— (1995b) 'The Macroeconomic Effects of Restructuring Public Expenditure by Function in South Africa', paper prepared for the African Economic Research Consortium Conference on Transitional and Long Term Development Issues in South Africa, 30 November–1 December, Johannesburg.

Hirsch, A. (1994) 'GATT – The Way Forward', *Indicator SA*, vol. 12, no. 1, pp. 43–8.

International Development Research Centre (IDRC) (1991) 'Economic Analysis and Policy Formulation for Post-Apartheid South Africa', Mission Report, Ottawa.

International Monetary Fund (IMF) (1977) *The Monetary Approach to the Balance of Payments,* Washington, DC.

—— (1987) 'Theoretical Aspects of the Design of Fund Supported Adjustment Programs', Occasional Paper no. 55, Washington, DC.

—— (1992) 'Economic Policies for a New South Africa', Occasional Paper no. 91, Washington, DC.

Kahn, B. (1995) 'An Analysis of Exchange Rate Policy and the Real Exchange Rate', *Centre for Research into Economics and Finance in South Africa (CREFSA) Quarterly Review* (July), pp. 1–9.

——, Senhadji, A. and Walton, M. (1992) 'South Africa: Macroeconomic Issues for the Transition', Informal Discussion Papers on Aspects of the Economy of South Africa no. 2, Washington, DC: World Bank.

Khan, M. S., Montiel, P. and Haque, N. U. (1990) 'Adjustment with Growth – Relating the Analytical Approaches of the IMF and the World Bank', *Journal of Development Economics*, vol. 32, pp. 155–79.

Macroeconomic Research Group (MERG) (1993) *Making Democracy Work: A Framework for Macroeconomic Policy in South Africa*, A Report to the Members of the Democratic Movement of South Africa, Cape Town: Centre for Development Studies, University of the Western Cape.

McGrath, M. and Holden, M. (1994) 'Economic Outlook', *Indicator SA*, vol. 12, no. 1, pp. 40–2.

Mills, C. A. and Nallari, R. (1992) 'Analytical Approaches to Stabilization and Adjustment Programs', EDI Seminar Paper no. 44, Washington, DC: World Bank.

Mosley, P., Harrigan, J. and Toye, J. (1991) *Aid and Power – The World Bank and Policy-Based Lending*, London: Routledge.

Nattrass, N. (1994) 'The RDP White Paper – A Cocktail of Confusion', *Indicator SA*, vol. 12, no. 1, pp. 36–9.

Naude, W. and Brixen, P. (1992) 'A Provisional CGE Model for South Africa Based on the 1988 SAM', *South African Journal of Economic and Management Sciences*, vol. 10, pp. 22–33.
—— (1993) 'On A Provisional Computable General Equilibrium Model for South Africa', *South African Journal of Economics*, vol. 61, pp. 153–65.
Ndulu, B. J. (1990) 'Growth and Adjustment in sub-Saharan Africa', paper presented at the World Bank Economic Issues Conference, Nairobi, June.
Nolan, B. (1995) 'Poverty, Inequality and Reconstruction in South Africa', *Development Policy Review*, vol. 13, no. 2, pp. 151–71.
Overseas Development Institute (ODI) (1994) 'Economic Policies in the New South Africa', Briefing Paper no. 21, April.
Padayachee, V. (1990): 'The IMF and the World Bank in Post-Apartheid South Africa: Prospects and Dangers', mimeo, Institute of Social and Economic Research, University of Durban-Westville.
Polak, J. J. (1957) 'Monetary Analysis of Income Formation and Payments Problems', *IMF Staff Papers*, vol. 6, no. 1, pp. 1–50.
—— (1990) 'A Marriage Between Fund and Bank Models? – Comment on Khan and Montiel', *IMF Staff Papers*, vol. 37, no. 1, pp. 183–6.
Republic of South Africa (1995) 'White Paper on Reconstruction and Development', *Government Gazette*, vol. 353, no. 16085, Cape Town: Creda Press for Government Printer.
Robichek, E. W. (1985) 'Financial Programming as Practiced by the IMF', mimeographed paper, pp. 1–13.
South African Reserve Bank (SARB) (various issues), *Quarterly Bulletin*, Pretoria: SARB.
Swiderski, K. A. (ed.) (1992) *Financial Programming and Policy: The Case of Hungary*, Washington, DC: IMF Institute, International Monetary Fund.
Tarp, F. (1993a) *Stabilisation and Structural Adjustment – Macroeconomic Frameworks for Analysing the Crisis in sub-Saharan Africa*, London: Routledge.
—— (1993b) *South Africa: Background and Possibilities for Danish Transitional Assistance*, Copenhagen: Danida.
Taylor, L. (1988) *Varieties of Stabilization Experience: Towards Sensible Macroeconomics in the Third World*, Oxford: Clarendon Press.
—— (1989) 'Gap Disequilibria: Inflation, Investment, Saving and Foreign Exchange', Working Paper no. 76, Helsinki: World Institute for Development Economics Research (WIDER).
—— (1993) *The Rocky Road to Reform: Adjustment, Income Distribution and Growth in the Developing World*, Cambridge, Mass.: MIT Press.
Toye, J. (1993) *Dilemmas of Development*, 2nd edn., Oxford UK and Cambridge USA: Blackwell.
World Bank (1995) *World Development Report 1995*, Washington, DC: Published for the World Bank by Oxford University Press.
Zarenda, H. (1992) 'An Evaluation of the IMF Mission Document on Economic Policies for a New South Africa', Working Paper no. 27, School of Oriental and African Studies, University of London.

INDEX